# HOT FLASH

# HOT FLASH

## HOW THE LAW
## IGNORES MENOPAUSE
## AND WHAT WE CAN
## DO ABOUT IT

Emily Gold Waldman, Bridget J. Crawford, *and* Naomi R. Cahn

STANFORD UNIVERSITY PRESS
Stanford, California

Stanford University Press
Stanford, California

Printed in the United States of America on acid-free, archival-quality paper

Library of Congress Cataloging-in-Publication Data

Names: Waldman, Emily Gold, author. | Crawford, Bridget J., author. | Cahn, Naomi R., author.
Title: Hot flash : how the law ignores menopause and what we can do about it / Emily Gold Waldman, Bridget J. Crawford, and Naomi R. Cahn.
Description: Stanford, California : Stanford University Press, 2024. | Includes bibliographical references and index.
Identifiers: LCCN 2024012356 (print) | LCCN 2024012357 (ebook) | ISBN 9781503636606 (cloth) | ISBN 9781503641563 (ebook)
Subjects: LCSH: Women—Legal status, laws, etc.—United States. | Sex discrimination against women—Law and legislation—United States. | Menopause—Social aspects—United States.
Classification: LCC KF478 .W35 2024 (print) | LCC KF478 (ebook) | DDC 342.7308/78—dc23/eng/20240325
LC record available at https://lccn.loc.gov/2024012356
LC ebook record available at https://lccn.loc.gov/2024012357

Cover art: Unsplash / Codioful (formerly Gradienta)
Typeset by Newgen in Cardea OTCE 10/14.5

*For Dan – EGW*
*For my sister, Maureen – BJC*
*For my family – NRC*

# CONTENTS

# HOT FLASH

# INTRODUCTION

This book has its origins in the first-ever law school symposium on menstruation held in 2021.[1] Two of us (Emily Waldman and Bridget Crawford) planned that conference as we were finishing the manuscript for a book that analyzed the many ways that menstruation intersects with all aspects of the law, including tax, education, employment law, prisoners' rights, poverty law, and the environment. When Naomi Cahn proposed a conference paper outlining a research agenda centered on menopause—clinically defined as the *absence* of menstruation for twelve months in someone who previously menstruated—it was immediately obvious that menopause is a significant part of the same picture and also presents its own distinct issues. The three of us embarked on a series of conversations and collaborations that ultimately became this book.

To be frank, none of us could have predicted that we would devote so much of our professional attention to the subject of menopause. Each of the three of us—cis women in our 40s, 50s, and 60s—had internalized to a certain extent the cultural expectations of silence and stigma associated with the aging female body. Up until recently, our anecdotal experience has been that menopause was one of the last great taboo topics—not typically the subject of conversation, even among close friends or family members, and certainly not at work. To the extent menopause was ever mentioned, it was often as part of a joke about middle-aged women.

So, we were not surprised when our announcement that we were writing a book about menopause generated more than a few raised eyebrows and quizzical glances from colleagues. Yet based on our individual areas of expertise including employment law, antidiscrimination law, family law, aging and the law, business and tax law, and feminist legal theory, we realized how much the law needs to change to take menopause into account. After all, approximately half the population will experience menopause during their lifetimes, and yet law mostly does not acknowledge the topic.

This book is part of a growing movement to change the silent approach to menopause. It turns out that we are writing the book at an opportune time: U.S. culture seems to be at an inflection point regarding menopause. Menopause is becoming more visible in popular media, such as in Michelle Obama's podcasts, under headlines like *Glamour*'s "10 Celebrities Who Have Spoken Out About Menopause,"[2] or in a session of Oprah Winfrey's "The Life You Want" subscription-only class featuring Drew Barrymore, Maria Shriver, and two doctors doing a "deep dive" on perimenopause and menopause.[3] The US government is undertaking new initiatives. Stories about ordinary people's experiences with menopause are appearing with regularity, too. And an increasing number of for-profit companies are selling products to address menopausal symptoms. Admittedly, though, this catalogue of menopause mentions reflects one of the occupational hazards of writing a book about menopause: we now notice the subject *everywhere*.[4]

Menopause is having a moment—or lots of moments, it would seem. In helping to create more moments for menopausal awareness, we started this project by looking at the law. Our initial guiding questions included: How have menopausal silence and stigma contributed to the conditions in which bias and discrimination can flourish in the workplace, doctors' offices, scientific research, and even courts of law? What role can the law play in breaking the silence and stigma? Of the many ways that menopause matters in everyday life, where and how is the law best able to effectuate change? In conducting our research, we uncovered how law frequently reflects and then reinforces cultural, social, and political currents. Understanding those currents is the starting point for mapping the way forward for legal change. Accordingly, our new guiding question became: How can a better understanding of menopause improve life and law for everyone?

To be sure, menopause is an extremely complicated topic. Our central inquiry is grounded in the belief that all people—not just those who will personally experience menopause—can benefit from learning more about the ways that menopause affects individuals, workplaces, health care, and society. Understanding menopause's multiple intersections with everyday life and law is crucial to achieve a more robust economy and inclusive society.

The book situates menopause uniquely at the intersection of gender, aging, medicalization, and disability—acknowledging that gender is complex, that not all menopause is age-related, that treatment for menopause's symptoms is often needed, and that menopause itself is not a disability. In the past, menopause was often viewed as a problem or condition depriving older women of some sort of feminine essence. The "cure" came in the form of hormonal treatments touted as both restoring women's femininity and preventing disease. Indeed, during the second half of the twentieth century, such hormone therapy became widespread in the United States. But that came to a crashing halt when, in 2002, the National Institutes of Health (NIH) suddenly announced that it was stopping its large-scale study of one type of menopausal hormone therapy due to concerns about breast cancer, heart disease, and other serious risks.[5] Recently, the tide has turned back in favor of hormone treatments and a more nuanced understanding of the data from the NIH study. But there is still a great deal that scientists, doctors, and members of the general public do not know about menopause or how to address its many symptoms, which can range from unnoticeable for some people to outright debilitating for others. Especially given the variability in experiences with menopause, there is still much to understand. Race and other identity factors often affect the experience, diagnosis, and management of menopause. In situating menopause as part of the reproductive lifespan, the book's goal is to draw in, and draw on, those interested more broadly in the relationship between biology and equality by showing how menopause provides an entrance point for exploring issues of gender, culture, equity, and medicalization.

## STRUCTURE AND ORGANIZATION OF THIS BOOK

Chapter 1 sets out the framework for the remainder of the book. It provides a basic overview of the biology of menopause. It then describes the three main themes that run throughout the book: the importance of dismantling the stigma and silence around menopause; the need to develop a more nuanced understanding of menopause; and the importance of law and legal reforms in ensuring that menopause is treated as an accepted and recognized part of the life course of approximately one-half of the population.

Chapter 2 delves into cultural tropes and stereotypes about menopause. The chapter begins with a look at how menopause has been portrayed in the media and literature and moves on to discuss societal and personal attitudes toward menopause. Generally speaking, menopause is negatively stereotyped and stigmatized, but there are some people who experience menopause as a liberating experience. Indeed, research shows that both societal attitudes and subjective experiences of menopause tend to vary across different countries and groups within those countries, emphasizing the need for more research on the ways that both culture and identity may shape the experience of menopause.

Chapter 3 turns to the questions and controversies that dominate medical discourse around menopause in the United States, focusing on the historic development of "cures." The very idea that menopause might need a cure suggests that this inevitable life stage is a problem or illness. Acknowledging that some people do experience severe physical, psychological, and cognitive symptoms, the basic notion that menopause requires medical intervention sounds in ageism. In one sense, medical treatments for menopause can be understood as akin to technologies like hair dye, plastic surgery, Botox, and the like that may be invoked as part of an effort to appear more youthful. At another level, though, medical treatments like menopausal hormone therapy should be understood as providing necessary relief to those who experience symptoms that may range from troublesome to severely hindering.

Chapter 4 turns its focus to the workplace, a common site of discrimination based on menopause. Drawing on actual cases, the chapter identifies the main categories in which claims arise for menopause-based discrimination in the workplace: discrimination based on menopausal stereotypes (e.g., when a supervisor repeatedly jokes about whether a particular employee is having hot flashes), discrimination based on menopause-related symptoms (e.g., when an employee is punished for unexpected perimenopausal bleeding), and a lack of reasonable accommodations (e.g., when a menopausal employee is not allowed to deviate from a dress code that exacerbates hot flashes). U.S. law is largely undeveloped in this area and provides remedies in only a narrow swath of cases.

Chapter 5 considers how U.S. workplaces might evolve to take into account the needs of menopausal employees, drawing on the approach to menopause in the United Kingdom. The chapter argues that employment discrimination law should be expanded to provide legal protections for menopause that are akin to those available for pregnant and breastfeeding workers. The law should do more than merely protect against the most egregious and blatant instances of discrimination. Furthermore, this chapter identifies steps that employers can take on their own to ensure that menopause does not unnecessarily limit the ability to remain and succeed at work.

Chapter 6 centers on the experiences of queer, trans, and gender diverse people. Not all who experience menopause are "women" and not all who experience menopause are those who have sexual or romantic attachments to cisgender men (or anyone at all). This chapter centers the voices of trans and gender diverse people, as well as lesbians and bisexual women of all gender identities, to offer firsthand accounts of experiencing and managing menopause. As is true for cis heterosexual women, the menopause experience for queer, trans, and gender diverse people is not uniform. Some experience it as a time of liberation; others experience menopause as an unwelcome reason to focus on their bodies.

Chapter 7 situates menopause in the larger culture of commerce that occurs in both physical and digital products. Menopause is not only an inevitable biological process but also a profitable business opportunity that has resulted in a growing array of menopause-related products and services including hormonal treatments, skin care, vitamins, clothing, and personal appliances. Digital technology companies market telehealth and peer support apps. We take a skeptical approach to what we label "menopause capitalism"—the marketing and selling of menopause-related products or services through messages that celebrate autonomy, community, or stereotypical femininity by entities that are, at their core, commercial enterprises. To be sure, many menopause-related products and services are beneficial. Increased access to hormone therapy, the development of new treatments, easier tracking of symptoms, and even some of the new merchandise means that more people can get help and support. But, as the chapter shows, the products do not necessarily deliver on their promised outcomes. There is also a particular need for greater legal protection for private health information that consumers voluntarily enter into health apps generally and menopause apps specifically.

Chapter 8, the final chapter, explores the conceptual and pragmatic challenges to reforming the contemporary approach to menopause in the United States. On the one hand, it is axiomatic that all people should receive equal treatment under the law. On the other hand, this book demonstrates the many ways that, in the case of menopause, the *failure* to take into account biological differences can be an obstacle to many people's health, well-being, and full participation in the workforce. To achieve meaningful reform, it is necessary to be more explicit and intentional about societal approaches to menopause, recognizing the tension between sameness and difference and also taking into account how menopause intersects with sex, age, disability, race, and gender. Advocates for menopause-related law reform may be able to win support from the business community by emphasizing the economic and psychological losses associated with menopausal employees leaving the workforce. We suggest lessons for menopause from disability rights advocacy, too—even though menopause is not a disability—and the goal of designing accommodating environments for everyone. Furthermore, we connect menopausal discrimination to age-based discrimination and the menstrual equity movements. All of these links can facilitate greater cooperation among those who are interested in making sure that menopause is not used as a vector of discrimination.

The topic of menopause takes on particular salience when viewed in the context of other reproduction-associated conditions and processes, especially those often shrouded in silence, from menstruation to infertility to miscarriage to abortion. The Supreme Court's opinion in *Dobbs v. Jackson Women's Health Organization*,[6] which overruled *Roe v. Wade*,[7] has brought reproductive life to the fore of national politics in a new way. To us, menopause is one part of that reproductive life. Knowledge and bodily autonomy are key elements of a more just and equitable society.

## NOTE ON LANGUAGE

Throughout this book, we deploy the words "trans" and "gender diverse" in the same way as the World Professional Association for Transgender Health does: to describe people who are "member[s] of the many varied communities globally of people with gender identities or expressions that differ from the gender socially attributed to the sex assigned to them at birth."[8] We use "queer" broadly throughout the book to refer to sexual orientations like lesbian, gay, bisexual, and asexual. In short, we use "queer" as an umbrella term for the many sexual orientations beyond heterosexual.[9]

In talking about menopause, it is important to use language that does not pathologize or "other" queer, trans, and gender diverse people. We strive throughout the book to chart a course for an inclusive and effective discourse around menopause. Nonetheless, there are times when we refer to "women's" experiences with menopause because we are describing older research that did not account for a full range of gender identities in surveyed populations, for example, or because another original source does. Indeed, we recognize that a particular context may require a speaker to talk about "women" and menopause to make themselves understood. Moreover, menopause has been understood as a gendered experience; we recognize that its treatment (and dismissal) by law, culture, and medicine is a reflection of that understanding and even misogyny at times. This book seeks to unpack and remedy the gender bias that drives stigma, shame, stereotypes, and ignorance about menopause. That being said, any such essentialism must necessarily be provisional and tentative. All people should have expanded protections against discrimination on the basis of menopause.

This book reimagines law and society to take into account the biological needs of all people. We invite you to consider the many intersections of menopause and the law in places ranging from the privacy of one's own bedroom to the doctor's office, workplace, and beyond.

# CHAPTER ONE

# PREPARING FOR THE INEVITABLE

In August 2020, former first lady Michelle Obama made headlines on her eponymous podcast when, in frank terms, she described her personal experience with menopause.[1] She recounted having a hot flash on Marine One, just before she had to appear at an event: "Literally, it was like someone put a furnace in my core and turned it on high, and then everything started melting. And I thought, 'Well, this is crazy. I can't, I can't, I can't do this!'" On that episode, Obama and her guest—her friend Dr. Sharon Malone, an obstetrician-gynecologist and leading expert in menopause—had a broad-ranging discussion about menopausal symptoms, the considerations surrounding hormone therapy (which both of them have taken), and how menopause can affect the workplace. Obama reflected:

> There's a lot of stuff that women need to talk about, so some of these cultural norms change, like how you dress [for work], the temperature in the room. . . . What a woman's body is taking her through is important information. It's an important thing to take up space in society, because half of us are going through this, but we're living like it's not happening.[2]

Obama's comment—"we're living like it's not happening"—reflects the silence and stigma that have long surrounded menopause. But the public nature of her statements, and the way in which she encouraged others to talk more openly about menopause, help set the stage for considering how we can transform workplaces, healthcare, and society, given that menopause is an inevitable biological process that is experienced by half the population.[3] This discussion is already beginning to happen, as society moves toward greater awareness of menopause as a significant life transition that can have wide-ranging effects. But there is much to explore, and much that needs to change.

This chapter describes some of the "stuff that women need to talk about," as Obama put it. After providing a basic overview of the biology of menopause, it articulates the three main themes that run throughout this book: (1) the importance of dismantling the stigma and silence around menopause; (2) the need to shift toward a more nuanced understanding of menopause; and (3) the importance of law and legal reforms.

These themes are mutually reinforcing. As stigma and silence around menopause are replaced by improved understanding and recognition of the diversity of menopausal experiences, the law can, and must, play an increasingly important role in ensuring that menopause does not hold people back from participating fully in all aspects of public and private life.

## THE BASIC BIOLOGY OF MENOPAUSE

At the outset of a book on menopause, it is helpful to establish some basic understandings. Although most people have heard of menopause, they may not know precisely what the term itself means. Technically speaking, menopause is the complete cessation of menstruation for one year in someone who previously menstruated. It is measured retrospectively, twelve months after the last menstrual period.[4] In the United States, the average age of menopause in the United States is 51, although there is wide variation.[5] Perimenopause (literally, "around menopause"), also sometimes called the "menopausal transition," typically begins in the mid- to late 40s and generally lasts four years, although it may be shorter or longer.[6] Perimenopause is often marked by a number of symptoms that can vary widely, as described below.

Biologically speaking, menopause results from a decline in the production of two reproductive hormones: estrogen, which promotes reproductive health and plays an important role in ovulation; and progesterone, which helps prepare the uterine lining for a fertilized egg. Due to this declining hormone production, the ovaries eventually stop releasing eggs into the fallopian tubes, and the uterine lining no longer builds up and sheds.[7] When the body produces less estrogen and progesterone, menstruation becomes increasingly unpredictable; not only can cycles become shorter or longer than in the past, with missed periods as well, but bleeding may be lighter or heavier than it had typically been before.[8] As Dr. Jen Gunter, menopause expert and author of *The Menopause Manifesto*, explains: "[M]enopause is puberty in reverse, a transition from one biological phase of ovarian function to another."[9]

Not all instances of menopause result from the natural aging process. Other factors may induce premature or early menopause and the corresponding lack of ovarian function, including the surgical removal of the ovaries as part of treatment for cancer, endometriosis, or fibroids.[10] Furthermore, certain chemicals, like those used in cancer-fighting chemotherapy, can also cause temporary or permanent menopause.[11] Symptoms from surgical or chemical menopause can differ from those of aging-related menopause and, rather than developing over time, the onset may be more sudden.[12]

Perimenopause and menopause should be distinguished from other medical conditions that involve irregular or missed periods. Adolescents, for example, may experience irregular periods in the first few years after beginning to menstruate.[13] Perimenopause and menopause are also distinct from other manifestations of secondary amenorrhea— that is, the cessation of menstruation for at least three months in someone who previously was having menstrual periods.[14] This may occur in people who lose weight rapidly, who suffer from disordered eating, or who exercise excessively.[15] Thus, not all absences of menstruation indicate menopause.

## MENOPAUSE'S MULTIPLE SYMPTOMS

On a taping of *The Drew Barrymore Show* in early 2023, while Barrymore was talking with actors Jennifer Aniston and Adam Sandler, she began to fan herself, took off her jacket, and exclaimed: "I'm so hot . . . I think I'm having my first hot flash!" Barrymore added that she was excited to share this information with Oprah Winfrey; the two had recently discussed hot flashes on a panel with Gayle King, who recalled "dripping, drenching sweats."[16] Barrymore's description of what she was experiencing also echoes Michelle Obama's account of her experience on Marine One, with which this chapter begins.

Vasomotor symptoms (VMS)—more popularly known as hot flashes and night sweats—are probably the most well-known symptoms of the menopausal transition. The descriptions offered by Obama, Barrymore, and King are typical: a sudden feeling of heat, sometimes accompanied by a red, flushed face as well as sweating.[17] Research suggests that up to 75 percent of North Americans who go through perimenopause experience hot flashes during that time, and nearly a quarter of that population discusses them with a clinician.[18] Hot flashes vary in length and intensity, and may occur a few times per week or numerous times each day.[19] Most commonly, hot flashes persist for six months to two years, but approximately 15 percent of women experience the most severe form of hot flashes, which can continue indefinitely.[20]

Although the precise mechanism of hot flashes is not well understood, they are likely connected to hormonal shifts and attempts by the hypothalamus to regulate the body's temperature.[21] Some behaviors, such as smoking, appear to be associated with a higher likelihood of hot flashes; however, researchers have not found a consistent relationship between the occurrence of hot flashes and diet, exercise, or alcohol intake.[22]

Other physical symptoms of perimenopause and menopause can include night sweats (i.e., hot flashes at night), unexpected heavy bleeding (sometimes called "flooding"), headaches, a feeling of electric shocks throughout the body, a sensation of burning in the mouth, tingling extremities, itchy skin, joint pain, muscular stiffness, panic attacks, dizziness, hair loss, weight gain, vaginal dryness, decreased libido, breast tenderness, urinary tract changes, bladder infections, increased risk of osteoporosis, and numerous others. Additionally, heart palpitations can be symptoms for as many as 40 percent of people during perimenopause.[23] In one well-publicized case, MSNBC television anchor Mika Brzezinski described going to the emergency room with intense chest pains, only to be diagnosed with a "perfect storm" of physical exhaustion, a busy work schedule, grief over a recently deceased parent, and menopause.[24] The physical exhaustion that Brzezinski experienced could also have resulted from poor sleep, which is itself a symptom for up to 60 percent of those experiencing menopause.[25] Not getting enough sleep can result in other health issues, including depression.[26]

During the menopausal transition, psychological and cognitive symptoms are also common. Brzezinski, for instance, described having "major brain fog" when on the air during a newscast, an experience that inspired her to call for greater awareness of menopause in the workplace.[27] Along with depression and anxiety, Brzezinski's sensation of "brain fog" is a common symptom of menopause.[28] Indeed, a 2021 study used neurological imaging to conclude that menopause "has pronounced effects on [the] human brain's structure, connectivity, and energy metabolism."[29] The researchers explained that many people going through menopause are vulnerable to "neurological shifts" and may experience "bothersome symptoms as well as a higher risk of depression, anxiety, and [Alzheimer's disease]."[30] The study's ultimate conclusion—headlined as "good news" by the *Wall Street Journal*—was that most women do not have lasting adverse long-term effects from the menopausal transition, given the brain's ability to compensate for changing estrogen levels.[31] As the study's lead author, Weill Cornell neurology professor Lisa Mosconi, put it, "Our study suggests that the brain has the ability to find a new normal after menopause in most women."[32] That said, the researchers' finding that many people going through menopause are vulnerable to cognitive and psychological symptoms, at least for a limited period of time, is significant. It also echoes the findings of researchers that for some, the rapid hormonal flux caused by reproductive transitions like the postpartum and perimenopausal periods can cause or exacerbate anxiety and depression.[33]

The compendium of symptoms described here represents, necessarily, a partial list. Browsing online for "menopausal symptom lists" leads to more than 19 million results, including articles, websites, and other sources describing 12, 34, 40, 42, or even a supposed "full list" of such symptoms.[34] In fact, more than a dozen standardized symptom lists are recognized by the medical profession.[35]

Just as there is an enormous range in defining standard symptoms of menopause, there is also a significant range in the frequency and length of these symptoms. While some people have few menopausal symptoms, others experience symptoms that can be both incapacitating and long-lasting. That said, many people fall somewhere in between.[36] So far, as noted above with respect to hot flashes, scientists do not completely understand why some people experience few, if any, symptoms of menopause, while others suffer from severe menopausal effects.[37]

There is, however, a growing body of work showing that Black Americans tend to experience more symptoms of menopause for longer periods of time and with less symptom relief than their white counterparts.[38] According to the twenty-five-year longitudinal Study of Women's Health Across the Nation (SWAN), which began in 1996, Black women experienced a median age of menopause that was eight-and-a-half months earlier than that for white women, and their symptoms were also more severe.[39] Among the women in the study who reported vasomotor symptoms, white women experienced hot flashes for a median duration of around 6.5 years, Latinas for 8.9 years, and, for Black women, it was 10.1 years.[40]

A separate study found that Native American women are more likely than women in any other racial or ethnic group to experience symptomatic hot flashes and night sweats: in the study of 1,513 women between the ages of 45 and 55, 66.7% of Native American women reported vasomotor symptoms compared to 61.4% of Black women, 58.3% of white women, and 45.5% of Hawaiian/Pacific Islander women (several other categories of symptoms were also broken down by race).[41] By contrast, a 2015 study found that "women of Japanese and Chinese descent had the shortest duration of hot flash symptoms."[42]

As a partial explanation for some of the variation, the SWAN study noted that, at least for some aspects, "racial health disparities could be accounted for by Black-White differences in risk factors that are associated with social disadvantages."[43] This observation alone indicates that, in the end, there is an urgent need for more research on how and why menopause impacts groups differently.

## WHY DOES MENOPAUSE EXIST?

It turns out that relatively few animals experience menopause: killer whales, short-finned pilot whales, and humans. Most other animals can reproduce until death.[44] Although the precise reason for menopause is still speculative, particularly given that male reproductive capacity does not decline nearly as precipitously, scientists and anthropologists suggest that the "grandmother hypothesis" provides a partial explanation. As historian Susan Mattern has explained, this hypothesis posits that older women, who can no longer produce their own children, ensure their genetic legacy by playing a critical role in helping to feed, raise, and nurture their grandchildren.[45] In support of this "grandmother hypothesis," Mattern points to the Hadza, a modern hunter-gatherer tribe in Tanzania. Among these people, the body weight of children and grandchildren varies based on their grandmothers' foraging.[46] Additionally, in many societies, grandmothers can and do serve as experienced babysitters, enabling their children to work and to grow their own families. Menopause may thus have been, in Mattern's view, "a critical component of the success of the species."[47]

On the other hand, some scientists have started to explore how to delay the age of menopause, or even end it altogether.[48] The goal of those who seek to "cancel" menopause is twofold: not only to promote "reproductive longevity," but also to delay age-related problems related to bone loss and cardiac function that may be associated with menopause.[49] This research, however, is still in its early stage; it is unclear when—or if—it may come to fruition. Menopause likely will continue to be a reality for approximately half of the population for many years.

The reality of menopause sets the stage for the book's three themes (discussed in the Introduction) of dissolving the silence and stigma around menopause, recognizing the complexities of the menopausal experience, and connecting menopause to the law.

## DISMANTLING SILENCE AND STIGMA

Silence and stigma around menopause are multilayered and deeply ingrained. This is true even though, as Jen Gunter has observed, "Every single person is on this earth because of the menstrual cycle."[50] One ingredient of this silence and stigma is a general discomfort with frank talk about bodily functions in general, an aversion that is particularly strong regarding the menstrual cycle. Professor Jill Wood has named this the "menstrual concealment imperative," explaining that girls and women often feel compelled to hide their menstruation in order to seem attractive, competent, and in control of their bodies.[51]

For this reason, students consistently express fear of other students, teachers, or administrators learning that they are menstruating. In fact, several studies show that fear of a period leak, either due to difficulty affording menstrual products or just being unprepared, is a significant cause of school absences.[52] The menstrual concealment imperative applies with equal, if not greater, force to menopause, which may come with its own uncontrollable bodily manifestations, including hot flashes or unexpected heavy bleeding. Add to this the particular negativity surrounding menopausal symptoms, which have long been fodder for jokes or caricature in cultural depictions, and self-imposed silences about menopause take on a self-protective hue.

Ageism, too, should be understood as a key factor in menopausal silence and stigma. In 1969, physician Robert Butler defined ageism as an attitude of "deep-seated uneasiness on the part of the young and middle-aged—a personal revulsion to and distaste for growing old."[53] Revealing one's menopause, then, may function as a sort of "tell" that many people want to avoid. Again, menopausal silence can essentially be seen as a form of self-protection.

Ultimately, however, silence around menopause has *not* been protective for those who experience it. The silence not only perpetuates the cultural stigma around menopause, but it also has problematic medical and legal implications. A "State of Menopause Study" released by the healthcare company Bonafide, for instance, found that only 31 percent of women discussed their menopausal symptoms with their healthcare provider and that only around half were even aware that perimenopause is distinct from menopause.[54] Even finding a knowledgeable healthcare provider can be difficult. As Dr. Mary Jane Minkin of the Yale Medical School has explained, "Not only are many women not aware of perimenopause, but unfortunately many physicians aren't aware of it." As a result, she notes, physicians may not think about perimenopause when trying to discern why a patient has missed a few periods and is having trouble sleeping.[55]

The silence also seeps into the law's approach to menopause. For example, federal antidiscrimination law explicitly recognizes pregnancy discrimination as a form of sex discrimination, while saying almost nothing about menopause-based discrimination. The law also provides little guidance on when employers must accommodate menopausal symptoms in the workplace, in stark comparison to the Pregnant Workers Fairness Act, which took effect in June 2023 and requires employers to make reasonable accommodations for pregnant employees. Unfortunately, there is also a dearth of law relating to other key aspects of the menopausal experience, such as privacy-related concerns.

## MOVING TOWARD A NUANCED UNDERSTANDING

As the silence and stigma surrounding menopause begins to crack, it is important to develop a more nuanced understanding of this bodily inevitability. Historically, menopause has been viewed as either a condition requiring medical intervention or—as is becoming increasingly common today—a problem to be mastered through technology, such as tracking apps or special cooling devices. A more nuanced understanding means challenging this reductive framing of menopause as a problematic condition, and examining the failures of outmoded ways of thinking: gaps in scientific knowledge; denial of full agency to those who experience menopause; and failure to account for diversity of all kinds.

Accordingly, a new baseline understanding of menopause is necessary. This will require contextualizing it alongside other reproduction-associated conditions or processes like pregnancy and breastfeeding, as well as life stages like puberty. A nuanced approach to menopause also must recognize the variations in individual and group experiences, while taking account of the broader cultural and medical contexts. To give just one example, one-third of incarcerated women over the age of 45 in U.S. prisons have reported that "menopause is an important health concern." The carceral setting raises unique challenges, from lack of access to care, to the fact women who roll up their sleeves in the midst of a hot flash might be threatened with a sanction for negative conduct.[56] Fully understanding menopause requires accounting for both its universality and its specificity.

## THE ROLE OF LAW

The first two themes—the need to dissolve silence and stigma and the need for a more nuanced understanding of menopause—help bring the final theme, the role of law, into clearer focus. As silence around menopause is replaced by increasing cultural openness and improved understanding, the law can play a significant role in ensuring that menopause does not hold anyone back from full participation in public and private life. For example, those who work through menopause can experience significant challenges, both because of outright menopausal discrimination and because of the lack of accommodation of menopausal symptoms. The law's failure to address these issues has real costs. According to a 2023 Mayo Clinic study, menopause causes an annual loss of workplace productivity in the United States of approximately $1.8 billion, in terms of missed days of work, reduced hours, involuntary or voluntary terminations, and retirement.[57] U.S. law could take a more expansive and proactive approach to menopause in the workplace, which has already been taking shape, for example, in the United Kingdom.

The new marketplace of menopause products and services also raises important questions about the role of law. Digital technology companies that offer services for tracking the menopausal experience typically collect personal information concerning symptoms, prescriptions, doctor visits, and unrelated health conditions. Given the inadequacy of current data privacy laws, we must enact comprehensive legislation on digital privacy to protect people's personal information, not only for menopause but also for other conditions.

To be sure, as the rest of the book addresses, there are complications and obstacles to garnering support for menopause-based reforms, given cultural stereotypes, the medicalization of menopause, the range of menopausal symptoms, and the uneasy fit of menopause into existing legal approaches. Developing appropriate recognition of menopause will require reenvisioning certain aspects of both public health and public policy. The following chapters set out strategies for continuing to break down the silence and stigma surrounding menopause while fully recognizing the complexities of actually experiencing it. These chapters also offer a call to action, encouraging thoughtful and thorough reforms to the legal system to recognize—and center—these issues.

## CHAPTER TWO

# THE DECAYING WOMAN
# VS. LIBERATED LADY

"For two years I didn't sleep well. Never a full night. No peace. Restlessness and heart palpitations were my steady companions at nightfall." This is how Oprah Winfrey, talk show host, actor, and entrepreneur describes her life from ages 48 to 50.[1] As her heart rate reached over 200 beats per minute, she filled her journals with her worries, including "I don't know if I'll make it till the morning."[2] Winfrey consulted multiple doctors, including a cardiologist, but no one could explain what was happening to her. Only when Winfrey came across a book that identified heart palpitations as one of menopause's symptoms did she self-diagnose her menopause transition. She later recounted, "Until that point in my adult life, I don't recall one serious conversation with another woman about what to expect."

But that was just the beginning of Winfrey's menopause transition. After she stopped menstruating completely, Winfrey said she had difficulty concentrating and began to lack interest in activities that she previously enjoyed: "I wasn't prepared to have such difficulty concentrating. Reading, my favorite pastime, became a chore. . . . My whole world dulled down a couple of notches." Only postmenopause, after she began using a prescription estrogen cream, did Winfrey begin to feel like herself again.[3] She has since called menopause a "blessing," saying that menopause represents "your moment to reinvent yourself after years of focusing on the needs of everyone else."[4]

The experience of Oprah Winfrey—not recognizing or being diagnosed with the symptoms of perimenopause, taking a while to feel like "herself" again, and then reinventing herself—is relatively common. Like Winfrey, many people fail to recognize menopause's symptoms, in part because of long-standing cultural expectations of silence and even shame around women's aging. Menopause often is not discussed openly, even among friends. The general lack of education about menopause is not limited to members of the general public, either. As discussed in Chapter 3, many physicians themselves do not receive much education about menopause, so they cannot necessarily guide patients like Winfrey who seek explanations for what is happening to them. Even those healthcare providers who do recognize the symptoms of menopause may face pressure from insurance companies to spend minimal time with patients, limiting their ability to make tailored recommendations for medications or other support. The fact that Oprah Winfrey, despite her celebrity and wealth, encountered obstacles to an accurate diagnosis, suggests that the challenges for everyday people are even greater.[5]

Until relatively recently, in the larger U.S. culture, if menopause was mentioned at all, it was often in furtherance of negative stereotypes or crude jokes about middle-aged women being moody, angry, or perhaps in the throes of a hot flash. This chapter explores cultural and individual attitudes toward menopause, primarily in the United States and the United Kingdom, where many view menopause with fear or dread; the chapter also tracks the phenomenon around the world.

Despite rampant negative cultural views on this topic, at least for some, menopause ultimately comes to represent a new and liberating stage of life, as Oprah Winfrey described. In addition, exploring research about the menopause experience in other countries provides comparative touchstones. Perceptions and portrayals of menopause are important not only in terms of understanding the larger culture, but also because there is evidence suggesting that such perceptions may influence the subjective experience of menopause itself. This chapter shines light on cultural attitudes toward menopause, a variety of individual perceptions and feelings about the menopause transition, the personal and social costs of persistently negative stereotypes about menopause, and the emerging contours of more positive approaches. Negative cultural attitudes and stereotypes are obstacles to meaningful change, particularly because those who experience challenging symptoms may alternately be mocked for being frank about their needs, or suffer in silence in order to avoid negative perceptions.

## PLAYING MENOPAUSE FOR LAUGHS

While treatments for menopause have been advertised in women's magazines since at least the 1930s,[6] one of the earliest mentions of menopause on national television did not come until 1972. During an episode of the popular television sitcom *All in the Family*, Edith Bunker experiences mood swings and hot flashes to the bewilderment of the men in her family. Archie, Edith's impatient and bullying husband, has no sympathy for Edith's condition, and exhorts her, "If you're gonna have the change of life, you gotta do it right now! I'm gonna give you just 30 seconds. Now, c'mon and change!"[7] Edith blithely responds, "Can I finish my soup first?"[8]

This particular episode is now understood as a watershed cultural moment. As one critic has explained, "It was a big deal to see the topic [of menopause] out in the open on television, as menopause was kept hush hush in the public eye. But *All in the Family* took a sledgehammer to that social barrier and the episode will live on forever because of it."[9] The episode of *All in the Family* won several awards and is widely credited as bringing greater awareness of menopause to a large number of American households.[10]

More than a decade after *All in the Family* smashed the menopause taboo on television, the menopause transition was being used as a comedy staple. For example, when the character of Blanche Devereaux on the 1980s sitcom *The Golden Girls* discovers that she is perimenopausal, she laments that her "life is over" and the laugh track kicks in.[11] An entire 1990 episode of the *Cosby Show* centered around Clair Huxtable's manifestations of signs of menopause. After the Huxtable children give voice to every negative stereotype about middle-aged women who are "crabby" and "moody," Clair plays a trick on the family by exaggerating the effects of menopause and pretending to be mentally ill.[12] The strength of the cultural view of menopause symptoms as akin to madness essentially became the foundation for an entire episode of a television sitcom.

Usually, jokes about menopause traffic in stereotypes. On a 2001 episode of the U.K. sitcom *Absolutely Fabulous*, Eddie and Patsy attend a fictional "Menopause Anonymous" meeting at which the other fictional middle-aged female attendees deliver self-deprecating one-liners about the horrors of hot flashes, bladder leakage, disrupted sleep, skin dryness, and hormone treatments.[13] Similar complaints are the common ground over which four women bond in *Menopause: The Musical*, a live theater show, which has traveled to over 500 cities around the globe. The *New York Times* praised the production as "against all odds, actually exhilarating."[14]

Stereotypes about middle-aged women, like those on television and even live theater, seep into advertisements as well. One survey of U.K. women 50 years of age and older revealed that over 40 percent feel "patronized" by advertising; 74 percent believe that advertising is insensitive toward older women. The most common negative media stereotypes, according to the survey, are that middle-aged women are incompetent when it comes to modern technology, frumpy, and mean.[15]

## MORE SERIOUSLY?

In the twenty-first century, some references in popular culture have evolved away from blunt comedic punch lines to more dramatic allusions. In a 2013 episode of the Netflix show *House of Cards*, for example, when a friend notices that Claire Underwood lingers in front of the refrigerator, presumably to cope with a hot flash, the friend tries to initiate a bonding-type conversation. Claire immediately changes the subject, although her doing so may be more indicative of her private, steely nature than any particular stigma around menopause.[16] Similarly, on a 2021 episode of another Netflix show, *Bombay Begums*, viewers see Rami, the CEO of a large bank, leaving a board meeting abruptly. In the next scene, Rami is in the bathroom splashing water on her face and using the hand dryer to lessen sweat stains around her armpits. The viewer is left to assume that the hard-charging, middle-aged executive is experiencing symptoms of menopause, although once again no explanation is given.[17]

Occasionally, menopause is discussed openly and even positively in public or in the media. When Emma Thompson received a drama award in New York, she commented on how grateful she was for her hot flashes on a cold evening.[18] In a 2019 episode of *Fleabag*, the character of 58-year-old Belinda extols the virtues of menopause, saying, "It is horrendous, but then it's magnificent." She explains: "[It's] the most wonderful f-cking thing in the world . . . . [Y]ou're free, no longer a slave, no longer a machine with parts. You're just a person."[19] In 2022, country-pop star Shania Twain, at age 57, posed topless for the cover art of a new song release, explaining that she was not just comfortable doing so, but also "was just so unashamed of my new body, you know, as a woman that is well into my menopause." Twain said that, earlier in her life, she had struggled with issues around her physical appearance and tried to appear less attractive to avoid abuse from her stepfather. As she aged, Twain decided to be "courageous" about the changes in her body.[20]

In the U.K., this commitment to openness undergirds a multiple-season podcast on "Menopause Whilst Black." From the first episode of this podcast developed by Karen Arthur, the function of the show is explained as "[o]pening a well overdue conversation about diversity in menopause."[21] While many examples of older television shows are still streaming—think *The Simpsons*[22] and *The Big Bang Theory*[23]—that play menopause mostly for laughs, some contemporary portrayals are also more nuanced or even affirming.

## THE MEANING OF MENOPAUSE

That menopause is the subject of jokes on television shows is not entirely surprising. While the symptoms of the menopausal transition vary, as discussed in Chapter 1, they tend not to be discussed openly. Menopause has long existed in a fraught cultural position: ubiquitous yet taboo. This "taboo" status largely derives from stigma and shame associated with the aging female body; it has often been perpetuated by men. For example, Sigmund Freud famously said that menopause made women "quarrelsome, vexatious and overbearing, petty and stingy,"[24] while Robert A. Wilson, the author of the 1966 book, *Feminine Forever*, declared that menopause was a "natural plague."[25] Even in the twenty-first century, scientific articles still talk about menopause as "ovarian failure."[26]

In a world that treats inevitable aging as undesirable, that negativity is amplified for women, as they are valued for their attractiveness and sexual availability, both of which function as a rough proxy for their ability to become mothers. Indeed, negative stereotypes about menopause stem in large part from its power as a symbol of the loss of reproductive capacity.[27] A persistent common cultural understanding is that the ability to conceive and carry a child is what makes "women's" bodies different from "men's" bodies. In other words, the paradigmatic female body is "reproductive," and the aberrant female body is not. The existence of the menopausal body, which is, by definition, incapable of reproduction, thus disturbs any seemingly settled distinction between "women" and "men." In turn, menopause gets marked as different, unattractive, and undesirable.[28] Menopause's negative status encourages silence and concealment, or "covering," on the part of those who are experiencing the menopause transition, as there is no need to draw attention to the fact that one's body has aged out of the fertile category.

Indeed, menopause can code women as "past their prime," as broadcaster Don Lemon labeled Republican presidential candidate Nikki Haley in 2023, when Haley was in her early 50s.[29] Lemon added: "A woman is considered to be in her prime in her 20s and 30s and maybe 40s. . . . I'm just saying what the facts are—Google it."[30] Although Lemon did not explicitly refer to menopause, the subtext was obvious: menopausal women are useless, expired, or lacking gravitas, even though male politicians of the same age or even older are considered at the peak of their careers. To be sure, Lemon's description of Haley was immediately called out by colleagues and critics alike as offensive and sexist, and he was terminated from CNN shortly thereafter. But his comments echoed ingrained stereotypes all the same.[31]

Indeed, research indicates that North American cultural attitudes about menopause among college students are persistently negative. In one study, researchers asked both Mexican and U.S. college students to describe menopausal women. The students used words like "bitter," "tense," "old," and "sensitive." Students in both countries associated menopause with terms like "old," "irritable," "angry," "depressed," "having hot flashes," with no noticeable difference in responses based on the students' gender or location.[32]

In another study, researchers presented undergraduate students with a series of vignettes describing middle-aged people by their gender and mood (e.g., "Bert, who is 50 years old, and is feeling calm"). In each description, researchers added information about one of four possible health conditions, so that the fictional character was experiencing arthritis, chronic back pain, high blood pressure, or menopause ("Ann, who is going through menopause, is feeling moody" and "Sally, who is experiencing arthritis, is being temperamental"). After viewing the vignettes, study participants were then asked to estimate the number of times they had seen "midlife men," "midlife women," and "menopausal women" paired with certain mood states. Study participants accurately estimated the number of vignettes involving menopausal women with good moods but uniquely overestimated the number of vignettes involving menopausal women with negative moods, without committing the same errors for midlife men or midlife women who were not described as menopausal.[33] Researchers thus concluded that study participants imputed negative moods to menopausal women in a manner that could not be explained by anything other than stereotypes.

## MENOPAUSE AS LIBERATION

Just as menopause symptoms range from person to person, so do individual perspectives on menopause writ large, particularly with the benefit of hindsight. As noted earlier, Oprah Winfrey ultimately embraced menopause as a time "to reinvent yourself."[34] After Elizabeth Gilbert, the author of *Eat, Pray, Love*, had a hysterectomy and entered menopause, she posted to Facebook a celebratory poem addressed to herself: "Full, and left alone at last with all the parts of yourself that you DO want and that you DO love—which is everything, and all the rest of it."[35] Actress Cynthia Nixon has described menopause as uniquely liberating, saying "the freedom that comes from no longer being fertile is huge."[36]

The experience of menopause can also encourage women to come together in community. One episode of *Inside Amy Schumer* featured an entire skit organized around the age-related freedoms for women of menopausal age. Schumer happens upon a picnic where Tina Fey, Patricia Arquette, and Julia Louis-Dreyfus are celebrating Louis-Dreyfus's "Last F-ckable Day" in her 50s, the day when "the media decides when you finally reach the point when you're not believably fuckable anymore." When Schumer asks whether this is upsetting, Louis-Dreyfus says, "I'm thrilled. Ecstatic. I mean, I don't have to deal with this, maintaining this anymore," gesturing at her body. She then chugs a pint of melted ice cream to the cheers of her friends.[37] This is just one (funny) example of women feeling "freed from societal pressure to live their lives"; in that freedom, some people find "that menopause might not be the negative experience that it presently is for many."[38]

The idea that menopause can be a time of liberation is not just a contemporary one. Nineteenth-century women's rights advocate Elizabeth Cady Stanton famously opined that "the heyday of woman's life is the shady side of fifty."[39] After women have finished having children, Stanton contended, "the vital forces heretofore expended in other ways are garnered in the brain" and women's "thoughts and sentiments flow out in broader channels" as they no longer have to focus as much attention on their families.[40] Indeed, in some traditional cultures, the belief is that women cannot fully become spiritual leaders until menopause, because only then do women keep their "wise blood" inside their bodies.[41]

Between Stanton's celebratory framing and these contemporary liberation-focused narratives are many thoughtful, positive, and often realistic, portrayals of menopause that have coexisted with the stigma, shame, and jokes. That said, frank talk about the real experience of menopause has been a long time coming. For example, although the first edition of the feminist healthcare bible *Our Bodies, Ourselves* did not include a separate chapter on menopause in 1970, the second edition in 1973 did. It approached the topic in a matter-of-fact way, beginning with what menopause is and continuing by exploring symptoms, potential treatments, depression, and sex during menopause.[42]

More than fifteen years later, in 1989, Barbara Raskin published *Hot Flashes*, a best-selling novel that describes female friendship during the menopausal transition. In discussing the title, Raskin explained, "It worked as a symbol, a trigger for hot flashbacks, and a metaphysical reawakening, as well."[43] That same year, the North American Menopause Society was founded—its goal was to provide information to both the public and those working in healthcare.[44] A few years later, in 1992, journalist Barbara Ehrenreich reviewed two menopause-themed books for the *New York Times*. Ehrenreich critiqued one book for treating menopause as a "panicky, weepy episode," and the other for being "too cheery."[45] Based on Ehrenreich's review, one senses that, even as recently as the late twentieth century, there was a profound need for more matter-of-fact treatments of menopause in accessible, popular literature.

## CULTURE-BASED DIFFERENCES IN MENOPAUSE

Culture plays a powerful role in how menopause is both perceived and experienced. A study of over 4,000 women from the United States, Canada, Great Britain, France, Italy, Sweden, Norway, Denmark, and Finland found the greatest prevalence of many postmenopausal symptoms among women in the United Kingdom, United States, and Canada, while Sweden and Italy had the lowest levels of occurrence. The researchers concluded that "there is a core set of symptoms experienced by postmenopausal women in which variations may be influenced by culture."[46] The study's lead author, Dr. Mary Jane Minkin, later elaborated that "[i]n societies where age is more revered and the older woman is the wiser and better woman, menopausal symptoms are significantly less bothersome. . . . Where older is not better, many women equate menopause with old age, and symptoms can be much more devastating."[47]

The fact that culture plays a role in the perceptions and experience of menopause is well illustrated by the results of a 2022 survey conducted by Ipsos, a market research firm. The company asked more than 23,000 adults in 33 countries how comfortable they felt talking about a variety of topics, including menopause. Worldwide, a lower percentage of all adults felt comfortable talking about menopause (53%) than topics like religion (74%), mental health (72%), sexuality (69%), politics (67%), and personal finances (59%).[48] Among women alone, the percentage who felt comfortable talking about menopause was significantly higher (64%), but rates varied dramatically by country.[49] Women reported feeling comfortable talking to friends about menopause at high rates in Great Britain (78%) and Ireland (78%) and at lower rates in Saudi Arabia (52%) and Hungary (28%).[50] Self-assessment as "very knowledgeable" or "fairly knowledgeable" about menopause varied by country, too, with high rates among women in India (75%), Turkey (75%), and the United

Arab Emirates (56%), and the lowest rates in Japan (37%), Malaysia (44%), and China (54%).[51] These statistics clearly suggest relevant cultural differences around menopause, although the study did not suggest reasons for the differences.

Research also suggests cultural variation in terms of which specific menopausal symptoms are considered most problematic. The Decisions at Menopause Study surveyed approximately 300 women experiencing the menopausal transition in four different countries: Lebanon, Morocco, Spain, and the United States. In all four countries, just under half of all participants reported experiencing hot flashes.[52] This was true even in Morocco, which the researchers called the "least medicalized" of the studied countries and where there is no traditional word for "menopause." The consistency in reporting suggests that hot flashes are fairly widespread. Notably, however, hot flashes were ranked as the most bothersome by participants in the United States and Morocco, while weight gain was reported as the most frequent and bothersome symptom in Spain, and emotional symptoms like impatience, nervousness, depression, and anxiety appeared more frequently and were identified as most bothersome in Lebanon.

All of that said, making comparisons across cultures is notoriously difficult. And as historian Susan Mattern cautions, "It's not unusual for studies of menopausal symptoms to get different results even when focusing on the same population." As an example, Mattern points to five studies from Thailand that had widely varying results, finding rates of prevalence of menopause symptoms ranging from 25 to 80 percent.[53] Some of the variations can be explained by difference in methodologies, but not all of them can. Within any particular study, whether a participant takes note of (and then reports) any particular symptoms of menopause may depend on larger cultural expectations for the appearance or behavior of women of perimenopausal or menopausal age. It is human nature to become more aware of symptoms that others have cautioned are problematic or undesirable, as compared to symptoms about which the larger culture has a more neutral attitude. That being said, Mattern reasons that "menopause is best understood as a cultural syndrome."[54] Other researchers agree that the convergence of the reported frequency of menopause symptoms and the subjective assessments of them does suggest that cultural context plays some role in how individuals experience those symptoms.[55]

To be sure, researchers have demonstrated that not all societies have negative views of menopause. One 2001 study of Japanese women and physicians, using research from the early 1980s, suggests that menstruation was "not a very potent symbol" in that country, and that attitudes about menopause were not appreciably negative.[56] Within the studied populations of Japanese women, social scientists documented what they called a "small but significant" difference in symptom reporting: those with elder care responsibilities tended to report more back pain and shoulder stiffness than those without these responsibilities.[57] The study also found that some Japanese physicians claimed that these are the most common symptoms of menopause in Japan, and did not ask patients about their hot flashes, suggesting that the questions that doctors and researchers ask may also play a significant role in what information is gathered.[58] A later cross-cultural study found that the most common symptom of menopause among Japanese women was fatigue, whereas the most common symptom among Chinese women was memory loss, and that Japanese women experienced their symptoms as more severe than Chinese women did.[59] Given the role of culture in determining what any person might notice as a symptom, though, it is difficult to know what reliable conclusions one can draw from comparative studies.[60]

In a survey of women in Taiwan ages 35 to 55, most respondents reported that they viewed menopause positively, as a time for "wisdom and maturation," "a symbol of achievement," or "a time to start enjoying life."[61] In another study, published in 2002, more than 40 percent of postmenopausal Taiwanese women said that they thought menopause did not change women's lives for the worse.[62] This positive attitude has been associated with a high degree of awareness of menopause, a general willingness to receive therapies, and lower reported rates of hot flashes, night sweats, and other symptoms than women in other countries.[63]

Similar positive attitudes toward menopause were observed in a 2004 qualitative study of all women ages 40 to 60 living in the Dhanas village in the city of Chandigarh, India. Almost all (over 94%) of respondents said they welcomed menopause for a variety of reasons, including less worry or bother, fewer restrictions in the clothes they could wear, a feeling of being clean, and the end of concerns about

unwanted pregnancies.[64] In a later study of twenty-eight women in
the state of Haryana, India, who belonged to the lower socioeconomic
strata, qualitative interviews revealed what the authors called three
common "co-occurring narratives." They found that women tended to
view menopause as simultaneously "a normal life transition," a source
of "distress because it's taboo," and a time of "freedom from monthly
distress and societal restriction."[65] Researchers suggested that menopause was normalized, at least in part, because it seemed less important than other significant life events like death of a spouse, marriage of
children, or birth of grandchildren. To the extent that these particular
Indian women experienced menopause-related distress, it was attrib-
utable to difficulties managing perimenopausal bleeding and exclusion
from social or religious events during menstruation. Eventual freedom
from menstrual management and these cultural taboos contributed to
menopause's perception as liberating. Placing this study in its larger cultural context, the researchers noted this was true especially because,
as other studies had found, "Indian women enjoy higher social status
in post-reproductive years due to freedom from the so-called 'pollut-
ing' menstruation and power dynamics."[66] The researchers contrasted
the experience of these study participants, whose menopause-related
distress was due primarily to handling the excessive bleeding of perimenopause and to cultural taboos, with any menopause-related distress
experienced by Western women, whose concerns arose out of being
viewed as less attractive or beyond their prime.[67]

## IDENTITY-BASED DIFFERENCES IN MENOPAUSE IN THE U.S.

Identity-based factors can also affect how menopause is experienced
in the United States. In terms of perceptions and attitudes, key socio-
demographic factors appear to play a role in feelings about one's own
menopause. For example, a large-scale study published in 2021 found
that compared to heterosexual women, lesbian and bisexual women
had "lower levels of regret" about menopause.[68] One possible explanation is that these women may feel freer from the expectation that they
become mothers, so fertility is less of a concern.[69] At the same time, it
is important to note the ways that lesbian women are denied the ability to become parents, whether through rules that prevent them from

fostering or adopting children, or lack of access to reproductive technology.[70] Issues at the intersection of sexuality and menopause are explored further in Chapter 6.

The 2021 study also found that negative feelings about the age-related cessation of menstruation were more common among U.S. women who did not have children than those who did.[71] This relationship between the presence (or absence) of children and negative feelings about menopause resonates with a similar study conducted in 2000 that found that menopause was a "bigger marker event" for single women without children than for women who were currently or previously married and who had children.[72] As one participant in the 2000 study explained, menopause had greater significance for those without children because "you don't have other marker events such as children's births, graduations, bar/bat mitzvahs and marriages, to help you mark important life transitions."[73] This makes intuitive sense: menopause is a visible marker of time passing, of the aging process, and of entering a new life stage.

That same small-scale study also found that African American women were more likely than white women to voice concerns about being able to find a partner after menopause. As one African American woman said, "I just think that . . . there are still men out there [who] want babies and stuff like that and if I was menopausal then they know definitely that I'm not the one. . . . I just hope that with all the changes that I don't lose all my femininity . . . you hear about women growing mustaches and beards." It is difficult to know how generalizable these findings are, though, given the small overall sample size, the fact that women of color represented just one-quarter of the study participants, and the methodological limitations associated with focus groups and interviews (the study's methodology). White women and other women of color in the study sample may have had similar views that were not elicited or captured by the study.[74] In any event, there is a tremendous need for more research on how women of different racial and ethnic subgroups in the United States view menopause.

Symptoms, too, can vary, particularly across race. There are some studies suggesting that Black women are more likely than women of other races to experience hot flashes and less likely to be offered treatment for them.[75] In one such study, Black and Latina women reported more hot flashes and night sweats than white women; their hot flashes tended to occur over a period of 10 years and 9.0 years respectively, compared to 6.5 years for white women.[76] A separate study of 1,513 women ages 45 to 55 showed that indigenous American women are more likely than women in any other racial or ethnic group to experience symptomatic hot flashes and night sweats: 66.7% of Native American women reported vasomotor symptoms compared to 61.4% of Black women, 58.3% of white women, and 45.5% of Hawaiian/Pacific Island women.[77] Based on a longitudinal study of a large cohort of women of different races, researchers have shown that Black women also are more likely than women in other racial groups to undergo hysterectomies, which surgically induce menopause, to treat heavy bleeding.[78]

Finally, Black and Latina women may also experience age-related menopause earlier than white women, although there is conflicting research on this point. According to one study, the average age for menopause for Black women is 49, whereas for Latina and white women it is 51. According to another study, however, there is no measurable racial difference in the average age of menopause.[79]

FRAMING MATTERS

Evidence that culture- and identity-based factors can influence the subjective experience of menopause has two significant implications. First, at least in the U.S. context, in order to fully understand menopause, there needs to be better and more research about how the menopause experience may vary based on identity factors such as race. This research is critical to a more nuanced picture of menopause. A deeper understanding of how these factors impact the presentation, frequency, and intensity of menopause symptoms will facilitate more accurate diagnosis. It will also enable doctors to tailor medical interventions, for patients who want them, to the specific needs of each individual.

A second implication of the culture-symptom connection is the imperative to move beyond the stigma, shame, and silence associated with menopause. As discussed in this chapter, when a person has negative perceptions of menopause, that may affect the ways in which they experience menopausal symptoms. Equally significantly, negative stereotypes ripple well beyond individual perceptions and symptoms, influencing how people—including employers and others in the workplace—deal with others whom they suspect or know are menopausal. At the extreme, such stereotypes can prompt overt harassment or discrimination, as Chapter 4 discusses in more detail with respect to the workplace. However, the difficulties that menopausal women can face at work can be more subtle but just as damaging. For example, stereotypes may cause employers to worry that menopausal employees will be less productive or will seek accommodations. Such concerns, in turn, may consciously or unconsciously influence hiring and promotion decisions. Another area of concern is that, in response to coworkers' or employers' negative perceptions about menopause, menopausal employees may consciously or unconsciously alter their own attitudes or behavior, whether by conforming to that expectation or trying to disguise their menopausal symptoms.[80] The stigma may also influence treatment options. When an employee is reluctant to discuss or minimizes symptoms, or is not properly educated about menopause, this may result in the employee's receiving inappropriate medical treatment, or none at all, when such care may well be warranted, if not necessary.

Understanding menopause as complex and multifaceted ultimately means that menopausal symptoms are not purely medical "problems" that medication will completely eliminate. Menopause is not necessarily or solely a medical condition to be treated or managed, though that is one aspect of it for many. Nor can menopause's symptoms be addressed only through positive psychology or lifestyle changes, though these too can be helpful for some. As menopause loses some of its negative connotations and becomes recognized as a more neutral or even positive and inevitable stage of life, the larger culture is beginning to change as well.

## CHANGING CULTURE

U.S. culture does seem to be moving toward more openness. In April 2023, Oprah Winfrey organized what she billed as an "unguarded conversation" about menopause that was featured on *Oprah Daily* and covered by many media outlets.[81] *USA Today*, for example, hailed that Oprah and her guests "get candid about menopause."[82] Just a few months before, the *New York Times* published an article under the headline "Welcome to the Menopause Gold Rush," noting that "the market is flooding with high-profile, well-funded menopause-related beauty products and telemedicine start-ups, as well as a growing roster of celebrities willing to admit it's happening to them." (Many of these products and services, along with the celebrities selling them, are discussed further in Chapter 7.) The article also suggested the potential for "a big cultural shift to happen."[83]

Indeed, if a 1972 episode of the TV show *All in the Family* represented one cultural marker,[84] a 2023 Superbowl ad may represent another. A commercial by Japan-based Astellas Pharma featured an actor conducting person-on-the-street style interviews in which she asked women (but not men) whether they knew what "VMS" meant. Only after the passersby gave quizzical responses did the interviewer reveal that it stands for vasomotor symptoms—also known as hot flashes and night sweats—associated with menopause.[85] In many ways, the ad was a far-reaching consciousness-raising exercise, bringing conversations about menopause into American living rooms, just as *All in the Family* did more than fifty years before.[86]

Yet if the Astellas ad was groundbreaking, further analysis of the ad also serves as a roadmap of potential complexities on the path toward transforming culture. Calling hot flashes and night sweats "vasomotor symptoms," while medically accurate, contributes to their framing as a uniquely medical problem—to be remedied by a drug offered by a for-profit company—when it is increasingly clear that symptoms of menopause are the product of not only biology, but also much more.

Similarly, the ad's use of a more clinical term for hot flashes reinforces the notion that the common phrase "hot flash" sounds trivial or even embarrassing. Yet by using a formal medical term, the ad marks hot flashes as symptoms to be taken seriously, rather than something to be dismissed.

Finally, the actor-interviewer's sole engagement of cisgender women interviewees might inadvertently contribute to the construction of menopause as a subject that does not concern anyone else, even as it takes the conversation "to the street." In fact, menopause's connections, implications, and importance are far greater. The ability of all people to fully participate in many aspects of public life depends on a more nuanced and widespread understanding of menopause.

# CHAPTER THREE

## MENOPAUSE CURES?

Donna Kendall began taking hormones in 1991 to help with menopausal symptoms that included hot flashes and mood swings. For more than ten years, Kendall took estrogen, progesterone, or a combination pill. When she first started the treatment, Kendall believed the marketing claims that the hormone pills would "be good for Alzheimer's, good for your teeth, good for your heart, colorectal cancer."[1] At her doctor's recommendation, Kendall initially took both Premarin, a mixture of estrogen hormones, and Provera, a synthetic progesterone. After six years, Kendall's doctor then switched her to Prempro, a combination estrogen-progesterone pill that had been approved by the FDA. In 2002, Kendall developed breast cancer. Kendall sued the drug manufacturers, alleging that they had negligently failed to warn her physician about the potential risks of developing breast cancer from using the hormones, and that the drugs either caused or promoted her breast cancer.[2]

In 1997, Connie Barton, a medical office assistant,[3] began taking Prempro at her doctor's recommendation.[4] The doctor prescribed Prempro to help Barton manage menopause-related hot flashes. The manufacturer claimed that the drug, in addition to being effective in addressing hot flashes, provided additional benefits such as protecting against heart disease, bone loss, and Alzheimer's disease, with few adverse impacts.[5] Like Kendall, Barton developed breast cancer after taking Prempro for several years. Barton then sued the drug manufacturer, alleging that the company either knew or should have known that patients who took Prempro had a higher risk of breast cancer, and had failed to warn physicians about this.[6]

After jury trials, both Barton and Kendall won their respective cases. Barton received almost $4 million in compensatory damages and $75 million in punitive damages.[7] A jury granted Kendall $6.3 million in compensatory damages and $28 million in punitive damages. In Kendall's case, some of the jurors later explained the size of the award by saying that the drug companies "had clearly put profits over safety."[8] The manufacturers initially appealed the verdict in Kendall's case, but later withdrew their appeal.[9]

Kendall and Barton are just two of thousands of women who have sued drug companies in connection with the companies' sale and promotion of menopausal hormone therapy (MHT). Such companies have faced more than 10,000 lawsuits and paid millions in damages on the grounds that, as the *Barton* court explained, they "distributed ghostwritten materials, tampered with the medical standard of care, and touted the benefits of unverified off-label uses."[10]

These lawsuits draw attention to the many promises and the downsides of MHT. On the one hand, MHT can provide desperately needed relief for those suffering from menopausal symptoms; indeed, current research suggests that it may be under-prescribed. On the other hand, the ubiquitous, incomplete, and even misleading marketing of MHT has long made the landscape difficult, if not dangerous, for health care providers and their patients to navigate. This tension exists against a larger backdrop of questions about how to conceptualize menopause in the first place. Is menopause a "problem" or "illness" to be treated under a doctor's supervision, or is it an inevitable process that should generally not require intervention? How can menopause be treated effectively? These questions—and their answers—implicate fundamental issues about the health of approximately half the population, along with cultural anxieties about aging and gender roles.

As this chapter illustrates, the history of treatments for menopause has been a twisting road, oftentimes featuring dangerous hairpin turns that have resulted in whiplash. The road includes medical opportunities and medical myopia (if not outright medical misogyny), overreaction to risks, and both overselling and underappreciating potential benefits.[11]

For much of the twentieth century, MHT was touted as a miracle cure that would keep women looking young and, at the same time, prevent them from developing heart disease. By the early 2000s, however, new studies suggested that those who took the hormones might face an increased risk of breast cancer, strokes, heart attacks, and blood clots. The resulting swift backlash created uncertainty for both medical providers and patients about the safety and advisability of MHT. Since then, scientific consensus has moved towards recognition that, under certain conditions, MHT can be used relatively safely, and that an individualized risk-benefit analysis is the most appropriate path forward.

This chapter offers a succinct history of hormone therapies for menopause in the United States, highlights the debates around MHT, and explains the newer guidelines recommending that hormones can be used safely to treat some of the most significant symptoms of menopause. The chapter also places hormonal treatments in context, noting the barriers to, and development of, other nonhormonal treatments for menopause. Underpinning this entire discussion is the past, present, and future role of law in ensuring that medical treatments for menopause are thoroughly researched, well regulated, and safe.

## MEDICAL "DISCOVERY" OF MENOPAUSE

References to the existence of menopause date back to ancient Greek physicians who prescribed "spices, fungi and herbs" for menopausal symptoms.[12] Aristotle himself remarked that "fifty marks the limit of capacity of reproduction in women."[13] Sixteenth-century Italian physician Giovanni Marinello took note of the troublesome physical symptoms that can accompany menopause, observing that "as soon as the period stops, pains arise."[14] The earliest known monograph on menopause was published in 1710; it focused on menopause's negative impact on women's health.[15] A little more than a century later, in the 1820s, French scientist Charles-Pierre-Louis de Gardanne first used the specific term "menopause" to describe the age-related cessation of female reproductive function, although the precise mechanics would not be understood for more than another century.[16]

The so-called godfather of modern menopause was Edward Tilt,[17] a nineteenth-century British physician who published the first

English-language book on menopause in 1857.[18] He sought to establish
menopause as a subject of legitimate medical inquiry—and this meant
diagnosing menopause as a disease.[19] To help with the symptoms of
menopause, a catalog diverse enough to include both "insanity" and
"pale complexions," Tilt suggested treatments ranging from taking chloroform to drinking sherry,[20] and from using camphor to setting leeches.[21]

By the time that the first American menopause book appeared, forty
years after the publication of Tilt's work, attitudes had changed enough
that its author, U.S. physician Andrew Currier, charted a different
approach to menopause. Currier wrote that menopause could be "un-
eventful," and even compared it to indigestion: "Errors of digestion are
certainly as common and as significant as anything that can be associated with the menopause."[22] In fact, the primary gynecology textbooks
during Currier's time barely mentioned menopause.[23] To the extent
that doctors at the turn of the twentieth century addressed menopause
at all, they typically followed Currier's path. They took the view "that
menopause was not in itself a cause for alarm, [but] they nevertheless
conceded that middle age heralded the onset of many illnesses" and
encouraged women to visit their physicians.[24] In other words, menopause was a sign of aging, but also might be analogous to a mild illness.
Nonetheless, there were treatments for menopause ranging from "The
Famous Specific Orange Blossom"[25] to Ovariin, derived from cow ovaries.[26] As a self-help measure, women might be told to add fresh cow
ovaries to their sandwiches.[27] Menopause "cures" were certainly not
ubiquitous, though, nor were they well understood.

## DISCOVERING ESTROGEN

In 1929, Edward Doisy—who subsequently won the 1943 Nobel Prize
in physiology and medicine for a different discovery[28]—and a colleague
identified estrone, a form of naturally occurring estrogen, as a hormone
distinctly involved in female fertility.[29] The discovery of estrone represented a foundational step toward understanding menopause as an
endocrinal condition, or "deficiency" for which replacement estrogen
could serve as a cure.[30] Doisy successfully applied for a patent on an estrogen compound developed from pregnant women's urine.[31] Commercial drug companies, including Abbott Lab and Eli Lilly, subsequently

formulated injectable estrogen preparations.[32] In the early 1930s, a Canadian firm began marketing a commercially produced estrogen pill called Emmenin that was formulated from human placental extracts and could be taken orally.[33] Demand for Emmenin was strong; it was surpassed only when the company subsequently developed a new commercial preparation of conjugated estrogen from pregnant mares' urine: Premarin.[34]

The modern era of hormonal treatment for menopause in the United States began when the Food and Drug Administration (FDA), an agency of the federal government that is empowered to oversee the safe development of pharmaceuticals, first approved the use of synthetic estrogen in the form of diethylstilbestrol (DES) in 1941.[35] DES was one of the first drugs approved by the FDA, which had been established in 1938.[36] While DES was initially used to treat menopause symptoms, it was also subsequently used widely to prevent miscarriages, until studies showed that it was associated with a higher risk for breast cancer and serious birth defects. DES was later linked to cancer and infertility in the children whose mothers had taken the medicine. For these reasons, the United States discontinued the use of DES in 1971; it has not been prescribed since.[37]

One year after the FDA approved DES, the FDA approved Premarin.[38] Premarin is still prescribed today, typically in either tablet or cream form (although it can also be injected). Premarin was intended to treat hot flashes, mood swings, insomnia, and other common symptoms of menopause.[39] In the decade after DES and Premarin were first approved, the medical establishment was largely ambivalent about hormonal treatment for menopause, recommending that it be used as a "short-term palliative for menopause-specific complaints."[40] One prominent physician, Emil Novak, opined in the *American Journal of Obstetrics and Gynecology* that some women might need such treatments, but most would not. Novak cautioned: "[I]t must be remembered that many symptoms frequently observed in menopausal women are not directly due to the endocrine readjustments of this period, but that they are more logically explained as due to environmental and psychogenic factors of one sort or another."[41] Many of Novak's colleagues advised that hormone therapy could be useful in the short term, but they were skeptical about long-term usage to guard against loss of estrogen.[42]

Notwithstanding the medical establishment's lukewarm reception of MHT as an anti-aging antidote, drug companies marketed these hormones directly to physicians and consumers as treatments for the "problem" of menopause, including issues that went beyond hot flashes.[43] Popular magazines were soon filled with ads and stories that portrayed the beneficial impact on menopausal-aged women once they had taken the hormones.[44] For example, a 1940s advertisement for Endocreme, an estrogen-based moisturizer, depicted a blonde-haired woman with an unlined face, and a man behind her, with the question, "How long since he said . . . 'I love you'?" The copy suggested that women could "cheat the years" and obtain "more youthful-looking skin" if they used the cream.[45] A 1960s ad for Premarin that appeared in an obstetrics journal depicted a middle-aged blonde woman facing out at the reader and smiling at—or possibly flirting with—two men; the caption simply urged: "help keep her this way."[46]

Given the spending on drug advertising, it is not surprising that consumers with financial means and access to healthcare began to seek out these drugs—and that physicians began prescribing them. In fact, menopause was sufficiently medicalized by the 1950s that it is estimated that up to one-third of middle-class women of menopausal age were taking either hormones or sedatives as a treatment for menopause.[47] This usage rate suggests that drug companies were quite successful in getting doctors (and their patients) to approach the menopausal body as a problem to be solved through medical interventions. By positioning menopause as a disease that required pharmaceutical intervention, the drug companies were developing for themselves a lucrative and long-term profit center in the bodies of approximately half the population. Significantly, one reason they were able to accomplish this is that their activities went largely unchecked by government regulation.

## MARKETING FEMININITY

Rates of MHT usage continued to increase during the 1960s, with physician-backed promises of "femininity forever."[48] The expansion dates, in large part, to an article published in a relatively obscure medical journal by Robert Wilson, a physician, and Thelma Wilson, his wife and a nurse.[49] They boldly asserted: "[A] man remains a man until the end. The situation with a woman is very different. Her ovaries become *inadequate* relatively early in life."[50] The solution, the Wilsons proclaimed, was estrogen therapy to cure this estrogen deficiency.[51]

Three years later, Robert Wilson published a book with a title that tartly explained his goal: *Feminine Forever.*[52] The book sold over 140,000 copies during its first year, and Wilson's message appeared in magazines ranging from *Science Digest* to *Good Housekeeping.*[53] Wilson proclaimed that menopause was a "tragedy" and a "living decay" that undermined a woman's attractiveness,[54] "destroy[ing a woman's] womanhood during her prime."[55] He pronounced that "a woman's awareness of her own femininity completely suffuses her character and . . . the tragedy of menopause often destroys her character along with her health."[56] And he touted estrogen therapy as the cure. He also claimed that it would prevent cancer: a "misconception concerning hormone therapy is the notion that estrogen predisposes toward cancer. The truth is exactly the opposite."[57]

In many ways, Wilson positioned himself as a friend of women. He suggested that menopause was a treatable chemical deficiency, and that through hormone treatment, "women may share the promise of tomorrow as biological equals of men."[58] At the same time, though, he played into negative stereotypes, calling older women "castrates" who could (and should) be cured.[59] Wilson's message was simultaneously empowering and degrading.

That message was not universally acclaimed by his medical peers. A review in the *Journal of the American Medical Association* said that Wilson's book promised "unattainable benefits from a form of therapy that has been in use a long time," and that in doing so, he was "taking advantage of a most susceptible group of women."[60] Reaction among feminists, meanwhile, was mixed. Some challenged the very premise of MHT, while others welcomed it as addressing symptoms that had long been dismissed or ignored.[61]

For many, the promise of "femininity forever" might have seemed too good to be true, but MHT was aggressively marketed by the drug companies that sought to benefit the most from it.[62] Representatives from the Wyeth company even distributed copies of Wilson's book to doctors' offices nationwide.[63] In fact, it was later revealed that Wyeth, the holder of the patent on the popular MHT drug Premarin, had financially sponsored Wilson's research and book.[64] The marketing campaign had its intended effect; by the mid-1970s, Premarin was the fifth most prescribed drug in the United States, with approximately 28 million women taking some form of MHT.[65]

By the 1990s, Wyeth was using commercials featuring a fictional "Dr. Heartman," who, garbed in a white coat, discussed connections between menopause and illnesses such as Alzheimer's disease. Dr. Heartman advised the public to talk to a doctor about how they could protect their health.[66] In 1992 alone, Wyeth spent more than $9 million for Premarin advertising in women's magazines. Another company spent $4.7 million marketing a competitor Estraderm patch: "Now the change of life doesn't have to change yours."[67]

## STUDYING MHT

While there was little dispute that MHT relieved symptoms for many people, there were questions about both its risks and its potential to treat other conditions. On the risks, scientists had been concerned about a potential link between estrogen and cancer since shortly after the isolation of estrone in the 1930s.[68] Part of the problem in studying the impact of MHT, however, was women's historical underrepresentation in clinical trials generally.[69] In 1977, for example, the FDA issued guidelines excluding women of childbearing capacity from participating in any clinical trials at their early stages because of fears concerning potential harmful effects to a fetus. Only in 1993 did Congress require that women be included in clinical trials that were funded by the National Institutes of Health, and, in 1994, it mandated that the FDA establish an Office of Women's Health to promote gender equity in health understanding.[70]

Prior to that time, there had been some efforts to examine MHT's impact. When two 1975 studies documented a connection between endometrial cancer and estrogen therapy, the FDA decided to take action.[71] In response to its 1976 request for comments on a proposed rule to require a package insert for all estrogen products, the FDA received almost 400 responses. The comments ranged from hostility to strong support.[72] The final FDA rule required manufacturers to supply, and pharmacists to deliver, information on the uses, risk, and side effects of estrogen.[73]

Both the FDA warning labels and emerging new research on the link between MHT and cancer appear to have had some impact, as the number of prescriptions for MHT declined from 30 million in 1975 to 15 million in the early 1980s.[74]

Nevertheless, prescriptions for MHT rebounded over the following decade and a half, around the time that Donna Kendall and Connie Barton, whose stories introduce this chapter, began taking MHT. Like millions of women, Kendall and Barton sought effective hormone treatments for menopausal symptoms like hot flashes.[75] Around this time, as more researchers studied MHT, they began to uncover its further potential benefits beyond the treatment of the symptoms of menopause.[76] Scientific studies suggested, for example, that hormone treatment played a positive role in preventing hip fractures and coronary heart disease.[77] As a result, in 1984, the FDA's advisory committee on fertility and maternal health drugs voted to recommend estrogen to prevent the development of, and to treat, osteoporosis.[78] The FDA did not, however, recommend MHT for reducing the risk of heart disease; indeed, the research on this issue has consistently been mixed, as discussed below.[79]

Drug manufacturers were quick to critique any negative studies and capitalize on any positive ones to spread the message that MHT was effective as more than just a treatment for menopausal symptoms. They actively claimed that it had broad benefits for women's postmenopausal health.[80] For example, Wyeth developed extensive campaigns to market Premarin in the 1980s and 1990s, even hiring ghostwriters to prepare materials that touted the benefits of MHT while minimizing its risks.[81] Its "educational" campaigns claimed that using Premarin could reduce the risks of osteoporosis and heart disease without increasing those of stroke or cancer.[82] By 1992, Premarin was the most frequently prescribed drug in the United States.[83] Estrogen replacement therapy, as a prescription to prevent heart disease, is an example of what two scholars have called "technology adoption catalyzed by industry promotional efforts, absent good scientific evidence."[84] Another glaring absence was, of course, significant government oversight regarding drug companies' activities in this area.

Wyeth's commitment to marketing its drugs was so strong that it even began using celebrities in its campaigns to drum up interest in MHT

among physicians and members of the public.[85] For example, Patti La-
belle "was an official Prempro spokesperson, promoting the drug in
television advertisements in which she sang of her 'new attitude.'"[86]
The company also actively courted women who were hesitant to use
MHT, and particularly sought to increase the rate of uptake among
Black women, a population that had lower rates of utilization of MHT
than members of other racial groups.[87] It is difficult to know whether
this aggressive marketing played any role in the FDA's 1995 approval of
the Wyeth drug Prempro, a pill that combined estrogen with progestin
(synthetic progesterone).[88] But by the late 1990s, a survey of gynecologists, family physicians, and internists found strongly favorable attitudes toward the use of long-term hormonal therapy for aging women.[89]
By 2002, doctors were writing 90 million MHT prescriptions a year.[90]

CONTINUED CONCERNS

The scientific evidence for this widespread use of MHT, however, re-
mained mixed. In 1998, the findings of a large-scale randomized,
placebo-controlled and double-blind study known as the Heart and
Estrogen/progestin Replacement Study (HERS) were released.[91] The
HERS study, coordinated by researchers at the University of California,
San Francisco, and funded by Wyeth, showed that not only did MHT
fail to protect against heart disease, but women who had received the
experimental drug had almost three times the risk of a blood clot as the
placebo group.[92]

By the time the HERS study's results were released, the National
Heart, Lung, and Blood Institute had already initiated a long-term national study of postmenopausal women that focused on strategies to prevent various diseases, ranging from breast cancer to heart disease. The
launch of this study, known as the Women's Health Initiative (WHI),[93]
was announced by Bernadine Healy, the first woman to head the National Institutes of Health, at a congressional hearing in 1991.[94] Investigators recruited more than 161,000 women for the WHI study, with
68,000 in the clinical trial and more than 93,000 in the control group.[95]
The study also sought to include people from different racial and ethnic
groups, and, although it enrolled women between the ages of 50 and 79,
the mean age was 63.[96] Its clinical trial placed women into three groups.

One group, which included women with a uterus, took a combination of estrogen and progestin; the second group, which included women without a uterus, took estrogen alone; and the third group received a placebo.[97]

The WHI study, which began recruiting participants in 1993, was supposed to be a fifteen-year clinical trial.[98] However, the arm of the study in which women received an estrogen/progesterone combination was stopped prematurely in 2002, due to concerning evidence that the risks to the women participating in the study exceeded the benefits.[99] Those taking the popular combination of estrogen and progestin for menopausal symptoms, the WHI study found, "had an increased risk for breast cancer, heart disease, stroke, blood clots, and urinary incontinence."[100] (The portion of the study involving women taking solely estrogen also ended prematurely, in 2004, because of concerns about an increased risk of stroke.[101])

Reaction to the WHI study's early conclusions about the combined therapy was swift and negative for MHT.[102] It "blew apart the widely-held belief that hormone replacement therapy protected women from heart disease and other chronic ills."[103] For the executive director of the North American Menopause Society, Dr. Wulf Utian, the 2002 announcement was "the biggest bombshell that ever hit in my 30-something years in the menopause area."[104] A clinical professor of obstetrics and gynecology at Yale, Dr. Mary Jane Minkin, similarly describes the moment when she learned about the study as one of the most memorable of her life; indeed, she groups it with remembering where she was when she learned that John F. Kennedy had been shot and when she heard about the terrorist attacks of 9/11.[105]

The news that the study had been halted—and the reasons for its sudden cessation—caused the number of women who used MHT for relief of menopausal symptoms to drop quickly by almost 50 percent.[106] An editorial in the Cleveland Clinic's *Journal of Medicine*, issued shortly after the study's halt, proclaimed that the "ground rules" for prescribing MHT had changed, while also noting that some types of hormone therapy might still be useful for managing symptoms of menopause.[107] And an American College of Obstetricians and Gynecologists task force, chaired by Harvard's Isaac Schiff, carefully summarized the risks and benefits.[108] That was in accord with the WHI study itself, which was not intended to evaluate MHT's usefulness in managing symptoms of menopause, but rather to investigate the role of hormonal therapies in reducing fractures, breast and colorectal cancer, and heart disease.[109] The FDA issued new indications for prescribing hormone therapy and other warnings, emphasizing that hormonal therapy had not been approved for the prevention of heart disease.[110]

No doubt spurred by the halting of the WHI study, approximately 10,000 lawsuits—including those of Connie Barton and Donna Kendall—were filed in the United States and in Canada against the drug manufacturers of MHT.[111] These lawsuits asserted claims of negligence, strict liability, breach of warranty, fraud, and more; there were also some specific claims under states' consumer protection laws.[112] For the most part, as was true for Kendall and Barton, the cases focused on MHT's possible connection to breast cancer, although there were other claims as well.[113] By mid-2012, the pharmaceutical company Pfizer had settled (or was in the process of settling) 60 percent of the lawsuits (or approximately 6,000 of them). Pfizer had already been found responsible for $896 million, and it had earmarked $330 million for future settlement costs.[114]

## CONTEMPORARY PERSPECTIVES ON MHT

Subsequent scientific analysis of the WHI data indicates that the early publicity in connection with the study's sudden halting overstated the risks of MHT, particularly for women in their 50s. As noted earlier, the WHI enrolled postmenopausal women, with an average study participant age of 63. Its goal was not to focus on how to relieve menopausal symptoms, but on the effect of MHT on heart disease, bone fractures, and cancer.[115] Dr. Jennifer Gunter, the gynecologist author of *The Menopause Manifesto*, has counseled: "The WHI data shouldn't have been extrapolated to all women." She explains, for instance, that "[c]ardiovascular disease increases significantly with age, so two-thirds of the women in the WHI who were 60 years or older were already at higher risk for estrogen-related heart complications. The risk of estrogen on the heart may not be the same for women who start MHT at a younger age."[116]

This failure to segment the risk, and the resulting "one-size-fits-all" message, unfortunately overshadowed the benefits that MHT can have in treating menopausal symptoms. Subsequent clinical trials have shown that MHT is of relatively low risk for younger, recently menopausal women, but that clinicians are reluctant to prescribe it.[117] That is still true, even though, as one of the WHI researchers wrote in 2023, MHT "is the most efficacious treatment for reducing menopausal vasomotor symptoms," such as hot flashes and night sweats.[118] For vaginal dryness, low-dose estrogen in the form of vaginal inserts or rings is also effective and safe when prescribed correctly, the authors noted. This vaginal estrogen can also be used to treat urinary symptoms; systemic estrogen, which contains higher levels of estrogen, can be used for hot flashes and other symptoms. Both require a prescription in the United States, although vaginal estrogen is considered safe enough in the United Kingdom to be available without one.[119]

In a 27-page position statement on hormonal therapy, issued in 2022, the North American Menopause Society (which changed its name to The Menopause Society in 2023) notes the importance of analyzing the risks and benefits of each type of therapy for the various symptoms of menopause.[120] The recommendations differ depending on whether women are under the age of 60 or within ten years of the onset of menopause. For such women, MHT can be particularly helpful in terms of reducing bone loss and vasomotor symptoms (hot flashes and night sweats).[121] Moreover, MHT has other health benefits, including preventing osteoporosis and reducing the risk of onset of type 2 diabetes.[122]

Further, for those experiencing early menopause, MHT can also be a recommended treatment to help with the impact of lost hormones, including the risk of developing osteoporosis.[123] Under a heading on its web page entitled "The Experts Do Agree About Hormone Therapy," The Menopause Society states that "most" people who have recently experienced menopause and are healthy can use MHT, although it also notes the risks of MHT, particularly with long-term use. It concludes that "[h]ormone therapy is an acceptable option for the relatively young (up to age 59 or within 10 years of menopause) and healthy women who are bothered by moderate to severe menopausal symptoms," concluding that "individualization is key in the decision."[124] In a widely read 2023 article for the *New York Times Magazine*, Susan Dominus reached a similar conclusion, contextualizing the risks of MHT as follows: "A woman's risk of having breast cancer between the ages of 50 and 60 is around 2.33 percent. Increasing that risk by 26 percent [the estimated risk of MHT] would mean elevating it to 2.94 percent. (Smoking, by contrast, increases cancer risk by 2,600 percent.)"[125]

These conclusions echo a 2019 editorial in the *Canadian Journal of Obstetrics and Gynecology*, which observed that "the pendulum has swung back in favour of hormonal replacement therapy for most symptomatic newly menopausal women."[126] In fact, Gunter herself—who has been hailed as an important social champion for "normalizing menopause"—uses an estrogen patch for relief of her menopausal symptoms. As is true for half of women, she has found that it cures vaginal dryness and helps with other symptoms.[127]

Like Gunter, approximately 4 percent of women in the United States take some form of MHT each year.[128] Compare that to the almost one-half of postmenopausal women who reported ever using some type of MHT, with 22 percent reporting "current" usage in a study from 1988 to 1994.[129] Indeed, there is certainly an argument that MHT is currently *under*-prescribed—and, at the very least, it seems clear that there is insufficient information for people to make the type of individualized cost-benefit assessment that is called for here. There are several reasons for this. In addition to the widespread fear prompted by the early WHI results, many physicians may simply not have the knowledge—or the time—for the detailed discussions necessary to prescribe MHT.[130]

The abrupt halt of the WHI study in the early 2000s meant that, in the years that followed, there was scant discussion of MHT in medical education. Less than 15 percent of medical residents specializing in obstetrics and gynecology reported that they felt either very well prepared, or even adequately prepared, to manage a patient experiencing menopause, according to a study published in 2019.[131] There also continues to be a lack of clarity about the appropriate length of time for taking MHT, given that "MHT allows women to bypass [. . .] extreme hormone fluctuations and step back in, as it were, after they have passed."[132] Research suggests that half of those who discontinue MHT may experience the reappearance of menopausal symptoms and that low and ongoing doses may help prevent osteoporosis, but that there remain risks of long-term use.[133] The recommendation, again, is individualized determinations.

There is a societal expectation that neither one's menopausal symptoms, nor the care one receives, should be discussed among friends or family, let alone in public. That silence and stigma have contributed to not only a lack of knowledge about menopause and its potential treatments, but also inadequate scientific funding for research into the safety and efficacy of various menopause treatments. That said, medical schools and hospitals are now recognizing and responding to the need for better menopause care. Among other initiatives, Harvard's teaching hospital, Brigham and Women's, opened its Menopause and Midlife Clinic, a department in the Fish Center for Women's Health, in 2020. UCLA Health opened its Comprehensive Menopause Care program in 2023. And Johns Hopkins provides its residents with detailed menopause training.[134] Congress has also been considering legislation to identify gaps in existing menopause studies and to promote further research.[135]

Because drug companies have a financial interest in defining menopause as a medical problem to be solved, the focus on profitable (patentable) forms of estrogen and progesterone therapies likely will continue. Yet, as this chapter has explained, there is a developing consensus on MHT's safety, so long as MHT is prescribed within certain guardrails, including careful monitoring, starting with the lowest possible dose, using MHT for a limited duration, and paying close attention to the age at which treatment begins. It also important to recognize the growing menu of treatment options. For some, bioidentical, or plant-based, hormone treatments provide some relief from menopause symptoms, although they are under-studied. Other approaches, ranging from cognitive behavioral therapy to antidepressants, can also be helpful, and are especially critical for those for whom MHT may be contraindicated.[136] Indeed, the antidepressant paroxetine has been approved since 2013 to treat VMS. New treatments are also appearing, ranging from alternative forms of estrogen to nonhormonal drugs, an example of which is fezolinetant (brand name Veozah), which works on brain cells to reduce the severity of hot flashes.[137] Because it is nonhormonal, fezolinetant is also helpful for those in older age groups who face increased risk when starting hormonal therapy. When fezolinetant was approved in May 2023, it was hailed as "groundbreaking and long overdue."[138] But it was also very expensive, as is often true when new drugs first appear. With more attention on menopause, even more treatments are likely to emerge and to become more accessible.

Ultimately, while this chapter has focused on the history of treatment for menopausal symptoms—thus foregrounding the medical model of menopause—it is important to contextualize the preceding discussion with the broader themes of this book. Menopause is an inevitable part of the aging process for half of the population, and it is experienced differently by each person, in connection with a wide variety of factors. Some people experience no negative physical effects at all from menopause.[139] Some may never need or want to consider any type of hormonal therapy. These varied experiences point toward the need for greater scientific research into menopause—which can benefit everyone—and the equally important imperative to emphasize individual agency, multiple perspectives, and self-determination.[140]

# CHAPTER FOUR

# MENOPAUSE AT WORK

On July 29, 2009, Georgia Sipple quit her job. It was not the outcome that she had wanted. She loved her work as a food product demonstrator in a retail store.[1] But Sipple had begun to experience intense menopausal hot flashes that were exacerbated by her employer's required dress code: a long-sleeve shirt, long pants, closed-toe shoes, an apron or lab coat, and a baseball cap. She sought an accommodation, submitting a doctor's note that explained that she was experiencing "menopausal hot flashes."[2] The doctor put it plainly: "Please allow her to modify the dress code with short sleeves, knee high skirt or pants and a hairnet with or without a visor. . . . These changes would minimize her symptoms allowing her to keep working." Her employer, however, said no. It concluded that menopause was not covered by the Americans with Disabilities Act, and that the dress code stemmed from health concerns, safety concerns, and the contract with the retail store to which Sipple was assigned.[3] When the HR manager told Sipple that her request was being denied, Sipple responded in surprise: "I'm not resigning but I can't do what you're asking."[4] Nine days later, Sipple emailed her supervisor, saying that she perceived that she was being forced out: "I wore the full dress code uniform last Friday and Sunday, and I came home sick both days from too much heat. I will no longer be able to come back to work."[5]

Shortly thereafter, Sipple sued her employer, claiming disability discrimination. But her case was dismissed, largely because the court agreed that her employer was not legally required to accommodate her. "This Court is not willing to recognize menopause as a disability per se. Menopause is a natural progression over time, like gradually losing one's keen sense of vision or hearing," the court wrote in its 2011 opinion. "It is an inevitable part of the human condition for women."[6]

Since the 2011 decision in Sipple's case, much has changed in the cultural landscape. As earlier chapters have described, menopause has become much more salient in public discourse,[7] and new scientific research is yielding a more nuanced understanding of menopausal symptoms and treatments. There is even growing awareness of how menopause can drive people from the workplace. In particular, a 2023 Mayo Clinic study estimated that the cost associated with lost work productivity due to menopausal symptoms (measured by missed days from work, hours cut back at work, being laid off or fired, and quitting or retiring) in the United States is approximately $1.8 billion annually.[8] Shortly after that study was released, Bank of America—in partnership with the National Menopause Foundation—released a report entitled *Break Through the Stigma: Menopause in the Workplace*, which surveyed 2,000 female employees and 500 human resources benefits managers about the impact of menopause at work.[9] Among other things, the study found that 51 percent of peri- and postmenopausal employees felt that menopause had had "at least a slight negative impact on their work life."

But so far, this increased attention to menopause has yielded no legal changes in laws that govern workplaces in the United States. If Sipple were in the same predicament today, perhaps the growing sociocultural awareness of menopause would prompt her employer to be more accommodating. If her employer chose otherwise, though, Sipple's path to legal recourse would be just as murky.

The failure of the U.S. legal system to address menopause-related issues in the workplace sits in the shadow of long-standing laws aimed at preventing sex, age, and disability discrimination in the workplace. Although menopause sits at the intersection of these three issues, it has long fallen into a legal void. This chapter begins by unpacking the challenges that menopausal employees can face at work, and then explores how employment discrimination law addresses those issues. As the chapter shows, U.S. law's inadequacy regarding menopause is itself a contributor to the lost work productivity highlighted by the Mayo

Clinic study. If, for instance, Georgia Sipple's employer had been legally required to modify the dress code to accommodate her hot flashes, she would not have needed to quit.

Although most of the chapter focuses on current U.S. law, it also includes a discussion of the United Kingdom's emerging approach to menopause in the workplace. The U.K. has increasingly come to see menopause as raising legal issues, and a growing body of U.K. case law shows how existing antidiscrimination laws can be interpreted to better protect against menopausal discrimination. The chapter thus concludes with a look at what the U.K. example suggests for potential future directions in the law in the United States and around the world.


## PHYSICAL SYMPTOMS AT WORK

Georgia Sipple's case represents just one employee's experience with menopause, but numerous studies suggest that she was far from alone in finding that hot flashes interfered with her work. In a 2020 U.K. study of approximately 1,000 perimenopausal, menopausal, and postmenopausal women, more than one-third described hot flashes as problematic at work, particularly when working in hot or unventilated spaces or in formal meetings.[10] Similarly, a large U.S. study using data from Fortune 500 companies from 1999 to 2011 found that women with hot flashes had significant work productivity loss, largely because of absenteeism.[11] Notably, a literature review published in 2021 found a distinction between job types, observing that menopause's impact differed between women who were formally employed and women in "casual," informal, or precarious positions. While menopausal symptoms affected both groups' work experiences, for "women in casual work, musculoskeletal symptoms of joint and muscle stiffness, aches, and pains, particularly in the legs, back, shoulders and neck, were the commonest and worst symptoms" of menopause, especially among those whose work featured "a strong manual or menial component." By contrast, "for employed women, hot flushes were slightly or significantly more prevalent" symptoms of menopause.[12]

The effects of hot flashes, in particular, show up not only in external measures of workplace productivity, but also in employees' self-assessments of their own work performance. One study of approximately

2,000 Australian women aged 40 to 65, for instance, found that having any vasomotor symptoms caused significant reductions in self-reported levels of workplace ability.[13]

The unpredictability of hot flashes is part of what makes them so challenging in the workplace. Baroness Sayeeda Warsi, a member of the U.K. House of Lords, has reflected: "I used to dread sitting in a meeting and thinking, 'God I'm going to burst into sweats, and this is really uncomfortable and it's probably visible on my face as well.' Oddly, the more you worry about it, the worse it gets."[14]

In addition to hot flashes, another unpredictable physical symptom of perimenopause that can negatively affect work is sudden heavy bleeding. In the 2020 U.K. study cited earlier, over 20 percent of the approximately 1,000 women surveyed described this issue, sometimes called "flooding," as problematic at work.[15] Such bleeding has even resulted in people getting fired. In one case, a Georgia call center employee, Alisha Coleman, experienced two instances of sudden heavy menstrual bleeding due to perimenopause.[16] The first time, she bled onto a chair. She was warned that if it happened again, she would lose her job, and she took extra precautions to try to prevent a reoccurrence. But the following year, Coleman stood up to walk to the bathroom, and blood leaked onto the carpet. She immediately cleaned the stain with bleach and disinfectant, and the incident in no way affected her actual job duties at the call center. Even so, she was fired for failing to "practice high standards of personal hygiene and maintain a clean, neat appearance while on duty."[17] Like Sipple, Coleman sued, but lost.

Sleep disturbances are a third common menopausal symptom with workplace implications.[18] In one study of nearly 2,500 women across the United States, researchers found that "new-onset sleep disturbances in midlife women" were associated with job loss and a reduction in hours worked, amounting to an estimated annual loss in productivity of $517 to $524 per woman, totaling $2.2 billion in the aggregate. This is consistent with a 2009 U.S. study of members of the National Association for Female Executives, which found that "insomnia was deemed the most problematic menopausal symptom, greatly affecting some women's daily lives by causing them to have a more difficult time carrying out daily tasks, creating more fatigue and irritability, . . . and preventing them from doing their jobs effectively."[19]

Pippa Marriott, a U.K. teacher who ultimately left her full-time teaching job due to menopausal symptoms, later recalled the central role of sleep disruptions in her decision to leave work. "I'd be waking up—often eight times a night—and lying there completely awake.'" she recounted. Marriott elaborated:

> The effects of sleep deprivation started leaking into my day—leaking in in terms of someone coming to my office for a meeting and me saying, 'Great, lovely to see you, sit down,' while thinking, I have no memory of booking this meeting! . . . Once I knew that my brain could forget I'd booked a meeting with someone, I lost confidence in my ability to retain all the masses of information I should have had at my fingertips.[20]

## COGNITIVE/PSYCHOLOGICAL SYMPTOMS

As Marriott's account underscores, menopause often causes not only physical symptoms like hot flashes, unexpected bleeding, and sleep disturbances, but also emotional, mental, psychological, and/or cognitive symptoms. These can include mood changes, depression, anxiety, irritability, forgetfulness, diminished concentration, and so-called brain fog. As Chapter 1 describes, neurological research confirms that menopause is not just a reproductive transition state, but also a "neurological transition."[21] For most, the brain ultimately finds a "new normal," but in the meantime, these symptoms can significantly affect work.

Indeed, research suggests that emotional and mental symptoms of menopause can be even more disruptive to workplace functioning than physical symptoms, particularly for salaried (as opposed to more contingent or casual) employees. A U.K. study examining the effects of early-onset menopause (before age 45) found that women's employment rates fell as their number of menopausal symptoms increased, while recognizing that "different types of menopause symptoms have different employment effects."[22] Hot flashes, the researchers found, "do not typically cause employees to leave work until they become 'bothersome.'" By contrast, "psychological health problems associated with menopause"— which the researchers defined as anxiety/depression, tearfulness, panic, forgetfulness, palpitations, and irritability—significantly lower

total employment and full-time employment rates, even when the employees do not report those psychological symptoms as "bothersome."[23]
The effect is even stronger when the psychological symptoms *are* reported as bothersome.

These findings are particularly important in light of the prevalence
of such symptoms. The U.S. study of the National Association of Female
Executives, for example, found that 79% of the women reported at least
some "emotional/mental symptoms (forgetfulness/diminished concentration, irritability, mood changes, and anxiety)."[24] A study of approximately 600 Japanese working women aged 45 to 65 similarly found that
82.5% reported experiencing psychological symptoms of menopause
(with 62.5% specifically reporting anxiety and 79.5% reporting depression).[25] Not surprisingly, the researchers again found that the more
severe the symptoms, the greater the reduction in work performance.

Firsthand accounts of menopause highlight the multiple ways that
cognitive or psychological symptoms can interfere with work. For example, one professor, Tania, told researchers in an Edinburgh study,
"I'm finding menopause means I'm more reactive, I'm more tired, I'm
less resilient and I'm more vulnerable."[26] Janelle Delaney, a partner at
IBM, noted that the start of her menopausal symptoms coincided with
the start of her interview process for partnership. "I was in the middle
of my preparation—which is, obviously, a stressful situation, because
it's something that I had been working towards for almost 30 years," she
recalled. "And I just fell apart—I was crying something like 10 times a
day."[27] She saw a doctor, who explained that she had entered perimenopause, but that just raised the question of what to do next. "For me, it
was like, well, what do I do? Do I tell somebody at work? Do I say to
them, 'Look, I'm sorry, but I might cry in this panel. And it's not that
I'm not ready for an executive role, it's just that my hormones have gone
crazy'?" Ultimately, Delaney reached out to a colleague who helped her
prepare for the interview, and she made partner.[28]

## HARASSMENT

Unfortunately for many workers, not all colleagues are as supportive as
Janelle Delaney's IBM colleague. On top of the internal challenges posed
by menopausal symptoms, employees sometimes have to contend with

an added external stressor: harassment. This workplace harassment can take multiple forms, from "jokes" to outright hostility to worse.

A common occurrence involves using the *concept* of menopause—and especially hot flashes—as a way of demeaning women (whether they are menopausal or not) at work. "You're not getting menopause, I hope," said the plaintiff's attorney to the defendant's attorney at one deposition, when she remarked that the room had become hot.[29] In another case, a dentist alleged that when her male dentist colleague indicated that he felt hot, their supervisor first joked to him, "Are you going through menopause?" then turned to her and said, "Right? You would understand that, right?"[30] Jackie Dault, a nurse at a Georgia urology clinic, faced an even more extreme version of this phenomenon; the urologist with whom she worked not only made negative comments about her appearance and age, but purposely turned the operating room thermostat to 80 degrees to try to induce a hot flash or at least make her sweat.[31]

In addition to hot flashes, the supposedly moody nature of menopausal women is a source of material for harassment. One plaintiff's lawsuit described how her supervisor asked her whether her "negativity was caused by menopause."[32] In another, a supervisor told his administrative assistant: "If your problem is PMS or in your case menopause, get on some meds!"[33] Similarly, when Vanessa Bailey, a clerk for the United States Postal Service, complained to her supervisors that her colleagues were harassing her, one supervisor advised another not to intervene because the situation involved "just some black women going through menopause."[34]

The menopausal symptoms and stereotypes of hot flashes, moodiness, and forgetfulness were all deployed together in the harassment inflicted on Deloris Paigo, a title clerk at a car dealership. When Paigo's colleagues learned that she was perimenopausal, they started making demeaning comments about her on a daily basis, including asking her whether "we [were] having any hot flashes today," commenting that Paigo was an "old lady" and getting "senile," and calling her an "old fat bag."[35] In her subsequent lawsuit for workplace harassment, Paigo described the emotional and physical toll these comments took on her: she became depressed, felt nauseous, broke out in hives, cried often, and dreaded going to work. Indeed, what can be so upsetting about menopausal harassment is that its themes—for example, symptoms like hot

flashes—center on genuine symptoms of menopause for many employees. This makes it harder to just ignore or brush off hurtful comments.

Indeed, research indicates that the workplace can be a significant
source of stress for menopausal women. And this workplace stress can
itself exacerbate menopausal symptoms. A 2020 survey of approximately 1,500 American women aged 35 to 55 found that, of the various
common stressors (work, partner relationships, family relationships,
other relationships, financial concerns, health, and overcommitment),
the median ratings of stress were *highest* for work.[36] Moreover, in a study
of 839 "midlife to older women" working in Australia, researchers found
that "work-related stressors were significantly associated with menopausal symptom reporting."[37] This suggests that menopausal symptoms
and the workplace environment interact with and reinforce each other.

On the positive side, the same study also found that greater supervisor support was associated with lower symptom reporting, noting
the importance of "feeling valued and understood by line managers."[38]
These findings track qualitative findings from U.K. researchers, who in
2017 spoke to 137 working women aged 45 to 65 about how they thought
employers should handle menopause. A common refrain was the importance of supportive, sensitive leadership—as opposed to, as one woman
put it, "not find[ing] it a joke amongst the male colleagues to refer to
the older women as having menopausal issues and the like."[39] Another
woman added that supervisors should behave "respectfully and not be
dismissive of the fact that these are real symptoms that make women
feel tired, ill, stressed out, depressed and not themselves."[40] Indeed,
helpful and sensitive managers and colleagues can make a real difference in how well an employee can navigate the workplace while experiencing menopausal symptoms.

## STIGMA AND SECRECY

Harassment of the type described above—or fear of it—is one reason
that many menopausal employees hesitate to disclose their menopausal
symptoms at work. Even the fear of being subjected to low-level joking
can prompt secrecy. Pippa Marriott, the teacher who later left her job at
a large U.K. girls' school, recalled that her main emotion around menopause was "embarrassment" and even "shame." She explained: "There

was a real element of not wanting to be associated with the menopause and the whole baggage of stuff attached to [it], the careless mockery and disrespect that went with it."[41]

But the prospect of harassment or jokes from others is only one reason why employees do not reveal their menopause. As Chapter 1 described, there is also an internalized stigma and silence that surrounds all aspects of the menstrual cycle. Menopause, in turn, implicates not only menstrual stigma, but also age- and disability-related stigmas. Those concerns are heightened in the workplace. The 2023 Bank of America study found that 58 percent of menopausal women reported not feeling comfortable discussing their symptoms at work, not only because it was "too personal," but also because of fear that colleagues would "perceive me as old," "treat me differently," "not think I can do my job well," and the like.[42]

Indeed, studies consistently show that significant portions of menopausal employees remain silent, even when experiencing symptoms at work. The mobile phone provider Vodafone interviewed more than 5,000 women in Germany, Spain, Italy, and South Africa, and found that approximately one-third had hidden their menopausal symptoms, even though 62 percent thought that their symptoms had affected their work.[43] These results are roughly consistent with earlier research from the U.K. and U.S., which found that workers are reluctant to discuss menopause at work, even when menopausal symptoms are the true reason for a particular day's absence.[44] (Indeed, the title of the small U.S. study published in *Harvard Business Review* was "Workplace Stigma Around Menopause Is Real."[45])

In addition to fear of harassment and sociocultural expectations of silence, the law—or, more accurately, the *lack* of law—may also play a role in reinforcing menopausal silence. Speaking up can feel daunting, even futile, when there is no clear legal path guiding the way toward remedies. And, unfortunately, U.S. employment law is largely undeveloped in this area.

## LEGAL RECOURSE?

There are three broad U.S. federal employment discrimination statutes, respectively addressing sex, age, and disability, that provide the key backdrop for menopausal discrimination cases.

First, Title VII of the Civil Rights Act of 1964 makes it unlawful for an employer to discriminate on the basis of sex (in addition to race, color, national origin, or religion).[46] Discrimination "on the basis of pregnancy, childbirth, or related medical conditions" counts as a form of sex discrimination.[47]

Second, the Age Discrimination in Employment Act (ADEA) of 1967 makes it unlawful for employers to discriminate on the basis of age (with respect to employees who are 40 or older).[48] Under the ADEA, acts that represent age discrimination not only include making age-based hiring and discharge decisions, but also "limit[ing], segregate[ing], or classify[ing] . . . employees in any way" because of their age.[49]

Finally, the Americans with Disabilities Act of 1990, as amended by the Americans with Disabilities Amendments Act of 2008 (together the ADA),[50] prohibits discrimination "against a qualified individual on the basis of disability."[51] Under the ADA, an individual with a disability "has a physical or mental impairment that substantially limits one or more major life activities, has a record of such an impairment, or is regarded as having such an impairment."[52] An impairment must be "substantial," and it must "limit major life activities such as seeing, hearing, speaking, walking, breathing, performing manual tasks, learning, caring for oneself, and working."[53] The ADA further provides that the failure to make "reasonable accommodations to the known physical or mental limitations of an otherwise qualified individual with a disability" counts as a form of disability discrimination, unless the accommodations would impose an "undue hardship" on the employer.[54]

None of these laws mention menopause. Newer federal laws now mandate accommodations for pregnant and nursing employees,[55] but while these laws address issues related to the female reproductive system, they do not mention menopause either.

The omission of menopause in any federal or state antidiscrimination laws has created a significant void. Consider Jackie Dault, whose employer harassed her by turning up the operating room thermostat in hopes of triggering a hot flash; Alisha Coleman, who was fired for unexpected perimenopausal bleeding; and Georgia Sipple, who was denied a dress code accommodation for her hot flashes. For each of them, the menopause transition was the vector through which they suffered severe disadvantage at work. Indeed, each ultimately left or lost their jobs as a result. Their situations represent the three broad categories into which employment discrimination cases involving menopause can fall: (1) discrimination (often taking the form of harassment) based on menopausal stigma and stereotypes, as Dault experienced; (2) discrimination based on menopausal symptoms that are not affecting workplace performance, as Coleman experienced; and (3) discrimination connected to menopausal symptoms that *are* affecting workplace performance—often by refusing to accommodate those symptoms, as with Sipple. And in each type of case, the path to legal recourse is narrow. In the last two categories, it is often murky as well.

## DISCRIMINATION BASED ON MENOPAUSAL STIGMA AND STEREOTYPES

As the above discussion shows, harassment based on menopausal stigma and stereotypes can take many forms. Sometimes it involves "jokes" about hot flashes or irritability, or crude commentary about menopause in general. Sometimes it involves speculation about whether a particular employee is menopausal. Sometimes it involves insults directed at a particular employee who is, or is regarded as, menopausal. And, as in Dault's situation with the thermostat, sometimes the harassment extends beyond verbal comments altogether.

When employees are subjected to harassment on the basis of a legally protected characteristic like sex, age, or disability, they can bring what is known as a "hostile work environment" discrimination claim. Although U.S. employment discrimination law does not prohibit harassment per se, the Supreme Court's 1986 opinion in the case of *Meritor Savings Bank v. Vinson* established that sexual harassment is a form of sex discrimination because it subjects employees to different terms and conditions of employment based on their sex.[56] This reasoning has been applied to harassment on the basis of other legally protected characteristics, like age or race, as well.

To win a discrimination claim based on harassment, however, the employee must show that the harassment was "severe or pervasive" enough to create a hostile work environment.[57] And courts have set the threshold very high. As Professors Sandra Sperino and Suja Thomas have observed, "[C]ases are dismissed where women allege that their bosses or their coworkers repeatedly touched their breasts or buttocks, supervisors regularly asked employees on dates or for sexual favors, or employees were continually the victim of unwanted sexualized comments and gestures. Federal courts have ruled that this conduct is not serious enough to be called sexual harassment."[58]

Menopausal harassment cases—whether framed as sexual harassment, age-based harassment, or both—often meet a similar fate. Consider the case of Cathy Burkhart, a manufacturing plant employee who brought a sexual harassment claim after experiencing persistent harassment by her boss. He forwarded graphic photos to her, told her that she "looked good on her knees" when she was on the floor taping up a box for mailing, and even sent her an email entitled "Why Women Are Crabby" that mocked various stages in a woman's reproductive development, culminating in "'The Menopause' where women either take hormone replacement drugs and chance cancer in those now seasoned 'buds' or the aforementioned Nether Regions, or, sweat like a hog in July, wash your sheets and pillowcases daily and bite the head off anything that moves." The court dismissed Burkhart's sexual harassment claim before a jury could even hear it. The court held that her boss's behavior was "boorish and offensive," but not severe or pervasive enough to create a legally actionable hostile work environment.[59]

A few menopausal harassment cases have, however, been extreme enough to meet the threshold for a hostile work environment. Deloris Paigo, who received a daily barrage of negative comments once she began going through menopause, succeeded in her age-based hostile work environment claim against her employer.[60] And in Jackie Dault's case, the court found that "intentionally increasing the temperature to physically harass" her was so extreme and outrageous that, in addition to her claims of sex and age discrimination, she could also pursue a claim for the tort of intentional infliction of emotional distress.[61]

Even when menopausal harassment is not severe enough to create a hostile work environment claim on its own, such harassment can serve as evidence for why an employer took a tangible adverse job action against an employee—like firing her. Becky White, for instance, had been a sex crimes investigator in Idaho for years before being terminated. The sheriff's office claimed that she had been fired for making untruthful statements on her time cards for two pay periods. White countered that she had merely underreported her time because her overtime had not been approved in advance, and that sex discrimination was the real motivation for her termination. To support her argument, White pointed to harassing comments that the sheriff had made to her, like "How's the menopause today?" "Why do you have to be such a bitch?" and "How's the hot flash queen?" The court agreed to take these comments into account, and ruled that her sex discrimination claim relating to her termination could go forward.[62]

Collectively, these cases show that the path to victory in a case alleging discrimination based on menopausal stigma or stereotypes is narrow, albeit clear. The employee must either prove that such menopausal stereotypes motivated the employer to take an adverse job action, or prove that the menopausal stereotypes were expressed or acted upon in an extreme enough fashion to create a severely or pervasively hostile work environment.

## DISCRIMINATION BASED ON MENOPAUSAL SYMPTOMS THAT ARE NOT AFFECTING PERFORMANCE

The path for proving discrimination on the basis of an employer's response to menopausal *symptoms,* as opposed to *stereotypes,* is murkier. Recall the case of Alisha Coleman, who was fired after her perimenopausal bleeding stained the office carpet. There was no question about what happened or why. Coleman had told her employer that she was going through menopause and struggling with sudden heavy bleeding, and her employer had responded that if it happened again at work, she would be fired. Sure enough, that is exactly what happened. Coleman's termination notice even stated that she was fired for "failing to maintain high standards of personal hygiene."

Nonetheless, the court dismissed Coleman's sex discrimination claim. The court did not disagree that Coleman had been fired for experiencing menopausal symptoms at work. Rather, the court's disagreement was over something more theoretical: whether the firing counted as sex discrimination at all. In the court's view, Coleman was not terminated "simply because she was pre-menopausal," but rather "for being unable to control the heavy menstruation and soiling herself and company property."[63] But this is a specious distinction, given that heavy bleeding is a common, known, and uncontrollable symptom of perimenopause.

Additionally, and rather oddly, the court suggested that the only way Coleman could win would be to show that "male employees who soiled themselves and company property due to a medical condition, such as incontinence, would have been treated more favorably."[64] This, too, makes little sense. In telling Coleman that she was being fired for perimenopausal bleeding, the employer was essentially admitting that it was firing her for an unavoidable manifestation of her sex. Coleman should not have needed to identify a comparator—that is, the court's hypothetical incontinent male employee who was treated more favorably—to prove the employer's motive here. Moreover, the very notion of a comparison between incontinence and menstrual/perimenopausal bleeding is problematic. Incontinence is a relatively rare medical condition; it is often covered by the ADA. By contrast, menstrual and perimenopausal bleeding are sex-linked phenomena experienced by approximately half the population (and, as the chapter later discusses, typically *not* covered by the ADA). Thus, even if the hypothetical incontinent employee *were* treated more favorably than the perimenopausal employee, the employer could theoretically justify the differential treatment by pointing to the ADA.

Unfortunately, the *Coleman* court's rationale has already influenced at least one other court. A Florida federal judge relied on *Coleman*'s reasoning to dismiss the sex discrimination claim of a female waitress who unexpectedly got her period and was denied permission to leave work to change her clothes and get menstrual supplies. That court, citing *Coleman*, rejected the claim on grounds that the waitress had not alleged that males were "treated more favorably while suffering from similar conditions involving bodily fluids."[65]

A later case from 2021 is more encouraging on this point. Joyce Flores, a perimenopausal dental hygienist, was employed at a Virginia correctional facility. She was terminated after a body scanner picked up an image of a "suspicious item in her vagina" (actually, toilet paper that she had put in her underwear as a stop-gap measure, because she had unexpectedly saturated the tampon she was previously using). The court recognized that "*but for* Flores's menstruation and use of a tampon [earlier in the day when she had first gone through the body scanner, such that the later image was different]—conditions inextricable from her sex and child-bearing capacity—she would not have been discharged."[66] The court added that requiring Flores to point to a comparator employee would be an illogical and nearly impossible hurdle. The *Flores* decision provides a much better path for courts to follow when faced with similar cases. Yet with so few menopause-related cases, it is not yet clear how the law will develop.

## DISCRIMINATION IN CONNECTION WITH MENOPAUSAL SYMPTOMS THAT *ARE* AFFECTING PERFORMANCE

In both the *Coleman* and *Flores* cases, the perimenopausal bleeding in question did not affect the employees' actual workplace performances as, respectively, a call center employee or dental hygienist. Similarly, the harassment based on menopausal stereotypes and stigma in *Dault* and the other cases were not related to the employee's actual job performance. In those situations, the issue was not a failure to *accommodate* menopausal symptoms. Rather, the issue was animus toward menopause that manifested in either harassment or punishment for "appearing" menopausal.

As this chapter (and indeed, this entire book thus far) illustrates, however, there are some menopausal symptoms that *can* end up affecting work. For example, hot flashes can affect employees' ability to follow certain workplace dress codes, or whether (and when) they can work in offices without air conditioning. Emotional symptoms like depression and anxiety can also affect work performance, as can cognitive symptoms like forgetfulness and brain fog. Sleep deprivation, which is both caused by and exacerbates menopausal symptoms, can make everything worse. These situations raise new questions: Is firing an employee whose work performance is affected by menopausal symptoms a form of sex, age, and/or disability discrimination? What obligations do employers have to make reasonable accommodations for those symptoms? These are complex questions as to which U.S. law is particularly murky and undeveloped.

The case of Georgia Sipple, the food product demonstrator discussed earlier in the chapter, exemplifies one such situation. Sipple was not harassed for being menopausal, nor was she terminated for menopausal symptoms. But the combination of her hot flashes and her employer's refusal to make any dress code adjustments forced her to quit. She then sued for disability discrimination. Another example comes from the case of Kia Baskerville, a longtime CBS news employee who was ultimately terminated in 2018. Baskerville transferred within the company to a position that involved managing CBS's internship program. She struggled in the job and took a short-term medical leave, seeking care for depression, anxiety, and insomnia. When she returned, she told her supervisor that she had "premenopausal dysphoric disorder," which she described as a condition that gave her anxiety, irritability, mood swings, and difficulty concentrating. After an incident involving a CBS intern who was taken to the hospital for a mental health episode, Baskerville was terminated. CBS claimed that the termination stemmed from Baskerville's "poor judgment" in handling the incident, as well as her history of "poor job performance"; Baskerville alleged that the termination was instead due to her "premenopausal dysphoric disorder," and sued for disability discrimination.[67]

Both Sipple and Baskerville lost their disability discrimination cases. Indeed, their claims were dismissed before ever reaching a jury. That is because in both cases, the courts concluded that menopause did not qualify as a disability under the relevant laws. (Sipple had sued under the California Fair Employment and Housing Act, and Baskerville had sued under the District of Columbia Human Rights Act (DCHRA); both laws have provisions that largely track the ADA.) Because neither Sipple nor Baskerville was disabled, at least according to the courts, they were not entitled to the relevant legal protections that prohibited disability discrimination and required reasonable accommodations for disabilities.

Indeed, it is not immediately obvious whether or where menopause fits into the disability framework set out by U.S. law. The ADA has long defined a disability as something that "substantially limits a major life activity." In 2008, the Americans with Disabilities Amendments Act (ADAAA) clarified that major life activities could include a wide range of activities, including lifting, bending, concentrating, thinking, and working. A major life activity also includes, in the ADA's words, the "operation of a major bodily function," including "endocrine" and "reproductive" functions. Not only does menopause involve a change in the operation of the endocrine function, but it ultimately effectuates a loss of reproductive function. That does not necessarily make menopause a *limitation* on one of those functions, though. (Indeed, this would mean that "reproductive" function means being able to reproduce throughout one's entire life, such that menopause always amounts to a disability.)

More straightforward, for ADA purposes, is to argue that specific menopausal symptoms like hot flashes or "brain fog" can—for some employees—substantially limit the major life activity of working. Both Baskerville and Sipple were unsuccessful in these arguments, however. In Sipple's case, the court ruled that Sipple's hot flashes did not render her disabled under the law. "Sipple provides insufficient evidence that she cannot work," the court said. "She only contends that she cannot work as a product demonstrator at Crossmark given the dress code."[68] Similarly, the *Baskerville* court did not agree that Baskerville's menopausal symptoms had substantially limited her ability to work. "Baskerville's argument appears to conflate her ability to work with her ability to do a good job," the court stated. "There is no dispute that Baskerville was able to work, despite her anxiety and depression."[69]

Even if Sipple and Baskerville *had* shown that their menopausal symptoms substantially limited their ability to work, it is still unclear whether courts would have found them covered by the ADA. The current doctrine suggests that "typical" symptoms of "normal" conditions cannot count as disabilities.[70] Consider the somewhat comparable situation of pregnancy. Guidance issued by the Equal Employment Opportunity Commission (EEOC) states that while pregnancy does not qualify as an impairment, "and thus is never on its own a disability, some pregnant workers may have impairments related to their pregnancies that qualify as disabilities under the ADA."[71] As examples, the EEOC guidance lists pregnancy-related anemia, pregnancy-related carpal tunnel syndrome, nausea that causes severe dehydration, and depression. Courts have relied on this guidance to hold that symptoms arising from a "normal" pregnancy are not covered by the ADA, and thus do not fall under its accommodation mandate. It took a new federal law—the Pregnant Workers Fairness Act,[72] which went into effect in 2023—to require reasonable accommodations for all pregnant women who need them, regardless of whether their pregnancy is "normal" or amounts to a disability.

By the same token, courts have been receptive to the idea that the ADA only covers symptoms caused by *atypical* menopause, not symptoms resulting from "normal" (i.e., age-related) menopause. Jessica

Mullen, for instance, began working as a stitcher for New Balance Athletics shortly after having her uterus and remaining fallopian tube and ovary removed for extremely painful ovarian cysts. This surgery put her into early menopause at the age of 35. As her doctor had advised was likely, Mullen started experiencing menopausal symptoms, including hot flashes, feeling emotionally overwhelmed, and crying. When Mullen had trouble mastering one of the stitching machines, she had an "abrupt exchange" with the trainer and began crying. The human resources managers then met with Mullen, at which point she told them she had undergone a hysterectomy, was having hot flashes, and was working with her doctor on medications because her emotions were "all over the place." One of the HR managers responded, "Maybe this isn't the right time for you at New Balance . . . instructions from your trainer should not have set you off as it did." By the end of the conversation, Mullen had submitted a resignation form, indicating that she was leaving for "emotional reasons." She later sued under the ADA, and the court allowed her case to proceed because "a reasonable jury could find that an impairment to the endocrine system sufficient to place the plaintiff abruptly into menopause at the age of 35 constituted a substantial limitation on that person when compared to an average person in the population."[73]

The implication of cases like Mullen's is that the type of menopause faced by an "average person" is *not* covered. And, indeed, that was the central holding in Sipple's case. In addition to finding that Sipple was not disabled because her hot flashes did not prevent her from working altogether (even though experiencing them in her uniform caused her body temperature to rise high enough to make her ill), the court approvingly cited cases suggesting that menopause is a "natural progression" rather than a "disability." As the court put it, menopause is an "inevitable part of the human condition for women."[74] This echoed another court's observation that "enlightened women have been espousing for centuries" that "menopause is not a disability."[75]

Even if menopausal symptoms like Sipple's and Baskerville's *were* covered under disability laws, there would still be some tricky questions to unravel. The ADA requires employers to make "reasonable accommodations," up to the point of "undue hardship," for "qualified individuals with disabilities." It states that a "reasonable accommodation" may include "job restructuring, part-time or modified work schedules, reassignment to a vacant position, acquisition or modification of equipment or devices, appropriate adjustment or modifications of examinations, training materials or policies, the provision of qualified readers or interpreters, and other similar accommodations," and that "undue hardship" means "an action requiring significant difficulty or expense."[76]

For some menopausal symptoms, like hot flashes, it is easy to envision reasonable (and often inexpensive) accommodations, like dress code adjustments or thermostat modifications. Sleep disruptions, too, might often be straightforwardly addressed with modified work schedules. Other menopausal symptoms, however, may be more complicated to address, such as "brain fog," anxiety, depression, and mood swings. Which types of accommodations for those sorts of symptoms are "reasonable," and which impose undue hardships on employers, are likely to be extremely job-specific and symptom-specific questions, just as they are for employees who experience these symptoms for reasons other than menopause.

Notably, Baskerville herself never officially asked for job modifications, so it is unclear what type of workplace accommodations (if any) she thought would help address her menopausal symptoms of depression and anxiety. Indeed, rather than alleging that CBS had failed to make reasonable accommodations for her menopausal symptoms, Baskerville alleged only that CBS had fired her for those symptoms. This, in turn, reduced the case to the overly simplistic question of whether CBS had fired her for being menopausal or for her poor job performance. The court quickly dismissed the case, attributing the firing to the latter.

## BINARIES AND IRONIES

Indeed, overly simplistic binaries run throughout the case law on menopause. In Alisha Coleman's case, the court suggested that it was deciding an "either/or" question: Coleman's termination was due either to sex discrimination or "for being unable to control the heavy menstruation and soiling herself and company property." In reality, though, the alternatives were inextricably linked. Coleman was experiencing heavy uncontrollable bleeding precisely *because of* her sex. Moreover, the employer's disgust over this particular bloodstain—which, it bears repeating, Coleman cleaned immediately—most likely stemmed from the sex-related stigma surrounding menstrual blood and menopause. It is difficult to imagine an employer firing an employee who accidentally cut his finger, bled onto a piece of office furniture, and immediately cleaned up the mess, even if it happened twice within two years.

Similarly, the binary approach to "normal" versus "abnormal" menopause—with only the latter being covered by the ADA—is problematic. In comparison to the (also problematic) distinction between "normal" and "abnormal" pregnancies, which focuses on the severity of the *symptoms*, the normal/abnormal divide for menopause typically centers on the symptoms' *cause*. The theme emerging from the case law is that early menopause caused by surgery or other medical treatments can qualify as a disability (if accompanied by severe symptoms),[77] but that "normal," age-related menopause cannot. It is true that medically induced menopause can sometimes trigger more acute symptoms than "natural" menopause, since the hormone shift is more abrupt. But all menopausal symptoms occur along a spectrum, and even age-related menopause can come with significant symptoms. Drawing a sharp binary between "normal" and "abnormal" menopause simply does not line up with how menopause actually affects workplace functioning.

Two competing impulses seem to drive the notion that the ADA only covers, and requires accommodation of, "abnormal" menopause among younger workers. The surface, ostensibly benign impulse is that it would be "unenlightened," and indeed ageist and sexist, to classify "normal," age-related menopause as a disability. After all, such a classification would potentially mark all women and people with ovarian systems above a certain age as presumptively disabled. Lurking beneath this "enlightened" approach, though, is its darker mirror image: the notion that older women with menopausal symptoms that are affecting them at work are not the concern of antidiscrimination law—that there is nothing that can or should be done for them, because menopause is simply an "inevitable part of the human condition for women," in the *Sipple* court's words. Far from being anti-ageist or anti-sexist, that reasoning has ageism and sexism baked right into it. There is a profound irony here: the supposedly empowering concept that menopause is not a disability ends up *disempowering* many menopausal employees from getting the very accommodations that they need to remain at work.

Other ironies abound throughout the cases involving menopausal symptoms. For example, consider the *Sipple* court's secondary conclusion that Sipple did not qualify as disabled, notwithstanding her severe hot flashes, because she had not provided sufficient evidence that she could not work or conduct any other major life activities. "She only contends that she cannot work as a product demonstrator at Crossmark given the dress code," the court reasoned.[78] In other words, because all that Sipple needed in order to keep working at her current job were dress code modifications—indeed, her doctor wrote that such changes "would minimize her symptoms allowing her to keep working"—she was not entitled by law to those very accommodations. Meanwhile, had Sipple's menopausal symptoms been so debilitating that they prevented her from working in any job at all, the ADA would have been more likely to cover her. But in that situation, there might not have been any reasonable accommodations that would resolve the issue. To be sure, this is a larger problem with the ADA's approach, not one limited to menopause. But the menopause context brings it into particularly sharp relief.

The juxtaposition of Coleman's and Sipple's cases highlights yet another irony in the developing jurisprudence around menopause discrimination: the notion that menopausal symptoms are too "medical" to be about one's sex, but too sex-related to be about disability. In *Coleman*, the linchpin of the court's reasoning was that firing Coleman for her uncontrollable premenopausal bleeding was not about her sex, but her medical condition. (Indeed, recall the court's suggestion that to win, Coleman would need to show that more favorable treatment was given to "male employees who soiled themselves and company property *due to a medical condition*.")[79]

The suggestion that menopausal symptoms are not about sex, but rather about a medical condition, might lead one to think that disability discrimination is the best framing for cases involving menopausal symptoms. And yet in *Sipple*, the court essentially held the reverse: that Sipple's hot flashes were not stemming from a disability, but from sex—that they were a manifestation of "an inevitable part of the human condition for women." This doomed her disability claim. Indeed, menopausal employees' difficulties in winning cases involving their symptoms amount to a "heads-I-win-tails-you-lose" situation for employers.

The reasoning expressed in these decisions also points to yet another false binary (or "trinary"): the idea that menopause cases are only about sex, or age, or disability—when in reality, they sit at the intersection of all three.

Professor Kimberlé Crenshaw's analogy to traffic, as a way of introducing the concept of intersectionality in her landmark 1989 article in the *University of Chicago Legal Forum*, is particularly helpful here. As Crenshaw put it, "Discrimination, like traffic through an intersection, may flow in one direction, and it may flow in another. If an accident happens in an intersection, it can be caused by cars traveling from any number of directions, and sometimes, from all of them."[80] Her foundational insight, which drew from the experiences of Black women, is that intersectional discrimination is not just additive, but synergistic. Similarly, ageism, sexism, and disability bias frequently come together and reinforce each other in overlapping ways in many menopausal discrimination cases. Current menopausal discrimination case law in the U.S., however, often fails to understand this complex interaction of age, sex, and disability.

## LESSONS FROM THE UNITED KINGDOM

A growing body of case law from the United Kingdom exemplifies how—in contrast to the U.S. approach—existing antidiscrimination law can be interpreted to better protect against menopausal discrimination. As in the U.S., the U.K.'s antidiscrimination law, known as the Equality Act 2010, does not explicitly mention menopause. But the Equality Act's text, and judicial interpretations of it, have made it easier for menopausal employees to succeed in claims involving harassment, failures to accommodate, and other forms of discrimination.

The Equality Act brought together different previous pieces of antidiscrimination legislation that had been enacted previously in the U.K. into a single, overarching law, in order to "harmonise discrimination law, and to strengthen the law to support progress on equality."[81] It is roughly analogous to a combination of Title VII, the ADA, and the ADEA in the U.S. context. The Equality Act first enumerates eight categories of legally "protected characteristics": age, disability, gender reassignment, marriage and civil partnership, race, religion or belief, sex, and sexual orientation.[82] As to these characteristics, the Equality Act prohibits discrimination, harassment, and "victimisation" (defined similarly to retaliation).[83] Harassment is defined as "unwanted conduct related to a relevant protected characteristic" that either has "the purpose or effect of (i) violating B's [the recipient's] dignity or (ii) creating "an intimidating, hostile, degrading, humiliating, or offensive environment for B."[84] In addition, the Act defines disability as a "physical or mental impairment" that has "a substantial and long-term adverse effect on P's [a person's] ability to carry out normal day-to-day activities," and imposes a duty on employers to make "reasonable adjustments" for disabled persons.[85] Employment discrimination cases brought under the Equality Act, like other employment cases in the U.K., are decided by Employment Tribunals, which are independent tribunals with the authority to make legally binding decisions.

Two features of the U.K. approach stand out in comparison to U.S. antidiscrimination law. First, the Equality Act's approach to harassment differs. Recall that Title VII, the ADEA, and the ADA do not explicitly prohibit harassment. Instead, U.S. courts have merely inferred as much from these statutes' general prohibition of discrimination, while adding the further gloss that the statutes only prohibit harassment that is truly "severe or pervasive." By contrast, the Equality Act not only explicitly prohibits harassment, but also defines it more expansively to include conduct that has the effect of violating the recipient's dignity. It is not surprising, then, that U.K. employment tribunals have been significantly more willing than U.S. courts to find legally actionable harassment in cases involving menopause.

Consider, for example, the 2019 U.K. case of *A v. Bonmarche Limited*.[86] There, the employee, referred to in the case as "A," had worked in retail for over thirty years when she began the menopause transition. At that point, A alleged, the manager began to "demean her and humiliate her in front of other staff" and called her a "dinosaur" in front of customers. Ultimately, she suffered a sudden panic attack, at which point the store's human resources department agreed that she could have a part-time schedule of only four hours per day. The manager, however, informed her that she would need to take the hours that she would no longer be working as "holidays"; he also told A that she was "pushing her luck" when she asked for a break to take her medications with a drink. Soon thereafter, A resigned from her job, and then sued for harassment, age discrimination, and sex discrimination.

The tribunal ruled for A on all three claims, concluding that the manager had treated her "less favourably than he would treat someone who was not a female of menopausal age."[87] The decision added that these "remarks would not have been made to someone who did not have those characteristics," that A was "clearly upset during the course of the hearing," and that A "felt [her manager] had created a hostile work environment for her and that this was related to her status as a woman going through the menopause," such that this "amount[s] to unlawful harassment on grounds of age and sex."[88] The outcome thus did not hinge on whether the harassment rose to the level of being objectively "severe" or "pervasive," the threshold that U.S. courts have imposed. Rather, the tribunal focused in large part on A's *subjective* reaction to the harassment and on whether she, as a menopausal woman, was treated less favorably than other employees.

Second, the U.K. also takes a more expansive view of what counts as a disability. The Equality Act itself defines a disability as having "a substantial and long-term adverse effect on P's [a person's] ability to carry out normal day-to-day activities," and U.K. employment tribunals have consistently found that menopausal symptoms can meet that threshold. Indeed, one tribunal judge specifically stated that "I see no reason why, in principle, 'typical' menopausal symptoms cannot have the relevant disabling effect on an individual." This markedly differs from the U.S. case law, which suggests that "typical" symptoms of "normal" menopause cannot count as a disability.

To be sure, there have been some U.K. cases in which the tribunal ruled that employee's menopausal symptoms did not rise to the level of a disability under the Act. But that happened because the U.K. tribunals engaged in a fact-specific inquiry of the specific menopausal symptoms at issue in each case, rather than resorting to an artificial binary between "normal" and "abnormal" menopause.

Particularly notable is the case of Maria Rooney, a longtime children's social worker for the Leicester City Council who began experiencing menopause symptoms that included, as she described it, "fatigue, sleep disturbances, anxiety, low mood, hot flushes, night sweats, brain fog and memory loss."[89] Rooney also experienced "work-related stress as a result of management bullying, harassment and intimidation," and ended up taking a sick leave. When she returned, she received a warning for having taken sick leave, and soon after felt forced to resign.

The employment tribunal dismissed Rooney's subsequent disability claim, finding that her symptoms did not amount to a disability for purposes of the Equality Act, in part because her symptoms were primarily mental rather than physical, such that she could still perform "normal day to day activities."[90] The Employment Appeal Tribunal, however, reinstated Rooney's case in late 2021. The appellate judge emphasized that Rooney's symptoms "demonstrate[d] an effect on day-to-day activities that was more than minor or trivial," and held that further "careful factual analysis" was required.[91]

Ultimately, a new employment tribunal judge ruled that Rooney was indeed "disabled within the meaning . . . of the Equality Act 2010 by virtue of a combination of symptoms of the menopause associated with symptoms of stress and anxiety."[92] Rooney's case—the first ruling by an Employment Appeal Tribunal as to whether menopausal symptoms can qualify as a disability under the Equality Act[93]—garnered wide attention from the U.K. bar and the press.

Indeed, the growing number of successful menopause cases brought under the Equality Act have raised general workplace awareness about menopause in the U.K. Numerous websites of U.K. solicitors who specialize in employment law now feature menopause-specific information and guidance.[94] The London-based Chartered Institute for Personnel and Development (CIPD), an association for human resources professionals, published a lengthy guide, entitled *Menopause at Work*, with detailed suggestions (and sample policies from U.K. workplaces) for how employers can support menopausal employees.[95] The U.K.'s Advisory, Conciliation, and Arbitration Service (Acas)—an independent public body that receives government funding and attempts to resolve employment disputes before they are brought to a tribunal—has also issued guidelines on the topic.[96] To be sure, there is still "highly variable workplace support" for those undergoing menopause in the U.K.,[97] but the conversation has advanced considerably in recent years.

This increased attention has sparked a national dialogue in the U.K. about how to further strengthen protections against menopausal discrimination. In July 2022, the Women and Equalities Committee of the

U.K. Parliament's House of Commons issued a lengthy report on this subject, entitled *Menopause in the Workplace*.[98] The report concluded by suggesting specific legal reforms, such as piloting a menopause leave policy, along with amending the Equality Act to include menopause as a protected characteristic, prohibiting "combined discrimination" based on multiple protected characteristics, and adding an explicit duty for employers to accommodate menopausal workers. The report explained that menopause-related discrimination cases were currently "being 'shoehorned' into claims based on existing characteristics of age, sex and/or disability," which failed to capture the intersectional nature of menopause or highlight the specific challenges faced by menopausal employees. "Menopause has been ignored and hidden away for too long," the report opined. "There is nothing shameful about women's health, or about getting older. Supporting those experiencing menopause makes sense for individuals, for the economy and for society."

In January 2023, however, the U.K. government issued a response to the committee report, stating that it agreed with some of the recommendations (like appointing a "Menopause Ambassador" to work with stakeholders from businesses, unions, and advisory groups to encourage and disseminate guidelines), but not others.[99] Most notably, the government rejected the ideas of producing model menopause policies to assist employers, amending the Equality Act to prohibit "combined discrimination," or launching a consultation on how to amend the Equality Act to introduce a new protected characteristic of menopause. The government asserted that it was unnecessary to add menopause as a new protected characteristic, reasoning that sex, age, and disability were already protected characteristics, and that to single out menopause for added protection might "inadvertently create new forms of discrimination, for example, discrimination risks towards men suffering from long-term medical conditions." The government also justified its rejection of a menopause leave pilot program on grounds that the government's aim was to "support menopausal women to remain in the workplace, and to ensure employers are well-equipped to support the workforce during menopause." It did, however, agree to bring forward legislation to "make the right to request flexible working a day-one right for all employees."

Even with the government's tepid response, the U.K—in its law and in its cultural discourse—is clearly ahead of the U.S. in approaching menopausal stigma and symptoms as raising not only social and/or medical issues, but *legal* issues. The next chapter builds on this idea, considering how workplaces—and employment discrimination law—can and should evolve to ensure that menopause does not unnecessarily limit the ability to remain and succeed at work.

# CHAPTER FIVE

# CHANGING WORKPLACES

On October 18, 2019—World Menopause Day—British television station Channel 4 made a major announcement. It was adopting a dedicated menopause policy, one of the first in the country.[1] "This is Channel 4 living its remit, normalising a taboo subject by making it more visible," said Channel 4's CEO, Alexandra (Alex) Mahon. The following year, on World Menopause Day 2020, Channel 4 published its finalized menopause policy, explaining that "the need to support women at work during menopause is now greater than ever, with 30% of women reporting that their menopausal symptoms have worsened during the pandemic . . . . We'd love you to take [the policy] and make it your own."[2] Channel 4's policy lists specific workplace adjustments for employees experiencing menopausal symptoms, such as desk fans, cool and quiet break rooms, flexible schedules, and use of paid sick days. The policy also emphasizes respect and support for menopausal employees, even requiring line managers to attend "mandatory menopause awareness training."

Shortly after World Menopause Day 2022, the U.K.'s largest employer—the National Health Service (NHS)—announced a menopause policy of its own: the NHS Menopause Programme, whose vision is to "create a supportive working environment that champions the wellbeing of women and others affected by the menopause transition, so they stay and thrive in the workplace whilst going through the menopause."[3] Like Channel 4's policy, the NHS menopause policy offers a mix of expressive messaging and tangible solutions, emphasizing the importance of an "open and receptive culture around the menopause" at work as well as "menopause-friendly uniforms" in breathable fabrics.

Employers like Channel 4 and the NHS are not anomalies within the U.K. The increasing receptiveness of U.K. employment tribunals toward menopause discrimination claims has yielded not only victories for individual employees, but also broader workplace reforms. A 2022 study indicated that nearly 30 percent of U.K. employers have adopted menopause policies, up from 10 percent in 2019.[4] A robust U.K. market of lawyers and consultants offering menopause-related guidance is flourishing. As of mid-2023, over 2,000 U.K. companies had signed the "Menopause Workplace Pledge," through which employers commit to actively supporting menopausal employees and talking "openly, positively and respectfully about the menopause."[5] And the U.K. government has itself developed a "Women's Health Strategy" that sets out specific goals for improving menopause-related support in the workplace and taking other actions in recognition of the significance of menopause.[6]

To be sure, just as in the U.S., no U.K. law explicitly requires employers to adopt menopause policies or sign menopause pledges. But concerns related to both business and liability have prompted many U.K. employers to become proactive in this area, to the point where they are now going beyond what the law mandates. The U.K. example indicates that raising awareness of menopause as a *legal* issue can be a critical step in prompting menopause-related workplace change. Indeed, it shows how law and workplace culture can exist in a feedback loop, with each pushing the other toward greater recognition of the challenges faced by menopausal employees.

These new menopause policies provide a window into how U.S. workplaces might evolve, too. Typically, the policies adopted by U.K. employers address the key challenges faced by menopausal employees—physical and mental symptoms; harassment; stigma; discrimination; and self-imposed silence—making them strong potential models for the U.S. workplace. Indeed, *Break Through the Stigma: Menopause in the Workplace*, a report released by Bank of America and the National Menopause Foundation in June 2023, found that 64 percent of the surveyed women wanted menopause-related benefits—including, most commonly, a clear menopause policy at work.[7] The increasing openness about menopause in U.S. cultural discourse suggests that the U.S. is ripe for such progress, especially if legal developments can now push the dialogue forward. What, then, might menopause-related legal reform—as well as more broad-based workplace reform—look like in the U.S.?

This chapter takes U.S. law's current approach to pregnancy and breastfeeding as a starting point in identifying a framework for change. Like menstruation and menopause, pregnancy and breastfeeding are directly connected to the reproductive system and the potential for childbearing. While not all cis women experience each of these processes, and not all who experience them are cis women, the processes are biologically and culturally linked to female sex. And all of the processes implicate common issues. Negative attitudes toward all of them—from stereotypes about "hormonal" or distracted employees to squeamishness about the processes' physical aspects—are all rooted in sexism and even misogyny.[8] The processes also share numerous symptoms that can be addressed by the same sorts of workplace accommodations. Unlike menstruation and menopause, however, pregnancy and breastfeeding are already visible in U.S. employment discrimination law. By understanding how U.S. law currently addresses them, we can more fully consider the possibilities for addressing menopause as well.

The chapter starts by explaining the current U.S. legal protections for pregnant and breastfeeding employees. It then unpacks why pregnancy and breastfeeding sit atop the socio-legal hierarchy of reproduction-related processes, and argues that this hierarchy needs to be dismantled: employment discrimination law should provide equivalent legal protections for menopause as well. This means recognizing that punishing employees for their menopausal symptoms (like unexpected heavy bleeding) is sex discrimination, just as the law has long recognized that punishing employees for pregnancy symptoms is sex discrimination. It would also mean requiring employers to provide reasonable accommodations for menopause, just as employers now must do for pregnancy and breastfeeding. Indeed, the shared symptoms cutting across pregnancy, breastfeeding, menstruation, and menopause point toward overlapping workplace solutions—and, even more broadly, toward the need for workplaces that are accommodating for all.

## PREGNANCY AT WORK

U.S. law has explicitly addressed pregnancy discrimination in the workplace since 1978, when Congress enacted the Pregnancy Discrimination Act (PDA).[9] The PDA was a direct response to a Supreme Court decision, *General Electric v. Gilbert*.[10] In *Gilbert*, the Supreme Court held that although Title VII prohibited sex discrimination, employers could still exclude pregnancy-related disabilities from general disability benefit programs. Congress disagreed. Through the PDA, Congress amended Title VII to state that discrimination based on sex includes discrimination based on "pregnancy, childbirth, or related medical conditions," and that "women affected by pregnancy, childbirth, or related medical conditions" should be treated the same as other persons "not so affected but similar in their ability or inability to work."[11] The PDA thus clearly established that pregnancy discrimination counted as a form of sex discrimination. That alone was a major step forward.

The PDA did not, however, guarantee any sort of *accommodations* for pregnancy. Unlike the Americans with Disabilities Act (ADA), which requires employers to make reasonable accommodations for employees' disabilities, the PDA stated only that pregnant women should be treated "the same" as other employees who are similar in their inability to work. This meant that if—and only if—accommodations were offered to other nonpregnant employees who were "similar in their ability or inability to work," such accommodations needed to be offered to the pregnant employees as well. Pregnant employees in workplaces that were generally unaccommodating, then, were out of luck. And, because (as discussed in Chapter 4) the ADA was interpreted by the Equal Employment Opportunity Commission (EEOC) as not covering "normal" pregnancies, the ADA did not provide most pregnant women with any legal entitlements to accommodations either. The effects were particularly devastating for pregnant employees who had physically strenuous jobs that heightened their risk of miscarriage.

But that picture changed in 2023.[12] After years of languishing in Congress, the Pregnant Workers Fairness Act (PWFA) was passed in December 2022 and took effect in June 2023. The PWFA created a new, stand-alone entitlement to workplace accommodations for *all* pregnant employees. It states that employers must make reasonable accommodations for pregnancy, childbirth, and related medical conditions, unless doing so would impose an undue hardship (defined, just as in the ADA, as a "significant difficulty or expense"). Importantly, there is no requirement that the pregnancies be "abnormal" to be covered; indeed, the PWFA does not do any line-drawing at all between "normal" and "abnormal" pregnancies. *All* pregnancies are included. And notably, the House Committee report that accompanied the PWFA listed, as examples of reasonable accommodations, numerous possibilities that could have been lifted from the menopause policies discussed above, like flexible schedules, rest times, water, and extra bathroom breaks.[13]

In addition to the PDA and PWFA's coverage of all pregnancies, and the ADA's coverage of "abnormal" pregnancies, pregnancy is also indirectly addressed by another federal workplace law: the Family and Medical Leave Act (FMLA).[14] The FMLA, originally passed in 1993, entitles eligible employees to take up to twelve weeks of unpaid, job-protected leave for several reasons, including a "serious health condition" and the "birth and care of [a] newborn child." This unpaid leave entitlement is thus another piece of the federal protection afforded to pregnancies.

## BREASTFEEDING AT WORK

Breastfeeding, too, is addressed in federal workplace law. As an initial matter, most courts now interpret the PDA's reference to "women affected by pregnancy, childbirth, or related medical conditions" to include breastfeeding.[15] The EEOC advises employers that lactation is a "pregnancy-related medical condition," such that the PDA prohibits discrimination and harassment based on breastfeeding in the same way it prohibits it against pregnancy.[16] By the same token, the newly passed PWFA—which copies the PDA's language of covering "pregnancy, childbirth, or related conditions"—would seem to cover breastfeeding as well. If this is the case, then employers must make reasonable accommodations for their breastfeeding employees, unless those accommodations would impose an undue hardship. That means accommodations on an as-needed basis, such as flexible work schedules, water breaks, and the like.

Apart from the implicit protections for breastfeeding provided by the PDA and now the PWFA, there is also explicit, stand-alone legal protection for breastfeeding in the workplace. Indeed, breastfeeding received independent workplace accommodation entitlements under federal law even before pregnancy did. As of 2010, Congress has required covered employers to provide lactating employees with reasonable break times to express breast milk for one year after their children's births, and also to provide them with a private place (other than a bathroom) to do so.[17] Then, in July 2019, Congress mandated that certain public buildings provide a shielded, hygienic space (other than a bathroom) that contains a chair, working surface, and electrical outlet for members of the public to express breast milk.[18]

In a subsequent development, on the same day (December 29, 2022) that the PWFA was signed into law, the Providing Urgent Maternal Protections ("PUMP") for Nursing Mothers Act[19] also became law. The PUMP Act covered additional employees who had not been included in previous breastfeeding laws. It also states that if employees are working while they are pumping, they must be compensated for that time (rather than having it count as unpaid "break" time).

## UNPACKING THE HIERARCHY
## OF REPRODUCTION-RELATED PROCESSES

When comparing employment discrimination law's treatment of pregnancy and breastfeeding to menopause and menstruation, it is hard not to discern a socio-legal hierarchy among the reproduction-related processes. Pregnancy and breastfeeding sit atop that hierarchy, receiving explicit legal protection and even accommodation mandates. Meanwhile, menopause and menstruation sit at the bottom, amid an absence of clear law. In thinking about how to make menopause more visible and protected in the law, then, it is helpful first to unpack why this hierarchy exists in the first place.

The long-standing sociocultural silence and stigma around menstruation and, especially, menopause certainly explain much of the legal silence around them. While pregnancy is often surrounded by public celebration—in the form of baby registries, showers, and the like— menopause is not.[20] Employees do not often discuss their menstruation or menopause with their colleagues or supervisors, even when dealing with symptoms that are affecting their work. Indeed, U.S. employers likely do not realize the extent to which employees are reducing their hours or quitting their jobs due to menopausal symptoms, although the 2023 Mayo Clinic study estimating the annual cost of such lost work productivity as $1.8 billion may raise some needed awareness.

Another key explanation for the law's differential treatment is the procreative aspect of pregnancy and breastfeeding. Federal and state laws that protect breastfeeding at work are often justified as promoting babies' nourishment and well-being. As Professor Elizabeth Hoffman has written, breastfeeding laws "enable[] very different kind of rights talk—the rights of the child, not the rights of the employee herself."[21] Professor Meghan Boone has likewise pointed out that "modern lactation laws are often conceived of and constructed as protective of an infant's right to breast milk, and not necessarily protective of an individual woman's right to lactate or breastfeed."[22] Similarly, even before the federal Pregnant Workers Fairness Act passed in December 2022, numerous states had passed such laws on fetal-protection grounds. State Senator Alice Forgy Kerr, a pro-life legislator, introduced Kentucky's pregnancy accommodations bill, and later told the *New York Times* that she had stressed to her fellow legislators that "this is a pro-life measure. . . . We want our women to have safe pregnancies so they can have healthy babies."[23]

Indeed, laws that protect and accommodate pregnancy and breastfeeding can also be justified in terms of *encouraging* those decisions. The House Committee on Education and Labor's report on the PUMP Act, for instance, emphasized the "health benefits of breastfeeding for both mothers and infants,"[24] implying that the Act was expanding accommodation mandates in order to enable breastfeeding. Similarly, although not all pregnancies are planned or chosen (especially in the wake of *Dobbs v. Jackson Women's Health Organization*), greater legal entitlements to workplace accommodations like light-duty work or flexible schedules may be seen as influencing the decision, for some, about whether a pregnancy is feasible.

These dynamics are simply absent from menstruation and menopause. When it comes to menstruation and menopause, there is no decision to incentivize, nor any baby or fetus to protect. By definition, both menstruation and menopause connote the *absence* of an impending baby. And they are entirely involuntary processes; employees have no choice about whether or when they will menstruate (apart from using certain forms of contraception) or enter menopause. Additionally, accommodations for pregnancy and breastfeeding may seem more straightforward because of their relatively predictable, time-limited nature.

All of these factors help to explain why menstruation and menopause are not explicitly addressed by U.S. employment discrimination law, even while pregnancy and breastfeeding are. But none of those reasons *justifies* the law's silence about menstruation and menopause. That employees have no choice about their menstruation and menopause certainly does not make these processes deserving of *less* protection. Nor does the non-procreative nature of those processes, or the greater variability surrounding them. These biological processes are all manifestations of the same underlying reproductive system, and they all implicate the same underlying concerns about ensuring equal opportunity in the workplace.

Employment discrimination law, therefore, has a key role to play in ensuring that none of these processes unnecessarily impedes employees' ability to remain at work. Indeed, the legal protections for pregnancy and breastfeeding can be used as a baseline that the legal treatment of menopause should also meet. The next part explores that issue, before turning to broader questions about how we might raise that baseline for all such processes.

## EXTRAPOLATING FROM PREGNANCY AND BREASTFEEDING PROTECTIONS TO MENOPAUSE

In measuring how employment discrimination law's treatment of menopause differs from its treatment of pregnancy and breastfeeding, it is helpful to return to the three basic categories of menopause discrimination cases discussed in Chapter 4: those involving (1) harassment or discrimination based on menopausal status; (2) punishment for menopausal symptoms; and (3) accommodation refusals for menopausal symptoms. Doing so helps highlight where the law's current treatment of menopause is lacking, as well as where there are particular needs for workplace change.

*Menopausal Status.* With respect to status-based harassment, there is not much difference—at least on the face of employment discrimination law—between the treatment of menopause-based harassment, pregnancy-based harassment, breastfeeding-based harassment, and other forms of sexual harassment. In all such instances, a "hostile work environment" claim of sex discrimination can be brought under Title VII. Such a claim would only be successful, though, when the harassment was severe or pervasive enough to change the very terms and conditions of employment. This high bar is not mandated by Title VII itself, which simply states that discrimination on the basis of sex is unlawful. Rather, it comes from Supreme Court precedent: the 1986 decision in *Meritor Savings Bank v. Vinson.*[25]

The most helpful legal change here would be a lowering of this steep threshold for harassment claims. That could happen either legislatively—akin to Congress's passage of the Pregnancy Discrimination Act in response to a Supreme Court interpretation of Title VII—or through the Supreme Court's reexamination of its prior precedents. Additionally, nothing prevents states or municipalities from adopting lower thresholds for what counts as actionable sexual harassment under their own employment discrimination laws. Indeed, New York State passed legislation in 2019 that makes harassment legally actionable in the state whenever it subjects an individual to inferior terms, conditions, or privileges of employment.[26] Essentially, any harassment that goes beyond "petty slights or trivial inconveniences" is illegal under New York law; it need not be "severe or pervasive."

Moreover, even without legal change, more could be done to raise awareness about menopausal harassment. As Chapter 4 describes, menopause-based harassment often intertwines aspects of sex-based, age-based, and disability-based harassment. In this way, it differs from more commonly recognized forms of sexual harassment, such as groping, repeated unrequited romantic advances, or lewd comments and pictures. The New York City Human Rights Commission, for example, developed a free online "Sexual Harassment Prevention Training" that employers can use to fulfill the city's requirement of providing annual sexual harassment trainings to employees.[27] The training video includes numerous skits dramatizing various forms of sexual harassment, such as a supervisor's threat to fire a subordinate who does not have sex with him, or a practice of holding work social gatherings at a strip club. But there is little focus on harassment connected to reproductive processes other than one skit. That skit involves a breastfeeding employee who receives suggestive comments when she takes a break to pump milk, like "How about you do one, and I'll do the other?" The training goes on to state that "offensive comments about pregnancy or breastfeeding are sexual harassment," but does not mention menstruation or menopause.

By including menopause-based harassment in sexual harassment training programs for employees, employers can raise awareness of this phenomenon—and, more broadly, challenge the silence around menopause itself. Indeed, one of the key recommendations offered by the European Menopause and Andropause Society in its 2021 "Global Consensus Recommendations on Menopause in the Workplace" is that employers and organizations should communicate a "zero-tolerance policy to bullying, harassment, victimization, or belittling of women with menopause symptoms,"[28] as many U.K. menopause policies now do. Bank of America's 2023 *Break Through the Stigma: Menopause in the Workplace* report likewise encouraged employers to "talk about menopause openly and often to help increase awareness and understanding of menopause and create a culture of caring."[29]

*Menopausal Symptoms.* In contrast to harassment, there is a clear disparity between the law's approach to menopausal symptoms and its approach to manifestations of pregnancy and breastfeeding. As noted above, the Pregnancy Discrimination Act specifically amended Title VII in 1978 to state that discrimination on the basis of pregnancy or related conditions is actionable sex discrimination. A pregnant employee who was fired because her water broke and she went into labor at work, or a breastfeeding employee who was fired for leaking milk, would therefore have a very clear sex discrimination claim.

That is not true for menopause. Recall that when Alisha Coleman's employer fired her for her unexpected perimenopausal bleeding, the federal district court accepted her employer's argument that this was not sex discrimination but merely a termination for "failing to maintain high standards of personal hygiene." Title VII certainly does not require that illogical result, as a different federal district court later recognized.[30] But this is an area where Title VII's silence about menopause (and menstruation), as compared to its explicit references to pregnancy and childbirth, has created legal confusion. More clarity here would be helpful, whether from courts, Congress, or agency guidance.

*Accommodations.* The gulf between the law's treatment of menopause on the one hand, and pregnancy and breastfeeding on the other, widens even further when it comes to accommodation mandates. Thanks to the 2022 passage of the PWFA and the PUMP Act, the workplace accommodation requirements for pregnancy and breastfeeding are now quite strong. But no such legislation requires accommodation of menopausal symptoms. Given the years that it took for the PWFA to become law, it seems unlikely that a parallel act for menopause will be passed in the near future, although that would certainly be one solution.

In the meantime, the EEOC could issue "best practice" guidelines for employers about how to address menopause in the workplace. Indeed, just as the U.S. Education Department's Office of Civil Rights has encouraged schools to go beyond legal mandates in supporting pregnant and parenting students—for instance, by designating lactation rooms for students and reaching out to "pregnant and parenting students who have dropped out of school and encourag[ing] them to return"[31]—the EEOC could encourage employers to proactively support menopausal employees.

As a starting point, the EEOC could advise employers to consider *having* a clear menopause policy—which, as Bank of America's *Break Through the Stigma: Menopause in the Workplace* report found, is the most commonly identified "menopause benefit" that employees want. The EEOC could then offer concrete suggestions for what such a policy might include. Here, the menopause policies from the U.K.'s private sector—along with the menopause guidance furnished by Acas (the U.K. entity that offers workplace guidance and mediation services)—provide useful examples, from climate-controlled break spaces, to dress codes that incorporate short-sleeve options, to flexible scheduling. Even though such EEOC guidance would not be mandatory for employers to follow, it would further challenge menopausal silence and help push forward workplace discussions.

Additionally, the ADA remains a potential source of accommodation mandates for menopause, at least in the case of significant symptoms. The first step is for the EEOC to revisit its 2015 "Pregnancy and Related Issues" guidance, in which it stated that pregnancy "is never on its own a disability," but that "some pregnant workers may have impairments related to their pregnancies that qualify as disabilities under the ADA."[32] The PWFA, which covers all pregnancies, has now rendered that guidance largely irrelevant to pregnant employees. But the guidance remains a problematic precedent for menopausal employees, who are still reliant on the ADA. As Chapter 4 explains, courts have used this guidance to hold that only "abnormal" menopause—that is, early surgical menopause—can be covered by the ADA.

The notion that menopause cannot be a disability for purposes of the ADA, unless it is "abnormal" in origin, is misguided. The ADA makes no reference at all to "normal" versus "abnormal" conditions. Rather, its text focuses on whether there is a substantial limitation of a major life activity. Even "normal" symptoms of menopause, such as hot flashes, can be significant enough to interfere with work, and should thus qualify for protection under the ADA standard.

Relatedly, as journalist Maya Dusenbery observes in *Doing Harm*,[33] the very notion of viewing reproductive processes in terms of "normality" has sexist undertones. As she puts it: "either women's reproductive functions are pathologized as innately abnormal—in which case any symptoms they bring are 'normal'—or else it is claimed that they're normal, so if they cause symptoms, it's only because an individual woman's response to them is abnormal—she's just especially sensitive or overreacting."

Dusenbery's focus is on the medical system, but her critique also applies to law. Menopausal symptoms that rise to the level of interfering with work should be reasonably accommodated, regardless of how "normal" they are. In connection with "best practices" guidelines regarding menopause, the EEOC should issue specific guidance that rejects the idea of an abnormal/normal binary. Such guidance would be consistent with the ADA's definition of disability, which does not include a prerequisite of "abnormality."[34]

## BROADER WORKPLACE SOLUTIONS

The above discussion has focused on menopause-specific approaches, in part by considering how the law's treatment of menopause could be put on the same footing with its treatment of pregnancy and breastfeeding.

Ultimately, however, the best solutions would be more systemic in nature.

Indeed, disability theory articulates two models for framing difference.[35] The first and more traditional model is the medical model, under which the analysis centers on whether the employee is impaired enough that the employer must provide accommodations within a workplace that is otherwise inhospitable. The second is a social model, which conceptualizes disability as constructed in the interaction between the workplace and the individual employee. The social model helps us see that challenges of menopause can be exacerbated precisely because workplaces are inhospitable, designed without taking menopause into account—for example, by not offering climate-controlled spaces or flexible dress code policies. Under the social model, the ultimate goal is not necessarily one-off accommodations for specific employees, but rather the redesign of the workplace environment to ensure integration for all.

Indeed, in the context of reproductive processes, the shared symptoms cutting across pregnancy, breastfeeding, menstruation, and menopause point toward overlapping workplace solutions that go beyond one-off accommodations. Hot flashes, for instances, occur not only during menopause, but also during pregnancy—due in both cases to significant hormonal shifts, particularly with estrogen.[36] Migraine headaches, too, are often linked to the hormonal changes associated with menopause, first-trimester pregnancy, and various stages within the menstrual cycle.[37]

Similar psychological symptoms, particularly those relating to depression and anxiety, are common across these processes as well. Indeed, psychiatrists Laura Miller, Christina Girgis, and Renu Gupta have explained that although "most women do not develop depressive symptoms during reproductive transition," the "evidence is accumulating to support the hypothesis that some women have a heightened vulnerability to emotional disturbance at a time of rapid hormonal flux."[38] Premenstrual dysphoric disorder and depression (PMDD), perinatal depression, postpartum depression, and perimenopausal depression all exemplify this phenomenon. So do anxiety disorders that start or worsen in connection with these hormonal shifts.[39]

Sleep deprivation is another common effect of pregnancy, menstruation, menopause, and breastfeeding. For pregnancy, menstruation, and menopause, this typically stems from the physical and psychological effects of hormonal shifts, back pain, and/or middle-of-the-night bathroom visits due to menstrual bleeding or frequent urination. For breastfeeding, it additionally stems from the concrete need to feed or pump in the middle of the night.

These common symptoms and effects indicate the potential for broadly applicable workplace adjustments. Workplace temperature control—particularly access to cool spaces—is one clear need that cuts across reproductive processes. Flexibility on dress codes and uniforms is another obvious solution, to address not only hot flashes but also varying needs for expandable waistbands, nursing-friendly tops, and stain-concealing bottoms. Extra bathroom access and break time, too, is important for those who are pregnant, menstruating, or going through perimenopause, in terms of both frequent urination (especially in the first and third trimesters of pregnancy) and potentially heavy menstrual bleeding. Relatedly, breaks for pumping are clearly essential for breastfeeding employees. Sleep deprivation similarly raises the need for break times, as well as for flexible schedules.

The fact that the PWFA and PUMP Act now require employers to implement these sorts of workplace changes as reasonable accommodations for pregnant and breastfeeding employees may well have beneficial spillover effects for menstruation and menopause as well. Once an employer is allowing pregnant employees to wear short-sleeve shirts to avoid overheating, for instance, it may become harder (at least practically, if not legally) for an employer to refuse the identical request from a menopausal employee who is experiencing hot flashes. After all, the notion of a uniform dress code for all has already been breached. Similarly, once an employer goes to the effort of developing a new flexible scheduling or break policy for pregnant and breastfeeding employees, it may not be as burdensome to fold additional employees into it.

While one approach is for employers to offer these sorts of changes on an as-needed basis, upon individual request, there are numerous benefits to making them available more generally, beyond those who disclose their pregnancy and breastfeeding—or, indeed, their other reproduction-related conditions—to their employer. Many people have physiological needs, unrelated to reproductive processes, that require cooler temperatures, dress code modifications, or regular bathroom breaks. Flexible schedules and remote options, too, tend to be widely desired.

Indeed, just as it is helpful to contextualize menopause among the other reproductive processes, it is also helpful to contextualize and broaden the very *concept* of workplace accommodations. Specific, one-off accommodations put the burden on the individual employee to request those accommodations. They can also make that employee stand out as "different," which is problematic for both individual and workplace morale. Transitioning to flexible policies that are more broadly applicable not only address such privacy concerns, but also reduce the potential for resentment about "special treatment" for certain employees.

Indeed, in a comprehensive study evaluating U.S. attitudes about the related topic of menstrual leave, researchers Jessica Barnack-Tavlaris, Kristina Hansen, Rachel Levitt, and Michelle Reno found that participants had predominantly negative reactions to the idea of such leave, particularly because of concern about unfairness to other employees.[40] Barnack-Tavlaris and Levitt thus suggest, in a subsequent work, that more effective strategies involve broadly applicable workplace policies that provide greater flexibility, as well as the reevaluation of "attitudes surrounding absenteeism and work ethic."[41]

In other words, it is the workplace that should itself change, as opposed to change that occurs on an ad hoc basis, one worker at a time. In addition to beneficial effects on workplace camaraderie, such policies may well have widespread appeal that boosts recruitment and retention.

In a 2021 *New York Times* opinion piece entitled *What If Disability Rights Were for Everyone?*, disability activist Ari Ne'eman traced the way that legal mandates and workplace culture build upon themselves and each other.[42] Ne'eman observed that although "[p]regnancy is not a disability under the A.D.A. . . . disability law has inspired a more expansive vision of workplace rights," leading to the passage of the PWFA. This observation suggests the possibility of future change: as Ne'eman puts it, "Can a movement born to address discrimination against a particular minority evolve into something greater—a larger push for rights for all?" This framing, of course, echoes and extends the social model of disability discussed above, whereby the individual and workplace are viewed in a more interactive, mutually constitutive way.

To be sure, legal mandates that *require* all employers to become broadly "accommodating"—as opposed to mandates that require "accommodations" for a potentially broadening pool of eligible employees— remain unlikely. That said, as the U.K. menopause policies illustrate, once the dialogue gets started, employers sometimes go beyond the minimum required by law. And the COVID-19 pandemic has opened the door to a reimagining of the workplace in numerous ways, particularly in terms of greater flexibility about where and when work gets done by some employees. Between the increased cultural visibility of menopause, the rise of workplace menopause policies, the new accommodation entitlements for pregnancy and breastfeeding, and the increased availability of remote work, we may well be at an inflection point whereby working through menopause—something that millions of employees already do—becomes more common and less challenging.

# CHAPTER SIX

## QUEER, TRANS, AND GENDER DIVERSE EXPERIENCES OF MENOPAUSE

Erica Rand, a college professor who is "a non-trans, white, non-precariously employed Jewish queer femme," writes of her experience of menopause as one of increasing unfamiliarity with her own body.[1] Menopause-related weight gain and fat redistribution left her with a sense of "deep loss" and "mourning the departure of my curvy hips within the queer erotics of butch/femme." Although Rand realizes that menopause is an opportunity to "remake or reinterpret [Rand's] relationship between [Rand's] body and [Rand's] gender," Rand said it felt like her body in menopause "was stealing my queer gender."[2]

—

Lisa Scheps, a 62-year-old trans woman, had been taking estrogen for twenty years when she needed to stop doing so in advance of a planned surgery. Describing that experience, Scheps said, "I wouldn't say that I've experienced perimenopause or menopause like a cis woman would have, but I certainly know what a hot flash feels like."[3]

—

Mike Funk, a 27-year-old trans man, describes his testosterone treatments as a reason he is "glad to live the life I get to live." After four years of taking these hormones, he has both a beard and a lower voice, and he does not get menstrual periods. Funk's network of trans friends is an important source of informal medical advice. Compared to when he first started hormone therapy, "Now I have a ton of trans friends, and any time I have a medical problem I'm just texting them about it."[4]

—

Bret, a 46-year-old nonbinary person who was assigned female at birth and uses they/them pronouns, self-reports that they did not receive adequate education about menopause, learning only that it was a time when "your periods stopped and you apparently lose interest in sex and your middle gets thicker . . . [and] you move into old lady phase." Bret reflected that, had they not learned more about menopause from a queer friend, "I [might] well be . . . thinking that I am developing mental health problems or my body is falling apart." When Bret participated in a menopause support group on Facebook, they did not self-identify to the group as nonbinary, for fear of being excluded. Bret's perception was that they were "doing stealth" (by not revealing their gender identity) and that menopause support was laden with "lots of gendered assumptions."[5]

—

While most people may think of menopause as a cisgender "women's" issue, not everyone who experiences menopause falls into that category. There are trans men and other gender diverse people with ovarian systems who experience menopause.[6] Trans women who stop taking hormones may experience menopause-like symptoms, too. To be complete and inclusive, any exploration of the experience and significance of age-related declines in sex hormone levels must account for multiple important identity axes. These axes include sexual orientation (a "person's enduring physical, romantic, and/or emotional attraction to another person . . . [that] may be straight, lesbian, gay, bisexual, pansexual, queer, asexual, etc."), gender identity (a person's "internal, deeply held knowledge of their own gender"), and/or gender expression ("[e]xternal manifestations of gender, expressed through a person's name, pronouns, clothing, haircut, voice, and/or behavior").[7] This chapter explores how each of these may impact the experience of menopause.

Using inclusive language allows for a complex and nuanced conversation about the relationship between and among hormones, sexual orientation, gender identity, gender expression, and the ever-changing language we use to talk about these issues. Throughout this chapter, and in accord with the language used by the World Professional Association for Transgender Health (WPATH), we use the phrase "transgender and gender diverse" to describe people who are a "member of the many varied communities globally of people with gender identities or expressions that differ from the gender socially attributed to the sex assigned to them at birth."[8] In this discussion, we follow suit, while recognizing that language itself is constantly changing.[9] We also use "queer" broadly in this chapter as an umbrella term for the many sexual orientations beyond heterosexual, like lesbian, gay, bisexual, pansexual, and asexual.[10]

After providing an overview of relevant hormones—including a brief discussion of so-called "male menopause"—this chapter centers the menopause-related experiences of queer, trans, and gender diverse people. Some of those experiences raise familiar issues of stigma, silence, and lack of basic awareness about menopause. In addition, queer, trans, and gender diverse people may face some more specific challenges: finding identity-affirming menopause care; having access to gender-inclusive menopause educational materials and support networks; and navigating frequent obstacles in accessing desired hormone therapies, whether in connection with menopause or other physical changes.

## HORMONES AND "MALE MENOPAUSE"?

All humans of all gender identities have what scientists call "sex hormones" in varying levels.[11] Contrary to what many people learn in high school science class, though, hormones are not "male" or "female." Ovaries (and other body parts) produce estrogen, progesterone, *and* testosterone. In bodies with ovarian systems, testosterone plays a role in sex drive, bone growth, and cognitive health.[12] In bodies with testicular systems, the testes (and other body parts) produce testosterone as *well as* estrogen and progesterone.[13] Estradiol, a form of estrogen, helps regulate erectile function and the creation of sperm.[14] As discussed in Chapter 1, fluctuating levels of estrogen are also what cause people to have less predictable or regular menstrual periods, until eventually the ovaries cease egg production and menstruation stops entirely.[15] Indeed, the consequences of that inevitable age-related loss of ovarian function are the focus of most of this book.

In people with testicular systems, testosterone levels usually begin to decline at a rate of approximately 1 percent a year beginning at age 40, absent medical intervention. For this reason, some people say that cis men experience a kind of "male menopause." But from a medical perspective, this moniker is misleading.[16] It implies a "male" analogue to the much steeper hormone drop that every person who possesses at least one ovary and a uterus will inevitably experience as a result of menopause. By contrast, in people with testicular systems, the testes will gradually produce less testosterone with age, but do not completely cease hormone production. Usually, testosterone levels remain in the "normal" range, rather than dropping below a particular "floor."[17]

That said, between 10 and 25 percent of all cis men do experience symptoms because their testosterone levels have dropped below the "normal" range for their age. Symptoms of low testosterone may include erectile dysfunction, reduced libido, loss of bone density, lack of energy or concentration, depressed mood, and even hot flashes.[18] Doctors diagnose late-onset hypogonadism when, due to declines in testosterone production, blood plasma concentrations of that hormone are "abnormally low."[19] In addition to age, factors that may contribute to late-onset hypogonadism include genetics, prior testicular trauma, obesity, elevated levels of alcohol consumption, or high amounts of stress.[20] In such cases, testosterone treatment is sometimes prescribed.

## CISGENDER, LESBIAN, AND BISEXUAL WOMEN AND MENOPAUSE

Regardless of one's gender identity, each person has a sexual orientation, in the sense of "physical, romantic, and/or emotional attraction" (or lack thereof) to others.[21] Multiple and shifting words describe the full range of human sexual orientations; these words are constantly changing. Common terms include straight, lesbian, gay, and bisexual.[22]

Historically speaking, most research on the experience of menopause has focused on cis women. Not only has that research sampled mostly a heterosexual population, too, when gathering data about the impact of menopause on "sex,"[23] but it has also generally taken a limited view of sexual activity (defining it largely in terms of heterosexual, genital-based intercourse). The limited amount of research on menopause in populations other than heterosexual cis women has focused on lesbian or bisexual cis women who have experienced age-related menopause (as opposed to medically induced menopause as a result of undergoing a hysterectomy as a part of cancer treatment, for example).[24] The voices of trans and gender diverse people—who also have a full range of sexual orientations—are largely absent in menopause research so far, including the research that has taken sexual orientation into account.[25] With those caveats, the existing research at the intersection of sexual orientation and menopause suggests three important points about the ways in which one's sexuality may affect the cisgender experience of menopause.

First, some limited data suggests that cis lesbian women may have lower rates of uptake of menopausal hormone therapy (MHT) compared to their heterosexual counterparts. One Australian researcher found that, of the 116 self-identified lesbians surveyed, only 15.9% of the study-participants were taking MHT, compared to 23.2% of Australian women between 47 and 52 years old who responded to a nationwide study.[26] Acknowledging that her sample was not necessarily representative of all lesbians in Australia (or elsewhere), Jennifer Kelly of the Murdoch Children's Research Institute posits that the low uptake of MHT among lesbians related to what she calls a rejection of "the male constructed ideal of beauty" and "feminist identity" among her survey participants.[27] To be sure, having a lesbian sexual orientation does not necessarily mean that one rejects conventional beauty standards or is a feminist. Nevertheless, on the whole, lesbian and bisexual women "often display more relaxed gender prescriptions and proscriptions (i.e., rules for what women should and should not be), embrace greater body size diversity, and take pride in their reputation for gender diversity."[28]

Given this greater flexibility, some lesbians may, as Kelly found, resist medical interventions around menopause. One survey participant, "Andy," framed it this way: "We don't give adolescents something to prevent puberty so why would we give something at the other end to prevent that? What [menopause without MHT] prevents is what the patriarchal society says we are supposed to continue in. We are supposed to stay sexually available to men, our breasts are supposed to stay firm. We are supposed to be available for serving men at any moment and menopause takes us out of that realm."[29]

Another survey participant, "Elizabeth," explained: "I've always seen it [menopause] as just another life stage and because I see it as a life stage[,] it's just[,] well . . . that's just what happens and there will be some inconvenient times and there may be times when you're not feeling very well but you just get on with it."[30] Elizabeth likened menopause to an obstacle to participation in sports: "I played sport for a lot of years and you just play with injuries, so things that are inconvenient, like you still swim if you've got your period . . . I can't allow issues around menopause or anything like that get in the way of my life."[31] As both Andy's and Elizabeth's comments illustrate, having some distance from conventional roles or behaviors expected of women may impact the decision to take MHT.

A second insight from research at the intersection of sexuality and menopause is that cis lesbian and bisexual women may experience less regret than cis heterosexual women do around menopause. A team of researchers at Penn State drew data from the *Midlife in the United States Study*,[32] and mapped participants' response to a question about the feelings associated with age-related cessation of menstruation (ranging from "great relief" to "great regret"). They also tracked responses to questions about attractiveness while aging ("Women sometimes worry about the future and getting older. How much do you worry about being less attractive as a woman?") and about fertility ("Women sometimes worry about the future and getting older. How much do you worry about being too old to have children?").[33]

The researchers, Mary Kruk, Jes Matsick, and Britney Wardecker, found that feelings about menopause did tend to differ based on sexual orientation. Lesbian and bisexual women reported significantly lower levels of regret than heterosexual woman about the cessation of menstruation, after controlling for age, whether the respondent had already stopped menstruating, and whether the respondent had children.[34] Lesbian and bisexual women also reported lower levels of what the researchers called "femininity concerns," or concerns about age-related attractiveness and fertility declines, compared to their heterosexual counterparts. In turn, researchers found a strong correlation between feelings about menstruation and femininity concerns. The lower one's "femininity concerns," the less likely one had feelings of regret about the cessation of menstruation, and vice versa.[35]

Kruk, Matsick, and Wardecker are careful to note that lesbian and bisexual women do not exist apart from society, and they are not necessarily uninfluenced by larger cultural attitudes about aging, beauty, and menopause. The researchers also acknowledge that, although there are lesbian and bisexual women with femme identities, those identities (which are not necessarily a function of appearance) "do not align with gendered roles in the same way as for heterosexual women."[36] The researchers posit that lesbian and bisexual women "as a whole are less likely concerned with heterosexual men's perception of their attractiveness than heterosexual women," and that this posture influences overall attitudes toward menopause.[37]

A third nascent insight from research at the intersection of sexuality and menopause is that the factors influencing how women experience sex after menopause may be more social than physical. Those who are best able to communicate with one's partner, and to define "sex" beyond the strict traditional parameters of heterosexual intercourse, report satisfying sex lives.[38] The research indicates that menopause-related changes to the physical body (such as vaginal dryness or altered libido) determine less about the nature of postmenopausal intimate life than whether (and how) one talked about those changes—or even understood them as impacting "sex" at all.

Researcher Julie Winterich conducted in-depth interviews of nineteen heterosexual women and eleven lesbian women, all of whom were postmenopause. She asked a variety of questions about the participants' relationships, sexual desires, and sexual activities. One 58-year-old woman said that her husband "really minded the dryness . . . [because] his penis would get irritated and then he would say it must be my fault."[39] The emphasis in heterosexual encounters, Winterich noted, tended to be on male pleasure and penetrative sex. Compare that with lesbians like Marcia, age 48, who described her partner's vaginal dryness; menopause had increased Marcia's own libido and decreased her partner's.[40] The couple handles it by taking a broader view of what sex is: "There are moments when we can be really loving, and I don't want to make it sound like we're not sexually into it. We really try to be . . . but we're just not to the point of orgasm all the time," Marcia explained.[41]

In introducing the study, Winterich suggests that, among heterosexual women, "cultural expectations about menopause, gender, and heterosexuality influence how women experience biological changes for sex."[42] Therefore, sexuality is likely a factor in many people's experiences of menopause. However, because Winterich's study was qualitative, not quantitative, and the study sample was small, these conclusions are necessarily circumscribed.

## GENDER IDENTITY AND MENOPAUSE

Pivoting to the ways that multiple gender-related identity axes may impact the experience of menopause, it is important first to note that no formal "transition" needs to occur for a person to be trans or gender diverse. For those who do choose to take externally discernible steps to align their gender identity and gender expression, such changes may be social (e.g., changing one's hairstyle, clothing, or pronouns), legal (e.g., changing one's name), medical (e.g., involving surgeries and/or hormones designed to change the physical body), or some combination of these.

For those who pursue medical changes, affirming healthcare often includes hormone therapies and/or one or more surgical treatments. In fact, WPATH and the Endocrine Society both recommend that doctors begin hormone therapy simultaneously with an adult trans patient's social change, if that patient desires to take hormones.[43] For many trans people, hormone therapy brings a welcome change in physical appearance that eases the social change.[44]

Apart from externally visible changes associated with hormone therapy, medications may enhance the quality of life for trans and gender diverse people in other ways. Researchers have reported that for both trans men and trans women, hormone treatments that are typically prescribed increase certain chemical binding in the brain—specifically, serotonin reuptake transporter binding—which has been linked to reduced levels of major depression, although the role of serotonin's precise involvement in depression is not straightforward.[45] Hormone therapy may also reduce stress levels and facilitate the desired physical changes.[46]

## TRANS WOMEN, HORMONES, AND MENOPAUSE

For trans women (i.e., those assigned male at birth [AMAB] with gender identities as women) who choose medically affirming care, hormone therapy is common. Such hormone therapy typically includes estrogen and other anti-androgens. Estrogen has the effect of reducing male pattern hair growth, contributing to breast development, redistributing body fat, and decreasing the size of the testes. Estrogen also naturally suppresses the production of androgens, like testosterone. As is true with MHT, estrogen may be administered in a variety of forms. Injectables, for example, typically deliver higher doses of estrogen needed for a "feminizing" effect.[47] Additional anti-androgen hormone therapy may also be a desirable option, as it works to minimize characteristically male physical traits like facial hair development, male pattern baldness, and erectile function.[48]

Trans women who take hormones may or may not take them for their entire lives. For example, some trans women—like Lisa Scheps, whose story is one of those that begins this chapter—in order to minimize the risk of blood clots, must stop estradiol therapy in the days or weeks leading up to some surgical procedures, although more research is needed to establish why this is necessary.[49] Some trans women, as they age, decide to take lower doses of hormones or stop taking them entirely, as the consequences of long-term use of this kind of use of hormone therapy is not well studied. Decreasing or ending the hormones may be accompanied by menopause-like symptoms, although negative symptoms are lessened by any testosterone that the body may be producing on its own.[50] Indeed, in one of the few studies of the expectations and experiences of transgender women, the researchers found that "[m]enopause was generally not considered to be particularly relevant."[51]

## TRANS MEN, HORMONES, AND MENOPAUSE

Trans men (i.e., those assigned female at birth [AFAB] with gender identities as men) who elect medically supported change often receive testosterone hormone therapies.[52] In the United States, testosterone typically is administered intramuscularly or subcutaneously, at least initially.[53] Testosterone therapy causes the cessation of menstruation, redistribution of body fat, changes to the skin, deepening of the voice, and increased libido, facial and body hair, muscle mass, and clitoral size.[54] From an externally visible and physical perspective, a trans man who receives hormone therapy will experience certain physical changes, such as increased hair on the face and body, greater muscle mass, altered distribution of body fat, and the cessation of menstruation.

As they begin taking testosterone, trans men with ovarian systems may experience menopause-like symptoms, such as hot flashes and night sweats.[55] They technically will not experience *menopause* as long as they continue taking the hormone.[56] However, in order to become pregnant or undergo certain medical procedures—or simply as a matter of personal choice—a trans man may discontinue taking testosterone at one or more points in time. At these times, the experience of coming off hormone therapy may bring about menopause-like symptoms, including fatigue, hot flashes, sweating, and difficulty sleeping or concentrating.[57] Eventually, a trans man with an ovarian system who does not take testosterone will experience menopause.

## GENDER DIVERSE PEOPLE, HORMONES, AND MENOPAUSE

Not all gender diverse people choose to (or can, based on their personal situation) take hormones. Additionally, some only take hormones on a short-term basis. For example, Simon Moore, a 27-year-old nonbinary person who uses they/them pronouns, had very specific goals in starting hormone therapy: "I never really wanted to be full-on masc, like go to the gym, get ripped, and get the whole beard. I wanted something in between. I wanted to be comfortable."[58] For that reason, Moore opted for "microdoses" of testosterone (fewer milligrams administered less frequently than a "standard" dose of testosterone) for just seven months, and then stopped when the treatment achieved their desired results. Moore likes the way they look now, but they remain open to a different course of action in the future.[59]

For those who are gender diverse, the most sensitive menopause-related care must transcend binary approaches to gender identity. For example, menopausal hormone therapy (MHT) typically involves estrogen, but some patients might be reluctant to take estrogen because of what Tania Glyde of the Queer Menopause Collective describes as "feelings of dysphoria and fear of being feminized."[60] For some of these patients, a microdose of testosterone might be a desirable path toward easing some of their symptoms while also being gender affirming. Yet, as Glyde explains, "Someone wanting to take T both for menopause and for gender affirmation may have to negotiate with multiple gatekeepers,"[61] including primary care providers and gender-affirming care providers, each of whom may focus on different aspects of the situation.

Notably, among health professionals who treat cis women patients who are going through menopause, there is also increasing interest in testosterone supplementation to address low libido, particularly if MHT is ineffective.[62] Testosterone also may be helpful for improving mood, cognition, and muscular-skeletal health.[63] For these reasons, microdoses of testosterone may become a more common aspect of menopause-related care in the future. If so, and as more doctors become comfortable with microdosing testosterone, it may also become a more common option for gender-affirming care, too.[64]

## ACCESS TO GENDER-AFFIRMING MENOPAUSE CARE

Given the range of experiences that all people, including queer, trans, and gender diverse people, have with menopause, menopause-related care needs to take into account various identity axes like sexuality, gender identity, and gender expression. By the same token, gender-affirming care should take the prospect of menopause into account.

Thus far, however, healthcare professionals who specialize in the health needs of trans and gender diverse people have not focused on menopause.[65] For example, the *World Professional Association for Transgender Health (WPATH) Standards of Care* (2022), which set the standards for gender-affirming care worldwide, curiously do not address how trans and gender diverse people may experience menopause; in fact, the standards make almost no mention of menopause at all. To the extent that the *WPATH Standards of Care* do reference menopause, they do so only in passing, such as by referring to the way that extant studies (or the lack thereof) about postmenopausal cis women inform gender-affirming hormone therapies for trans and gender diverse patients.

Reading the *WPATH Standards of Care*, one would have no idea that menopause is part of the inevitable lived experience for many trans and gender diverse people, just as it is for cis women. Of course, the *WPATH Standards of Care* are not meant to address all "routine" health needs that trans and gender diverse patients have. Yet because of the role of "sex" hormones in both gender-affirming care and menopause, the omission is notable.

To be sure, finding providers who are well informed about menopause can be challenging for all people. But these challenges may be amplified for queer, trans, and gender diverse people. According to the *2015 U.S. Transgender Survey*, the largest population-wide study of its kind, 23 percent of all transgender people did not seek out healthcare at all because they feared mistreatment. One-third of trans people who did seek care reported being harassed or even refused treatment because of their trans identities.[66]

Although one would hope that increased trans visibility since the time of the *2015 U.S. Transgender Survey* might be causing rates of such harassments and refusals to decline, it is not clear that there has been much improvement. Indeed, queer people of all gender identities report persistently negative interactions with healthcare providers. This is happening despite the visibility of lesbian and gay people reaching an all-time high, which perhaps has been driven by the Supreme Court's 2015 decision in *Obergefell v. Hodges* affirming the constitutional right of same-sex couples to marry.[67] According to a nationally representative survey conducted by the Center for American Progress in 2017, among all queer respondents who had visited a healthcare provider in the past year, 6% reported that they were refused care because of their actual or perceived sexual orientation, 9% reported healthcare providers using "harsh or abusive language" during treatment, and 7% reported that healthcare providers refused to recognize the patient's family members (such as a child or same-sex partner).[68] Visibility and legal victories, unfortunately, do not necessarily protect queer people against discrimination in the healthcare system.

Add to this fraught landscape the possibility that, in the case of providers who offer gender-affirming care to trans patients, the importance of that care may lead the provider to ignore menopause entirely. In other words, a focus on a patient's *transness* might mean overlooking "basic health needs," ranging from routine health screenings to menopause.[69]

The lack of attention to menopause may result either from inadvertence or intentionality. One transmasculine patient, for example, described how a clinic seemed to overcompensate by not even using the word "menopause," because "its feminine implications could be alienating to transmasculine clients."[70] Yet Sam, a 36-year-old trans man, reports that accessing any healthcare around what historically is called "women's health" is, for him, "awful." As Sam explains, "I'm forced to confront the fact that my body doesn't naturally produce testosterone, but it does produce oestrogen. I experience a lot of dysphoria about that."[71]

Conversely, among providers who do have menopause expertise, a lack of sensitivity and competence in the specific needs of queer, trans, and gender diverse patients may mean that these patients remain untreated. For example, as one transgender woman explained, "I've had the experience of doctors refusing to treat me because they didn't know enough about 'transgenders' [a term of ignorance]."[72]

Adding complexity to the analysis is the fact that the language, conversations, and procedures that may distress one person do not necessarily distress others. That is, "menopause" might be an unwelcome term for some because it calls to mind a "connection with what is known as feminine." For someone else, menopause might mean an end to a familiar experience of bleeding and a loss of a "connection to that part of themselves."[73] There is no one-size-fits-all experience of either menopause or gender-affirming menopause care.

The multiple negative interactions that queer, trans, and gender diverse people have with the healthcare system were illustrated by a 2021 study by Tania Glyde, a London psychotherapist. Glyde conducted in-depth interviews with twelve people of varying sexual orientations and gender identities, asking them about their experiences of menopause care with both mental health professionals and general healthcare providers.[74] Glyde's study participants reported multiple negative experiences. For example, when a 46-year-old nonbinary patient assigned female at birth approached their doctor to talk about menopause, the doctor immediately insisted on prescribing antidepressants, despite the patient's concerns that they might cause a loss of libido. The doctor did not listen to the patient's concerns or treat the patient as having a stake in their own treatment. Keeping patients in the dark about their own care reinforces a hierarchical model with the doctor as the "expert" and the patient as a non-agentic actor who does not deserve to understand their own health.

Likewise, Glyde recounts the experiences of one lesbian with a genderqueer identity who was assigned female at birth. In seeking medical care for perimenopause-related symptoms, the patient consulted several doctors, an experience that is not uncommon, as discussed in Chapter 1. Once the patient mentioned their prior breast removal (top surgery), the conversation with the doctor changed:

> [One GP] started asking what genitalia I was born with, and whether I was born with normal genitalia. . . . I had [another GP] say "I don't understand what genderqueer is," and get quite aggressive with me, and just not seem to understand whether I was taking hormones or not, and when I said no, they were like, "Why are you not? You are not transitioning then? Are you a man or a woman?" . . . The medical facts seemed almost impossible for them to grasp without me being humiliated and interrogated.[75]

Negative interactions like these—infantilization, bullying, unnecessary questioning, and shaming patients—understandably leave many queer, trans, and gender diverse people reluctant to seek menopause-related care, if they seek healthcare services at all.

## HYPER-GENDERED AND HETEROSEXIST MENOPAUSE INFORMATION

Another significant obstacle that queer, trans, and gender diverse people face in accessing quality menopause care is its highly gendered and frequently heterosexist nature. For example, Bret, the 46-year-old nonbinary person assigned female at birth introduced at the beginning of this chapter, talked about their experience of "doing stealth" (i.e., not revealing their nonbinary gender identity) in menopause support groups. In these environments, Bret has observed a dominant narrative that women should be "able to deliver what is expected of them by their boyfriends or husbands, and that inevitably involve[es] intercourse."[76]

Tania Glyde has commented on the "pinking-and-purpling-and-flowering of things, whether decor, leaflets or products" related to menopause.[77] Glyde particularly objects to menopause messaging addressed to "ladies" as being both non-inclusive and patronizing: "The word . . . conjures up a kind of bum-patting old-fashioned sexism. There is enough misogyny, ageism and mockery—not to mention infantilisation—directed towards people in menopause to know that adding to it does not feel helpful."[78] While some people do not object to being addressed as "ladies," or may even like it, for others the term is alienating. To be misaddressed or misdescribed can be distracting, distressing, and draining, as Glyde explains.[79] Given that menopause is already a topic about which there is a great deal of apprehension and misunderstanding, the hyper-gendered nature of even well-intentioned communications can be an actual obstacle to receiving effective and truly compassionate menopause care.

The best menopause care should—indeed must—account for the full range of human sexual expression and relations. As described in Chapter 1, declining hormone levels during perimenopause may lead to changes in sexual drive. Around and after menopause, there may be changes to the genitourinary system, including vaginal dryness, pain, or urinary symptoms—all of which can impact one's intimate life.[80] Medical providers may frame symptoms as obstacles to "sex," narrowly defined as penis-in-vagina intercourse, with little or no mention of other types and forms of sexual intimacy. For example, in its public-facing medical information, Johns Hopkins Medicine provides information about "How Sex Changes After Menopause," explaining factors that may affect desire: "the vaginal canal [may become] less stretchy and you may experience dryness, which can cause intercourse to be painful."[81]

This information, however, might not be helpful for patients for whom intercourse is not the center of their sex lives. For example, a 52-year-old woman named Jane reflects that, although she and her wife have maintained a regular sex life during menopause treatments, "if we were having any problems with sexual stuff, I'd be more inclined to see a therapist and access my own information online. I can't see me sitting [and talking to a doctor]—and I am quite confident and assertive."[82] This is because, according to Jane, most menopause advice "is more about penetrative sex, and obviously lesbian sex isn't just around that at all."[83] Jane observes that "I've not had anything that's said: 'We appreciate all women are different' or 'All women will have different relationships.' There isn't an acknowledgement."[84] Heterosexual presumptions or biases may mean that many menopause resources will not be relevant or helpful for queer patients. Broadening the lens—of what counts as "sex" and what "sex" is—will make menopause care more accessible, relevant, and helpful for everyone.

For centuries, conversations about biology-based conditions have been framed in gender binary terms that presume heterosexuality. Changing long-standing ways of thinking and talking about human bodies is difficult, for sure. This may seem especially true with a topic like menopause, which many people are uncomfortable discussing in the first place. Understanding the full range of individuals who can experience menopause helps identify the shared experiences and needs of people of different sexual orientations, gender identities, and gender expressions. Ultimately, everyone should have access to information about menopause and care that encourages human flourishing.

CHAPTER SEVEN

# MENOPAUSE CAPITALISM

"I've been looking for a menopause company!" That was the reaction of entrepreneur Ankur Jain when he heard about Alloy, a menopause telehealth company cofounded by Anne Fulenwider and Monica Molenaar.[1] Jain, a cisgender man who was then 29 years old, was not drawn to Alloy for personal health reasons, though. His interest was financial. Jain is the cofounder and CEO of Kairos, a multibillion-dollar venture fund that became a major investor in Alloy's $3.3 million seed funding in October 2021.[2]

Alloy is just one of many new companies offering products or services related to menopause. Indeed, menopause has become a big business with significant profits at stake.[3] Venture funds, traditional corporations, and individual celebrity investors, including Drew Barrymore, Gwyneth Paltrow, Cameron Diaz, Abby Wambach, and Glennon Doyle, are all seeking to profit from what has been called the menopause "gold rush."[4]

That menopause represents a lucrative business opportunity is simple math. Worldwide, roughly 6 percent of the entire population falls in the demographic band of cis women aged 40 to 49—the group most likely to be perimenopausal.[5] Women between the ages of 45 and 54 represent almost 10 percent of the workforce in the United States. Overall, women constituted more than 45 percent of the country's workforce in 2022.[6] Given the sheer number of people experiencing the menopausal transition each year, investors estimate that by 2025, there will be a $600 billion worldwide market for menopause-related goods and services.[7] Indeed, according to a 2019 survey conducted by AARP (formerly known as the American Association of Retired Persons), a full 93 percent of menopause-aged women expressed interest in "non-invasive, technology-related solutions" to help address the symptoms of menopause.[8]

A 2019 article in the *New Republic* identified menopause-related products, from clothing and devices to lotions and apps, as the latest entrants in an industry devoted to the "wide array of products and services that are advertised as helping women along the path to self-determination and healthy, sustainable lifestyles," at every stage in their life cycles, starting with menstruation.[9] Many business journalists refer to the collective purveyors of these uniquely twenty-first-century products and services as the "femtech" industry. This book, however, mostly eschews that term, for four principal reasons. First, "femtech" is primarily an investor-driven term that neither has been adopted by consumers nor has any legal significance. Second, the term incorporates the root of the word "female"; however, it is important to recognize that users of products and services labeled as "femtech" have a full range of gender identities. Third, the term is a shorthand that could have the un-intended effect of stigmatizing so-called women's products or services, as well as companies that create and invest in them.[10] Finally, reflecting the book's subject, the focus of this chapter is on enterprises focused on menopause specifically—not the whole of "women's health." In fact, start-up funding for menopause-related companies is a comparatively small segment of the overall sector.[11]

This chapter examines menopause using a market-focused lens. It surveys the landscape of menopause products and services, which range from skin-care products, creams, and nutritional supplements to clothing, personal devices, and digital products and services, all of which are marketed primarily to perimenopausal and menopausal cis women. Here, we apply a critical lens to what we call "meno-pause capitalism"—that is, the marketing and selling of menopause-related products or services by commercial entities, typically through messages that celebrate autonomy, community, or stereotypical femininity.[12]

The examination that follows illuminates two of the paradoxes that recur throughout this book. First is the need to avoid pathologizing menopause as a "condition" or "illness," while simultaneously acknowledging that, for many people, the physical and psychological effects of menopause merit serious attention and treatment. Numerous businesses have now been founded on the premise that the treatment of menopause involves using a range of products, including but not limited to the creams, lotions, vitamins, clothing, devices, and digital services discussed in this chapter. Second is the importance of greater awareness and openness about menopause, on the one hand, and the imperative for more robust privacy protections for personal data, on the other. The growing number of menopause apps that prompt users to submit and log their menopausal symptoms, often in combination with receiving individualized health advice and/or connecting with other users, typify this tension. To illustrate and assess how these two paradoxes play out, this chapter takes a closer look at particular menopause-related companies as representative of larger trends or examples of salient issues.[13]

In one sense, menopause capitalism is long overdue. Diversity in both information resources and products not only increases consumer choice, but also allows for greater flexibility in addressing menopause. The proliferation of menopause-related offerings means that managing its symptoms need not be reduced simply to a decision about whether to take MHT or not. For customers who may be concerned about the possible side effects of MHT, nonprescription products that take the familiar form of topical applications and vitamins have tremendous appeal. Encouraging treatment free from stigma or shame is a salutary shift in both culture and commerce, too. At the same time, however, many aspects of menopause capitalism rely heavily on gendered and ageist stereotypes, tend to associate wellness and comfort with spending, and raise significant privacy concerns. This chapter explores those themes as well.

## LOTIONS AND POTIONS

"A peri/menopause self-care kit we only dreamed about until we decided to get together and actually make it. Treat yourself to sweet relief and proactive daily support inside and out."[14] This is how Kindra, one of several menopause-oriented companies that offer products for aging skin and bodies impacted by the menopausal transition, advertises an "Essential Bundle" of vaginal lotion and a "body-balancing" daily supplement that it sells for $98.[15] Kindra also sells treatments that target the face and other visible skin,[16] creams that promise relief for vaginal or vulvar dryness,[17] and nutritional supplement pills that allegedly address a range of menopausal symptoms including low libido, brain fog, fatigue, night sweats, difficulty sleeping, and depressed mood.[18] With its tagline, *"Feel Like You Again,"* the company's menopause topical products and supplements are advertised as "hormone-free relief that makes a difference on day one."[19]

Kindra's embrace of multiple products is, in some ways, typical of one segment of menopause-wellness companies. The company Stripes, which bills itself as a menopause brand of "scalp to vag products," also sells an array of face creams (that promise to brighten, hydrate, and plump) for approximately $85,[20] a "Vag of Honor" gel advertised for "dry vaginal skin" for $50,[21] and vitamins that are "specially formulated for those experiencing (peri)menopause symptoms including hot flashes and brain fog" priced at $40 for 60 pills.[22]

Indeed, vitamins and other dietary supplements, which are largely unregulated by the Food and Drug Administration, are a notable segment of the menopause market. The company Wile, in which tennis star Serena Williams is one of the investors, is devoted entirely to vitamins for women over 40.[23]

Much of the advertising for lotions, creams, and dietary supplements aimed at menopause-aged consumers conveys a shame-free attitude toward aging generally and menopause specifically. For example, the tag line for the Stripes brand is "Welcome to a world where menopause isn't a dirty word."[24] Kindra's website features the prominent headline "Embracing the Change" and describes the company's mission to "empower people who experience the hormonal changes of menopause to care for their bodies—naturally, safely, and holistically."[25]

Many menopause-oriented companies also lean into personal messaging, even holding out the promise of finding community through the purchase of the company's products. Kindra's website features a picture of the company's female CEO, next to which is a callout box saying that menopause "should not be like Fight Club. The first rule of menopause should be TALK about menopause."[26] Under the heading "Girlfriends and Guidance," Kindra's website includes a link to a members-only Facebook page billed as "Menopause Support & Straight-Talk."[27]

Personal storytelling and the presence of a discernible company story, or "face," at least on the firm's website, are central to many menopause companies' marketing strategies. For example, the advertising for Stripes emphasizes that the company was founded by actress Naomi Watts to offer "holistic menopause solutions" like creams and vaginal lubricants. On social media, Stripes asks potential consumers, "Curious why @naomiwatts founded Stripes? She did it for YOU!"[28] This question is followed by a link to personal video testimony from Watts herself, who recounts feeling "completely lost" when she entered menopause. She says that her goal is for any woman going through menopause to feel supported by both the company's products and "a community to wrap their arms around her and feel like she is being seen and her specific needs are being addressed."[29]

This empowerment and sisterhood rhetoric tends to downplay the fact that menopause-oriented companies like Stripes are profit-seeking ventures at their core. Indeed, menopause companies often seek to project an "indie" image through web presences and marketing that includes information about the company's origins, pictures of the people in leadership positions at the company, and even humorous or irreverent product names or advertising.[30] All of this does not necessarily present a full picture of what the company is, however. Kindra's website, for instance, does not mention that Kindra actually is backed by Procter & Gamble, the international consumer goods company that also sells well-known products like Always and Tampax brands of menstrual products, Head & Shoulders shampoo, and Gillette razors and skin-care products.[31]

## HIGH-TECH CLOTHING

For some people, "dressing for menopause" (with tongue-in-cheek) might mean novelty T-shirts with slogans such as "In menopause and hotter than ever,"[32] or "When I asked for a smoking hot body, menopause wasn't what I had in mind."[33] For others, dressing for menopause is a practical consideration that involves choosing lightweight fabrics or layers that can be removed easily during a hot flash or that will dry quickly after night sweats. Although people almost certainly have been dressing with menopause in mind for centuries, there are now entire companies devoted to selling menopause clothing lines (i.e., "cool clothing for hot moments"[34]), often touted as having the ability to "control hot flashes and night sweats."[35] This is, of course, a misleading promise. No clothing can *control* the *symptoms* of menopause. That said, certain garments may feel more (or less) comfortable or make it easier for the wearer to cope with the symptoms of menopause.

Advances in the development of synthetic fibers and moisture-wicking fabric have allowed menopause-oriented businesses to craft a message that customers need special clothing at this stage of life. Because the clothing is advertised as special—and even technologically advanced—companies feel entitled to charge a premium for it, which some people seem to have no problem paying.

As is true in the multibillion-dollar maternity clothing business, "menopause" clothing tends to be more expensive than nonspecialty garments. But unlike purchasers of pregnancy clothing, who may need specialty clothing only for a limited period with a fixed end point, those experiencing the menopause transition might have symptoms that last for years or indefinitely, as discussed in Chapter 1. That often translates into high prices for consumers over a much longer term. For example, on the website of Fifty One Apparel (so named for the average age of menopause in the United States),[36] a basic pajama short set sells for more than $80.[37] The company appears to justify its prices by reference to technology; the pajama short set, for instance, features "Thermocules Technology" and "Outlast Temperature Regulating Fabric." Fifty One Apparel describes these technologies under the headline "The NASA Technology Behind 51 Apparel."[38]

Another company, Become Clothing, sells moisture-wicking underwear (to "leave you feeling confident and fresh throughout the day") for $17 a pair, presumably with the promise that the wearer will feel drier after a hot flash or night sweats.[39] At a slightly higher price range, starting at $25, Become Clothing also sells absorbent underwear designed for those with irregular menstrual bleeding, bladder leakage, or urinary incontinence associated with the menopause transition.[40]

Once again, an examination of the marketing of menopause shirts, sleepwear, and undergarments reveals how companies craft messages of allyship and empowerment to encourage purchases. For example, the company Cucumber Clothing uses messages of solidarity: "Rampaging hormones can whip up a whirlwind of menopausal symptoms. . . . Well, Cucumber Clothing has your back."[41] Fifty One Apparel, the purveyor of "menopause day, lounge and nightwear," proclaims on its website, "You should never be held back by your menopause symptoms."[42] Hazel, a company that sells menopause underwear, hygiene wipes, and an "Anti-Stick Stick" to reduce "rashes and irritation causes by leaks and sweat," explicitly uses marketing language that rejects negative associations with menopause. "For far too long," the company's website reads, "the incontinence category has made women feel ashamed and alienated (hello adult diapers); our products are all about . . . making you feel like your marvelous self at every age."[43] The implicit promise is that by buying these products, one can be "marvelous" and free from shame that may have plagued past generations. Spending money is positioned as the pathway for "treating" menopause, controlling one's body, and improving one's sense of self.

## CHEMICAL CONCERNS

Given the positive messaging that dominates menopause clothing advertisements, consumers may not be aware that potentially harmful chemicals may be present in these products. Like exercise clothing, menopause clothing is advertised as having antimicrobial and odor control features. These qualities likely depend on the use of silver nanoparticles, which are small microscopic particles that have been identified as chemicals of possible concern for human health and are commonly referred to as "nanosilver."[44] Nanosilver can be absorbed through the skin, lungs, and mouth. In animal studies, nanosilver exposure has been shown to have a negative impact on organs such as the brain, liver, kidneys, spleen, and heart.[45]

Furthermore, given recent disclosures about the presence of per- and polyfluoroalkyl substances (PFAS) in so-called "period underwear," it is quite possible that menopause underwear contains them as well. PFAS have been linked to a variety of health concerns, including cancer, thyroid disease, liver damage, and hypertension.[46] In February 2023, European regulators proposed a gradual phaseout of all PFAS in all chemicals, mixtures, and products ranging from contact lenses to food packaging.[47] In the United States, some PFAS are no longer produced because of their potential hazard to human health.[48] Maine, Washington, and California, for example, have enacted strict rules on PFAS; several other states are considering legislation that would ban or sharply or limit them.[49]

In response to concerns about the dangers of PFAS, researchers at Emory University and the Chemical Insights Research Institute announced in 2023 the launch of a first-of-its-kind comprehensive study designed to precisely identify which PFAS are in certain clothing and furniture, whether and how PFAS are absorbed by the human body from consumer goods, and the impact of PFAS on human health.[50] The results of that study, combined with negative publicity around chemicals in menstrual underwear, may impact the future shape of the market not only for menopause clothing, but also for garments and textiles more generally. Perhaps in anticipation of these developments, Become Clothing's absorbent underwear are now advertised as PFAS-free.[51]

Although there are no publicized consumer tests for the presence of PFAS and nanosilver in menopause underwear specifically, there have been tests of menstrual underwear that show the presence of these chemicals.[52] In 2023, the underwear company Thinx, which markets absorbent period underwear primarily as an alternative to tampons and pads, settled a class action lawsuit that alleged deceptive marketing practices concerning its menstrual underwear. The company previously advertised its underwear as "organic, sustainable, and nontoxic."[53] In connection with the 2023 settlement, Thinx claimed that PFAS were not part of the underwear's "product design" but agreed to ensure that PFAS are not *intentionally* added to the underwear.[54] Relatedly, the company also agreed that it will "not refer to the anti-microbial components of Agion," which uses nanosilver and other particles for odor control, as "non-migratory," or staying entirely on the clothing.[55] In other words, the underwear does contain nanosilver; the company will simply limit its claims about the nanosilver's staying in place.

Neither the complaint nor the settlement in the PFAS class action litigation made any mention of the company's Speax product line of incontinence underwear (now known as Thinx for All Leaks), which can be useful to people suffering with menopause-related bladder issues, even though Speax was advertised as having the same absorbent and odor-reducing properties as the company's menstrual underwear.[56] Furthermore, Thinx is not under any obligation, either by statute or terms of the settlement, to make an affirmative showing of the absence of PFAS or nanosilver in its absorbent underwear.[57]

Thus, despite claims by Thinx and other companies that their absorbent underwear is "ecofriendly,"[58] consumers have every reason to take a more cautious approach. Indeed, it is notable that a significant portion of the customer base for menopausal products has already expressed concerns about the possible side effects of MHT, which suggests that they may well be concerned about the prospect of chemicals in menopause underwear as well.[59]

## MENOPAUSE-RELATED DEVICES

The market's selection of technology-related products to "treat" menopause goes beyond creams, supplements, and clothing, and increasingly includes special devices as well. One such product is the "Cube Sleep System," formerly called the "Chilipad," a mattress topper that promises to "reduce hot flashes' symptoms in both severity and duration by regulating your bed's temperature" for about $700.[60] Another device is the Embr Wave 2 wristband, which—also "at the touch of a button"—generates "precisely calibrated cooling or warming sensations to [provide] more control over your hot flashes and related menopause symptoms," at the cost of $299.[61] A different "smart" wristband (not yet available for sale to customers) is supposedly able to *itself* detect the onset of a hot flash and preemptively apply coolness to the wearer's arms.[62]

In 2021, the Food and Drug Administration even approved an at-home ultrasound device to treat menopause-related vaginal dryness, without the use of hormones.[63] The small handheld device is designed to stimulate blood flow to the vaginal canal to treat vulvovaginal atrophy[64]—a condition characterized by a shortening and tightening of the vaginal canal, vaginal soreness, vaginal dryness, and painful intercourse, and caused by low estrogen levels in the body.[65]

The promotional materials for these devices echo some of the same themes discernible in advertising for menopause clothing, skin-care products, and vitamins. Madorra, the maker of the ultrasound device, proclaims that its corporate goal is "to empower people to live fuller, healthier lives," adding that its device is the first to provide a nonhormonal alternative to MHT for "post-menopausal people and breast cancer survivors." In this way, Madorra embraces the familiar trope of empowerment, saying that "[a]ll people have the right to choose" how to address their symptoms of menopause.[66] Relatedly, Embr Wave touts its "exclusive technology" that is "grounded in thermal science," mirroring the language used to market high-tech menopause clothes that use "NASA" technology.[67]

## CURING THROUGH SPENDING?

Menopause capitalism is propelled by creating a perceived need for expensive products to cope with inevitable bodily functions. Indeed, what all these menopause products—from skin care, creams, and vitamins to clothing, pillows, and devices—have in common is marketing that relies on the notion that menopause is a "problem" with a "solution" that can be achieved through spending. The notion that exclusive, NASA-level technology is necessary here is striking. No doubt, many of these products do provide relief to their customers, and it is certainly positive that menopausal symptoms are being recognized and taken seriously by the market. However, fans, ice packs, or other inexpensive options may also be effective in addressing many menopausal symptoms (although not necessarily vaginal atrophy).

Moreover, the promotion of these products sometimes implicates stereotypes of menopause as embarrassing, shameful, or even mysterious. The promotion of cooling wristbands with electronic sensors because hot flashes "are uncomfortable, embarrassing and above all inconvenient, striking day and night," for example, goes beyond characterizing hot flashes as uncomfortable or inconvenient by also describing them as "embarrassing."[68] Relatedly, the advertising for a cooling pillow insert that touts a "machine learning model to make sure the temperature is right for you"[69] suggests that the symptoms of menopause are unknowable or mysterious, even though many people likely already know—without reference to computer-gathered biometrics—what their "ideal temperature profile" is.

The ability to know and understand the human body, with the hope of easing menopause symptoms, is the implicit premise of many of these menopause products. That premise becomes more explicit in yet another segment of the menopause market: businesses that sell primarily digital products that purportedly enable people to understand and address their symptoms by intensively tracking them.

## MENOPAUSE APPS AND PLATFORMS

There are a variety of apps and platforms that offer menopausal symptom tracking, often in connection with providing users with healthcare support and/or connection with others who are having similar experiences.[70] Stella, for instance, is an app created by Vira Health that describes itself as an "online clinic for menopause support." It encourages users to log their symptoms and medical history, at which point they can receive prescriptions for MHT, together with other "personalised lifestyle advice specific to [their] symptoms and the products [they] need." Additionally, through group coaching sessions, Stella users can "interact with other Stella users and get direct support with [the] plan's techniques and habits."[71] Copenhagen-based Femilog is also an app that offers daily menopause symptom tracking. Its stated goal is "providing women with a broader and clearer menopause health picture," in order to "decrease feelings of stress and anxiety and make them feel understood."[72]

Such apps often present symptom tracking as a sort of medical self-monitoring project. The mySysters app, for instance, permits users to track their symptoms and then print out charts with that data, presumably for personal consultation or to facilitate communication with a healthcare provider.[73] Similarly, the MenoLife app bills itself as "the most advanced menopause health tracker app ever built," offering users the ability to track their perimenopause and menopause symptoms along with their menstrual cycle, ovulation, weight, water intake, sleep, and mood, such that they can then review their 7-day, 30-day, and 90-day trend lines.[74]

As with so much about menopause capitalism, there is a "double-edged sword" aspect to these apps. There is no doubt, for instance, that the act of tracking one's symptoms may lead users to have an increased sense of control and understanding; it may also improve their ability to identify and describe trends to their healthcare providers. That said, such tracking apps should also be understood to be part of what anthropologists Andrea Ford and Giulia de Togni, together with student coauthor Livia Miller, have called the "neoliberal self-management project." Both menopause and period trackers "facilitate the integration of medical and non-medical approaches to health within a broader framework of approaching one's life as a personal management exercise."[75] Indeed, such trackers walk a fine line: they encourage health and well-being, but the focus on "symptom tracking" can simultaneously position menopause and menstruation as sorts of problems or illnesses that must be managed and monitored.

Related to the self-monitoring facilitated by the apps, many of these digital menopause platforms also offer peer support and connection. The mySysters app, for example, describes itself as both a "social and self-care mobile platform" that not only offers symptom tracking, but also enables women to "share advice with other women in discussion forums." Similarly, the perry app (tagline: "Menopause Sisterhood Support") connects all users in a "Sisters Chat" group, and then allows users to join separate groups with names like "Work & Peri," "Excessive weight, WTF?," "I don't feel like myself anymore," and "Sex or no SEX?"[76] Another app, Peanut, which was initially a networking app for new mothers, added a "Peanut Menopause" digital community.[77] Members can join groups like "fit at fifty," "M-brace The Change," "Midlife Pleasure & Power—Sex, Cycles Education & Empowerment" and "Product Feedback."[78]

No doubt, there is value in the peer support that many connection-focused menopause apps offer. Peer communication helpfully enables those who are experiencing the menopause transition to come together and discuss symptoms, challenges, and strategies for coping with common occurrences such as hot flashes, mood changes, or sleep disturbances. It also provides emotional support. Being present in a community, whether digital or face-to-face, can be an antidote in a culture that otherwise treats menopause as either something to be hidden or the butt of jokes.[79] The community also serves a powerful normalizing function. The perry app, for instance, reminds users that "85% of women experience symptoms of menopause: Yes! It's normal. No! You're not alone."[80]

At the same time, these platforms occasionally demand a flattening of the menopause experience. On Peanut, one's profile must include a user's life stage (with the only choices being "trying to conceive," "mama-to-be," "mama," "perimenopause," and "menopause"), even though one can, of course, be in two categories at once (such as a "mama" and "trying to conceive" or even "mama to be" and "perimenopause").[81] On perry, one's profile page asks for the user's "biggest WTF peri/menopause symptom," but the user is only given sixty characters to describe it.[82] In other words, to fully enter the community, a user must identify and share her symptoms, rank them, and then choose the most problematic. This forces users to fit their experiences into predetermined categories, and to define themselves in terms of their "worst" perimenopause symptoms.

In addition to these concerns about the apps' messaging, a separate issue lies in the substance of the apps themselves. One of the few studies of menopause apps found that just over a quarter had been developed with the benefit of professional medical involvement, and less than 25 percent featured "evidence-based practice," which took "the form of guidelines or treatment protocols."[83]

A related concern stems from the various ads (from third parties) for menopause-related products that often appear on these apps' websites. Given that people typically seek out the apps in the first place for health-based information, they may think that the products for which they encounter ads have been vetted or approved by the app itself. This is not necessarily the case, however, and such a disclosure might be made only in an app's legal fine print. A careful review of the terms and conditions of the U.S.-based menopause app Caria, for example, reveals that the company disclaims responsibility for any material made available by third parties such as advertisers.[84] Thus, an advertiser on that site might promote herbal supplements, to give just one example, as an appropriate treatment for symptoms of menopause, without necessarily being required to provide any backing for its claims.[85]

## PRIVACY BREACHES

Digital menopause-related products and services raise serious privacy concerns. To be sure, privacy concerns are present even with purely analog menopause-related products. For instance, to take advantage of discounts, bonuses, and loyalty programs, consumers may unwittingly share private information with businesses. But in the digital sphere, the privacy concerns run even deeper. Products like the Embr Wave 2 bracelet, for instance, come with an optional app; users are encouraged to "track your usage and learn from your patterns over time" to "get more options for relief that's just right for your body," like choosing "specially designed waveforms."[86]

In "helping" users track and share data about their perimenopausal or menopausal symptoms, digital technology companies are gathering extraordinary amounts of personal information that is itself a valuable commodity. For example, the privacy policy that accompanies the Embr Wave app states that its services "enable third parties to collect information through cookies, web beacons, and device identifiers, such as IDFA or Advertising ID, for use in online interest-based advertising," and that "we or our third-party advertising networks might use information about your use of the Services to help target non-EMBR Labs advertisements to you on unaffiliated websites or mobile apps based on your online activity in general."[87] Embr Wave also notes that it will use "commercially reasonable physical, electronic, and procedural safeguards" to ensure information is protected, but also notes that "no security program is foolproof."

The information that a company gathers and how secure that data is vary for every digital product and service. The story of Flo Health, a period tracking app, provides a cautionary tale. Launched in Minsk, Belarus, in late 2015, Flo Health had 22 million monthly users by 2018 and claimed to be the "number 1 female health product by active audience in the USA."[88] Flo's privacy policy at the time promised that it would not share details about "cycles, pregnancy, symptoms, notes and other information that is entered by you and that you do not elect to share, with third party vendors."[89] This information included users' answers to highly personal questions like, "Have you noticed a decrease in sexual desire?" and "Are you sexually active during your period?"

Only a few months later, however, the *Wall Street Journal* investigated Flo's Period & Ovulation Tracker. Reporters found that the app was indeed sharing information on periods and pregnancy intentions with Facebook and that there was no "apparent way to stop that information from being sent to Facebook."[90] After the newspaper article ran, Flo stopped disclosing the data, but hundreds of users complained to the United States Federal Trade Commission (FTC), which enforces federal consumer protection laws.[91]

In 2021, the FTC filed a complaint against Flo, alleging that the company had not kept its promise to keep private data private and had instead shared health information about its users with other companies, including Google and Facebook.[92] Without admitting any wrongdoing, Flo entered into a settlement agreement with the FTC, agreeing to notify users whose information had already been disclosed and to tell the companies that had received the data to destroy it. In addition, Flo promised to obtain consent from future users before sharing their health data.[93] Subsequent to the FTC settlement, a consolidated class action complaint was filed against Flo on behalf of individual plaintiffs who brought claims including breach of contract and invasion of privacy.[94] The suit is still ongoing as this book went to publication.

Whether users have changed their behavior in response to news of Flo's privacy breaches is unclear. Despite the negative publicity around Flo's privacy's policy, the company appears to have grown. It still claims to be the "#1 period and ovulation tracker worldwide," with 250 million users. In addition, Flo has expanded its reach by explicitly incorporating menopause into its offerings and messaging. The company describes itself as "supporting women during their entire reproductive lives through tracking menstruation, sharing cycle predictions, or preparing for conception, pregnancy, early motherhood, and menopause."[95]

## SELLING MENOPAUSE SUPPORT AS AN EMPLOYEE BENEFIT

If the story of Flo highlights the privacy risks associated with using menopause apps and platforms, those concerns may be heightened in the context of companies that are selling menopause support as a benefit that employers can offer their employees. The U.K.-based company Peppy, for example, has created an app that employees can use to access educational materials, and to either text, or meet via video conference, with a menopause healthcare specialist.[96] Peppy markets itself as a way that a business can "give your people access to personalized support through the phone, anytime, anywhere."[97] Likewise, Barcelona-based B-wom ("your coach for intimate and feminine health")[98] partners with insurance companies, drug companies, or doctors that seek to "be part of the shift toward self-care" by providing support for patient-consumers. B-wom also works with employers that wish to offer "preventative health plans and welfare improvement" for employees.[99]

In the United States, Massachusetts-based Ovia Health, a digital health company that works with health insurers and employers, as well as individuals, expanded into the menopause space. Employers can partner with Ovia to provide their employees with health plan care management, health coaching, and—not surprisingly—personal health tracking. At the end of 2022, Ovia Health announced its new "menopause support program," through which users can download an interactive tool in which they submit and track their menopausal symptoms so that "Ovia Health Coaches" can reach out "to offer support and connect members to resources." Ovia Health advises employers, meanwhile, that providing these sorts of benefits to employees can "help you contain medical costs, improve overall experience and satisfaction, and drive productivity."[100]

Digital menopause platforms like Ovia that position themselves primarily in the business-to-business (B2B) market are responding to recent, unprecedented attention that has been paid to the real economic costs of menopause for businesses.[101] As noted in Chapter 4, researchers at the Mayo Clinic estimated in 2023 that menopause-related absenteeism in the United States costs $1.8 billion annually in lost workplace productivity.[102] The reality of menopause-related absenteeism is not limited to the United States, either. A 2009 study of a Japanese company, for example, found that after offering increased health support for all female employees—including private consultations with an on-site occupational health nurse—fewer menopause-aged women took sick days. Those who did take sick days took fewer of them. Fewer workers took early retirement because of menopause-related symptoms as well.[103]

In the employment context, these menopause apps and platforms present unique privacy concerns. As Ovia explains to its users, "if you are receiving Ovia premium features through a health insurer or employer health plan"—like health coaching or alerts based on data that the user has logged—that data is protected by HIPAA and can only be used for "proper healthcare purposes," like treatment and payment. Even so, that anonymized health data can get shared with employers for "care and benefits management."[104] This means that employers are able to look up aggregate data on their employees' usage of Ovia's various services, and—depending on how many employees they have—may even be able to track such data back to individual employees.[105] As reporters at the *Washington Post* observed in the context of examining Ovia's pregnancy-tracking app, Ovia has thus become a "powerful monitoring tool for employers and health insurers," enabling them to gain significant amounts of data about their employees' reproductive lives and health.[106] The concern is that employers might use data to take negative, discriminatory employment actions against employees known or suspected to have certain health-related conditions.

## SELLING MENOPAUSE TELEHEALTH SUPPORT TO CONSUMERS

A distinct segment of digital menopause-focused companies relates not to symptom tracking, but to specialty telehealth services, such as virtual medical appointments and access to prescription medication. These are mostly advertised as for consumers, but one could imagine an employer suggesting these services to employees or even offering to cover costs as a kind of employee benefit.

One such company, Gennev—which bills itself as "the largest virtual clinic for menopausal care"—boasts that it has "helped thousands of women improve their quality of life in menopause."[107] With just a few clicks on the website, users can self-schedule a consultation with a physician or dietitian who is authorized to provide services in the state where the patient is located.[108] An initial thirty-minute telehealth consultation with a board-certified ob-gyn takes place via Zoom and costs $120.[109] Although Gennev does not take insurance, the website advertises that its appointments "are reimbursable through most insurance plans."[110] Based on the patient's medical history and menopause symptoms, the provider then creates a health plan "with evidence-backed treatments" designed to "alleviate . . . symptoms and improve . . . quality of life." That plan may include MHT, other prescription medications, and recommendations for dietary supplements and lifestyle changes, all of which cost extra.[111]

Through the Gennev website, users can also access free menopause-related educational materials and occasional fee-based group educational sessions about menopause.[112] Consumers also can purchase products like body wash, vitamins, vaginal moisturizers, and hygiene wipes.[113] The one-stop-shopping aspect of the Gennev website makes it a convenient and desirable platform for those patients whose doctors lack menopause-specific training, although the care it offers will still be out of reach for those who cannot afford it.

Another growing menopause company is Alloy, the start-up that had attracted the attention of 29-year-old investor Ankur Jain, as recounted at the beginning of this chapter. Alloy advertises "Menopause Relief, Delivered Right to Your Door" and makes more explicit appeals to potential customers. For example, the Alloy website proclaims: "Our current healthcare system isn't doing enough. Only 6% of women seeking treatment for menopause actually get it! Menopause is inevitable, but suffering through it isn't." The site also includes customer comments in praise of the company's offerings, such as "I'm feeling great! So much less moody and irritable and I'm sleeping through the night like a teenager!" and "I wish I had access to Alloy's advice and prescriptions 20 plus years ago."[114]

Would-be customers complete an online assessment, which is then reviewed by a physician. A user starts the assessment by clicking a button that leads to a survey. This survey prompts the user to check boxes to indicate all menopausal symptoms "bothering you most," with no limitation on the number that can be selected. After the user answers a series of health-related questions, the screen advances almost instantaneously to a list of recommended prescription and nonprescription products with prices. Depending on how the customer answers the screening questions, the recommended products may include MHT, antidepressants, estrogen creams for vaginal symptoms, face cream to address dry skin and wrinkling, or dietary supplements. To actually receive a prescription, though, customers must provide a credit card and verify their identity by showing, for example, a driver's license or passport. Only then does a physician review what medications have been recommended by the web's diagnostic tool and write a prescription, if any. Once they have received a prescription, customers can pay $35 for a follow-up appointment to talk to a physician. The website does not provide any statistics about how many times customers are denied access to MHT.[115]

Curiously, the main Alloy website (as of early 2024) boasts, "Our treatments work, are recommended by the North American Menopause Society, and approved by our Chief Medical Officer, Dr. Sharon Malone, and our Medical Advisory Board."[116] However, the actual Terms and Conditions of Service to which a customer must agree before making a purchase state that "Alloy does not make any representations or warranties about the training or skill of any [medical] Providers who deliver services" obtained through the website. Medical providers are independent: "Any information or advice received from a Provider comes from them alone, and not from Alloy."[117] Alloy does not accept insurance; customers are encouraged to submit receipts to their health savings account or flexible spending account, and the site does not mention the possibility of using Medicaid or Medicare.[118] Because not all people have these accounts, Alloy's services are likely out of reach for many.

Websites like Gennev and Alloy normalize the need for menopause-specific care and prescription medications to help manage menopause's symptoms. And the ability to receive medications with (Gennev) or without (Alloy) a telehealth visit undoubtedly offers relief for real symptoms. Alloy's seeming use of algorithms in making diagnoses signals the potential that treatment might become more widely available and easier to obtain. At the same time, however, given the absence of research about the appropriateness of MHT for all patients, it is reasonable to ask questions about the ability of a "smart" diagnostic tool to assess and suggest the appropriate treatment for more complex cases. Furthermore, consider the relationship of any digital menopause company to the prescriptions or products it recommends. Gennev, for example, allows customers to use any pharmacy to fill prescriptions recommended by a Gennev physician.[119] Alloy, on the other hand, offers home delivery of prescription medication subscriptions, as soon as they have been approved by a doctor with whom the patient likely never meets, even virtually, making the medicine itself a likely profit center for the company.[120]

The founders of companies such as Gennev, Alloy, and similar businesses are undoubtedly passionate about their work.[121] Pro-woman messaging, indicating that the products are created "by women for women" (Alloy),[122] or that there are significant, real-life "challenges faced by women who need menopause treatment" (the now defunct London-based Bia Care),[123] helps to destigmatize menopause and reduce the culture of shame and silence that surrounds it.

That said, it is important for consumers not to be blinded by the halo effect that this type of advertising engenders, and to make sure that they do their own independent research about what makes sense for them. If in-person physician interactions and digital prescription services do not feature strong counseling components, the pendulum may swing too far in the direction of leaving consumers without reliable, informed advice, notwithstanding the many peer-to-peer forums that provide menopause support.

## ADDRESSING THE LACK OF PRIVACY PROTECTIONS AND INACCURACY

Whether sold directly to customers or in a B2B model, the privacy and accuracy concerns associated with digital menopause products point to notable gaps in U.S. law. In terms of privacy, current U.S. federal and state laws provide only limited and scattered regulation of the disclosure of personal information. The Health Insurance Portability and Accountability Act of 1996 (HIPAA), for example, protects private health information, but it only applies to a specific set of entities: health plans (such as health insurance companies and employer-provided health plans); clearinghouses that process health information; and healthcare providers (such as doctors, psychologists, and pharmacies).[124] This means that information entered into most menopause apps that are downloaded directly by consumers is not covered by HIPAA. The most relevant rules come from the consumer protection field, but even there, protections are not especially robust.[125]

Under federal law, app users are entitled to notice of an app's data privacy policy and any breach of sensitive health information.[126] The overall "notice and consent" model is woefully inadequate, however. In the separate but related context of menstruation-tracking apps, Professor Michele Gilman has argued that such products should only be permitted in a nonprofit context in which companies are prohibited from sharing data with for-profit, third-party entities.[127] At a minimum, consumers should receive more than a one-time notice that their data is being collected. This could take the form of pop-ups at the time when collection occurs, or an avatar or symbol indicating when active data collection is occurring.[128]

Reforming digital products so that they serve as supportive tools, rather than solely as profit centers, might well start with adding protections for intimate data, meaning information "about our bodies, health, sex, gender, sexual orientation, close relationships, online searches, reading habits, and private communications."[129] Individual users can try to wade through the tangle of consents and information, or install plug-ins to limit tracking, but these actions are piecemeal and time-consuming. An alternative is to create a right to intimate privacy, as legal scholar Danielle Citron proposes. To ensure that companies collecting digital data serve as protectors of that information, rather than as conduits to third parties,[130] Citron envisions a future legal regime with four pillars: (1) companies should collect information only for a legitimate reason, and only then if the benefits outweigh the risks; (2) companies must ensure that they receive meaningful consent to the collection of this data; (3) the law should enforce both an obligation of nondiscrimination and a duty of loyalty that requires companies to put users' well-being first; and (4) there must be procedures that allow users to hold a company accountable.[131] These principles provide a framework for safeguarding user privacy on apps and platforms that address menopause as well as other sensitive and personal areas.

Another way to enhance the integrity of menopause-related apps and products would be to require that content and claims are truthful and subject to scientific validation. The FTC regulates deceptive advertising, but it does not provide much guidance for digital health developers beyond nonbinding guidance related mostly to data security, rather than truth-in-advertising.[132] Developing administrative rules that limit apps to making evidence-backed claims and to continuing clinical trials where appropriate, along with ensuring enforcement, would both strengthen the integrity of their claims and make the apps themselves more reliable.

Unless and until reforms occur, users of menopause apps and platforms should carefully read the fine print of the privacy policies before sharing any health data. These users should also remain aware of the potential for privacy breaches and perform additional checks of the veracity of evidence-based claims. As Citron has explained, the notion that a privacy policy necessarily means that a company will protect information, rather than sharing it, is a "myth of epic proportion."[133] And while some of the health claims made by menopause companies are not myths at all, consumers also should apply a degree of skepticism to advertising.

## SELLING MENOPAUSE "CURES"

Purveyors of the full range of menopause products and services—from clothing to creams and dietary supplements, from purely analog products like pillows to "high-tech" bracelets and handheld ultrasound devices, from digital trackers to online prescription services—have a financial interest in positioning menopause as a condition or disease that needs tracking, monitoring, and treatment. While the messaging behind these products may use language of empowerment, it fundamentally serves the goal of maximizing profits.

Given that each person's experience of menopause is different, consumers should educate themselves and critically evaluate claims that particular products or medicines are effective "cures" for menopausal symptoms. Similarly, users of menopause-related products or services that involve *any* submission of personal information, from symptom logging to questions or conversations, should in no way assume that the data will not be shared further.

Ultimately, this chapter's exposition of the operations of menopause capitalism is not a critique of capitalism as a whole, but a call for much greater balance and awareness. Menopause capitalism has a role to play in eliminating some of the invisibility, stigma, and shame that have been associated historically with menopause. Companies selling menopause-related products and services have the potential to create communities and sources of peer support, however virtual and somewhat contrived they may be.

## CHAPTER EIGHT

# MAKING A MOVEMENT:
# GENDER, DISABILITY, AGING,
# AND FEMINIST THEORY

On June 12, 2023, the United States Department of Labor Women's Bureau—an agency charged with championing policies that safeguard the interests of working women—held its first-ever public program on menopause. Entitled *Roundtable: The Menopause Transition and Work*, the event featured a broad discussion among healthcare professionals, law and workplace experts, and researchers from the AARP (formerly known as the American Association of Retired Persons), a membership organization focused on advocating for the interests of people aged 50 and over.[1] The program came on the heels of two significant publications that made national news: first, the Mayo Clinic's April 2023 study estimating the cost of menopause-related lost work productivity as $1.8 billion annually in the U.S.; and second, the *Break Through the Stigma: Menopause in the Workplace* report (discussed earlier) published on June 1, 2023, by Bank of America in partnership with the National Menopause Foundation, which surveyed thousands of U.S. employees and employers about the impact of menopause at work.[2]

One important finding of the *Break Through the Stigma* report was that 89% of employees and 67% of human resource officers who responded to a 2023 poll said that they view menopause as a life stage rather than a medical issue.[3] Additionally, 51% of human resource officers said that it was the employer's responsibility to address the impact of menopause in the workplace. The Mayo Clinic report, meanwhile, highlighted the "bidirectional" relationship between menopause symptoms and work outcomes, with each influencing the other.[4]

Taken together, these developments show that the United States is entering a new phase in its approach to menopause—an appropriate parallel to menopause's inauguration of a new phase of life. Menopause has not only become increasingly visible in culture and commerce, but—as these reports and this book show—it is starting to be recognized as raising *policy* issues as well.

This book has identified the key components of a policy agenda for menopause: (1) dismantling the long-held silence and stigma surrounding menopause; (2) contextualizing menopause as an inevitable life stage with commonalities but individual variations; and (3) pursuing specific reforms to workplace, healthcare, and commercial approaches to menopause through the law, media, and advocacy. In this chapter, we explore the conceptual and pragmatic aspects of building a movement for menopause-oriented reform. The chapter starts by outlining multiple possibilities for an agenda for a menopause advocacy movement. It then turns to considering where that movement might be located, drawing connections and comparisons to the current menstrual advocacy movement, which has achieved significant success since 2015. Menopause advocacy, we suggest, both overlaps with and is distinct from that movement.

The chapter then considers other theoretical and movement-based frameworks that are relevant to charting a course and building a broad coalition of support for menopause advocacy going forward. Feminist legal theory examines concepts such as sameness and difference, equality versus equity, reasoning from the body, and the challenge of comparators.[5] From disability and aging jurisprudence, there are insights into how to define and theorize "impairments," "disability," accommodations, and structural designs.[6] Poverty studies inspire focus on the particular challenges that low-income people face in accessing healthcare and material resources in connection with menopause. Finally, intersectionality provides an apt lens for viewing menopause along all of those dimensions, while also bringing in considerations of race, class, and gender identity.

The goal of exploring these perspectives is to show how they might provide guidance for a vision of "menopause equity" that parallels the current movement for menstrual equity. Theoretical approaches illuminate the interests at stake in the various—and sometimes dichotomous—characterizations of menopause: limiting yet liberating; stigmatized yet universal; hidden but inevitable. By exploring these tensions, theoretical insights reveal the complexities involved in building a movement for menopause equity, and ultimately show how such a movement can be both inclusive and transformative.

## GOALS OF A MENOPAUSE ADVOCACY MOVEMENT

Transforming the approaches of law and society to menopause has the potential to impact public spaces, workplaces, healthcare, and culture. In charting a path forward, there are concrete steps that individuals, schools, communities, businesses, and governments can take. Here are some initial efforts and goals to consider:

1. People should feel comfortable speaking, without stigma or shame, in both public and private spaces, about menopause as an inevitable stage of life.
2. As part of sex education, secondary schools should include a discussion of menopause.
3. In the healthcare field, both medical students and nursing students should receive formal instruction on menopause. Continuing medical education requirements for primary healthcare professionals and those who specialize in obstetrics/gynecology should include instruction on menopause.
4. The U.S. Equal Employment Opportunity Commission (EEOC) should promulgate guidance clarifying that, while menopause is not in itself a disability, some workers experiencing perimenopause and menopause may have symptoms related to those life stages that qualify as disabilities under the ADA. Relatedly, the EEOC should promulgate guidance for businesses on how best to accommodate workers experiencing perimenopause and menopause.

5. Congress should pass a Menopause Equity Act that parallels the Pregnant Workers Fairness Act by requiring reasonable accommodations for all people experiencing perimenopause and menopause who need them, regardless of whether they have symptoms that rise to the level of a disability. Until Congress acts, state legislatures should pass their own Menopause Equity Acts.

6. The federal government should provide funding for more menopause-related research, including treatments, to support "a new comprehensive reproductive-health initiative that can inform us of the long-term benefits of hormone therapy and accurately assess its risks."[7] In March 2024, important progress was made on this front when President Biden issued an executive order focused on advancing women's health research.[8] The order specifically called for "future investments in menopause-related research" and "new resources to help women better understand their options for menopause-related symptoms prevention and treatment."[9] As journalist and former first lady of California Maria Shriver observed, this executive order is unprecedented in many ways; she noted that it was likely "the first time a president of the United States has ever signed an executive order that mentions the words 'menopause' and 'women's midlife health' in it."[10] That said, the executive order should be understood as more of a starting point than an end point. A future president could overturn the executive order, or Congress could fail to fully fund the initiatives President Biden has identified.[11]

7. The EEOC should promulgate guidance providing that menopause-related discrimination—whether related to menopausal stigma and stereotypes, or to menopausal symptoms—is discrimination on the basis of sex, and that plaintiffs are not required to point to nonmenopausal employees as comparators in order to prevail in such cases. A Menopause Equity Act could make this clear as well.

8. Employers should provide training to managers and employees to increase awareness of menopause, and make available to employees menopause-related resources, such as referrals to qualified healthcare professionals who specialize in menopause and whose services are covered by the employer's provided health insurance.

Health insurance should cover hormonal therapies as well as alternative treatments.

9. Nonprofit organizations that focus on menopause awareness and advocacy should offer training, consultations, and even certifications for employers that wish to make their workplace menopause-friendly.

10. Menopause advocacy should include fighting for safe, affordable, and easy access to products that are needed to manage menopause in a safe, affordable, and accessible way, including pads and tampons (which are necessary in cases of perimenopausal bleeding).

11. Inclusive design principles should take menopause into account (by including, for example, functioning thermostats and other temperature control options).

12. New legislation should provide stronger privacy protection for data submitted to healthcare apps and platforms, including menstrual and menopause "tracking apps."

These measures, while not an exhaustive list of all that menopause advocacy could entail, would provide a foundation for moving toward a more just society that accounts for menopause as an involuntary and inevitable stage of life for roughly half the population. Successfully advocating for and implementing this agenda involves drawing lessons from numerous other theoretical and advocacy perspectives.

## THE MENSTRUAL ADVOCACY MOVEMENT

With antecedents in the women's health movement of the 1970s, the contemporary menstrual advocacy movement in the United States dates back to roughly 2015. That year, New York lawyer Jennifer Weiss-Wolf—who coined the phrase "menstrual equity" and has become one of its leading advocates—joined with *Cosmopolitan* magazine to launch a Change.org petition to "Stop Taxing Our Periods. Period!" in the United States.[12] The petition, aimed at the many states that imposed sales tax on menstrual products (often even while exempting other "necessities" from taxation), drew on similar petitions that had recently been brought in the U.K., Canada, and Australia. Shortly after the circulation of the petition—which garnered over 50,000 signatures—class action lawsuits were brought to challenge the tampon taxes in New York and Florida, arguing that comparatively unfavorable tax treatment of menstrual products amounted to an unconstitutional form of sex discrimination. Both states then changed their laws to eliminate the tampon tax, at which point the lawsuits were withdrawn.[13]

As a whole, the success of the tampon tax repeal effort has been striking, with numerous states legislatively eliminating the tax. Indeed, as of mid-2024, only 20 states still impose state sales tax on menstrual products, as compared to 40 in 2015. The tax has been eliminated in "blue" states like New York and California, "red" states like Texas and Nebraska, and numerous states in between.[14]

The tampon tax served as a gateway issue for the U.S. menstrual advocacy movement, which has since pursued a broad vision of "menstrual equity" on a number of fronts involving the accessibility and affordability of menstrual products. In addition to targeting the tampon tax, menstrual equity advocates have pushed to make menstrual products available for free in schools and correctional facilities. Students at both secondary schools and universities have emerged as leaders in urging the provision of free menstrual products at their institutions, an effort that largely began at the university level and then percolated to the school district level. Between 2015 and 2023, 15 states passed laws requiring some or all of their public secondary schools to provide free menstrual products, and others passed laws providing funding for schools that wish to do so.

Notable progress related to access to menstrual products has also been made in correctional facilities: the federal First Step Act of 2018, a sweeping criminal justice reform bill, included a mandate that federal prisons provide to prisoners "for free, in a quantity that is appropriate to the healthcare needs of each prison . . . tampons and sanitary napkins" that "conform with applicable industry standards."[15] Numerous states then followed suit with respect to their own correctional facilities.[16]

In keeping with the goals of affordability and accessibility of menstrual products, U.S. Representative Grace Meng (D-NY) has repeatedly proposed a Menstrual Equity for All Act, which she describes as a "whole-of-government approach to eradicate period poverty and achieve menstrual equity."[17] Her bill would, among other things, prohibit sales tax on menstrual products, require Medicaid to cover the cost of menstrual products, direct large employers to provide free menstrual products for their employees, and require all public federal buildings to provide free menstrual products in their restrooms. Although this bill has not moved forward so far, some of Representative Meng's more targeted initiatives—such as treating menstrual products as qualified medical expenses for reimbursement from health flexible spending arrangements—have been successful.[18]

In focusing on these issues, the menstrual advocacy movement has helped effectuate real legal change. And, more broadly, it has chipped away at the silence and stigma that has historically surrounded all aspects of the menstrual cycle, by bringing phrases like "period poverty" into the popular lexicon. That dialogue, in turn, has helped set the stage for franker discussions about menopause as well.

Indeed, there is a strong overlap between menstrual and menopause advocacy. Menstruation and menopause are tightly linked, with menarche (the first menstrual period) and menopause serving as bookends of reproductive capacity in approximately half the population. Some cases—like those in which employees are terminated for unexpected perimenopausal bleeding, as described in Chapter 4—are simultaneously menstruation and menopause cases. Moreover, some of the menstrual equity initiatives, such as allowing for reimbursement for menstrual products, also benefit those experiencing perimenopause. Additionally, in contrast to pregnancy and breastfeeding, both menstruation and menopause signal the *absence* of procreation, a dynamic that has unfortunately contributed to their lack of prioritization within the law.

But menopause is not just a subset of the menstrual equity agenda (and in fact, has been largely absent from menstruation-related advocacy to date). Rather, menopause raises unique issues of its own. The contemporary menstrual advocacy movement has largely been product-based. It kicked off with a focus on repealing the tampon tax, and expanded to other issues involving the affordability and accessibility of menstrual products, particularly in institutional settings like schools and correctional facilities. This emphasis is understandable: the product-based issues are salient, straightforward, and have clear solutions, like eliminating the tampon tax or providing free products in the settings in question. To be sure, menstrual advocacy is increasingly encompassing other issues, such as menstruation-based discrimination and menstrual education, but the clear "wins" so far have centered on products. Such products are not irrelevant to menopause; indeed, the menopausal transition is often marked by heavy and unexpected bleeding. But once that transition is complete, menstrual products are no longer needed.

Additionally, the menstrual advocacy movement has been somewhat youth-dominated. In fact, Representative Meng has stated that her own focus on menstrual advocacy began when she received a letter from a high school student from her congressional district in Queens about the lack of menstrual products in homeless shelters.[19] To be sure, advancing the menstrual equity agenda has also required sophisticated legal advocacy and lawmaking by professionals, and the movement is an intergenerational one. But it has a youthful energy. And, of course, menstruation itself is associated with fertility and the potential for pregnancy. By contrast, menopause has different associations, sitting squarely at the intersection of infertility, aging, and, at least to some extent, disability. Situating menopause as a movement more broadly in the overall justice project, as well as within equality jurisprudence, thus involves exploring a variety of theoretical intersections that can offer insight for advocacy.

## FEMINISM

Multiple feminist perspectives can inform an agenda for menopause equity. First, feminism invites scrutiny of the biases and assumptions that have long played a role in defining norms.[20] It reveals the silence about menopause within workplace law as a reflection of gendered male assumptions about who the "typical" or "ideal" worker is. And it sheds light on how menopause is viewed in the healthcare setting as well, from the 1960s characterizations of menopause as a "tragedy" that robbed women of their feminine essence, to the current lack of attention to menopause within the medical education curriculum. Feminism supports reframing menopause as *expected* instead of unusual or problematic. Furthermore, in light of its grounding in lived experience, feminist theory emphasizes practical reasoning, calling for close attention to individual variations in the menopause transition.[21]

Additionally, feminist legal theory's attention to what is sometimes referred to as the "sameness-difference" debate is especially helpful in thinking through an agenda for menopause equity. That debate asks whether the appropriate focus is on formal equality between men and women (a "sameness" approach), or on the need to accommodate differences, particularly biological differences (a "difference" approach). That debate particularly comes into play with reproduction-associated conditions like pregnancy, breastfeeding, menstruation, and, of course, menopause. Formal equality has intuitive appeal: everyone is treated the same, without regard to biological differences or gender identity.[22] The problem with formal equality, however, is that it fails to address unequal baselines. This failure has been explored in earlier chapters, particularly in the workplace context. If, for example, the design of the physical workspace does not include easy access to restrooms, or the design of mandatory uniforms does not take hot flashes into account, that leads to differential impacts. Indeed, if approximately half of the population will experience menopause at some point, but the workplace is not designed with that in mind, treating all employees the same way will disadvantage many menopausal employees. The Mayo Clinic's estimate of a $1.8 billion annual loss in work productivity from menopausal symptoms, due to fewer hours worked, resignations, and terminations, shows the magnitude of that gendered disadvantage.

In contrast to formal equality, "difference" theories acknowledge that people are not situated equally.[23] Here we refer not to the claim that women have values that are different than men's,[24] but rather to the ways that gender functions as a vector for disadvantage.[25] As Catharine MacKinnon has explained, biological differences should be the "first to trigger suspicion or scrutiny . . . . [I]s not the structure of the job market, which accommodates the physical needs, life cycle, and family expectations of men but not of women, integral to women's inferior status?"[26] Indeed, while helpful in framing the issues, the sameness-difference debate can sometimes risk diverting attention from the shared underlying goal of feminists of all perspectives, which is to call attention to "the deep structural factors that systematically disadvantage women," as well as all other minoritized people.[27]

If one understands that power differences based on gender identity are baked into human relations (and the law itself), then it becomes clear that, in the context of menopause, consideration of biology-based distinctions is critical. The notion of individual one-off accommodations for those who are menopausal, however, raises concerns of its own. Design inclusivity, which grows out of disability theory (discussed next), responds to this tension and offers a pathway forward. Closely related is vulnerability theory, which focuses on the social construction of disability and other "intersecting forms of oppression" and recognizes the need for society to move toward universal accommodation of human embodiment.[28] Ultimately, if the workplace is intentionally designed to take into account the full range of human needs and vulnerabilities, then the debate between sameness and difference becomes less relevant.

## DISABILITY THEORY

Disability jurisprudence provides a helpful lens for moving past the sameness-difference debate described above. This is not because menopause qualifies as a legal disability for all who experience it, or even because all symptoms of menopause are impairments. Rather, it is because disability jurisprudence offers a different model for framing menopause and thinking through workplace approaches to it.

As Chapter 5 describes, disability theory provides two models for framing difference. The first is the medical model, under which disability is framed as an individual deficit that needs not just diagnosis and treatment, but also remediation. Under that view, disability is an inherently limiting condition that must be legally accommodated in certain contexts and settings. The second is a social model that conceptualizes disability as constructed in the environment itself, not the individual.[29] Pursuant to the social model, the goal of disability policies is not necessarily "accommodation," but rather the redesign of the surrounding environment to ensure integration of all, without the need for special accommodation.[30] In this way, disability theory echoes the feminist legal method of challenging certain norms (e.g., able bodies, cis male bodies) as default expectations for everyone.

Applying the social model of disability might mean considering how to use Universal Design, which involves designing and building environments that are accessible by anyone, regardless of age, sex, or

disability.[31] With respect to menopause, Universal Design in new construction or retooling existing buildings could mean, for instance, ensuring better climate control—whether through air conditioning, desk
fans at each workstation, or cool break rooms—to enable employees to
better cope with hot flashes.[32] Flexible scheduling that takes potential
sleep disruptions into account is another example that moves beyond
physical design.[33] In other words, the challenges of menopause can be
addressed if workplaces and policies presume menopause's existence—
an approach that requires shifting baseline assumptions about who the
typical worker may be.

## AGING

The field of aging studies provides an additional lens for analyzing
menopause, which is stigmatized in part because of its association with
a loss of youth and fertility. Aging theories consider "how the law shapes
aging," how to allocate rights and responsibilities to respond to differing
age-based needs, and how to analyze "what the legal significance of age
is."[34] These theories also challenge society to consider healthcare challenges associated with aging, and to address ageist stereotypes, both by
reducing their salience and by providing redress when they produce discrimination and disadvantage.

On a practical level, AARP's growing interest in menopause is an
encouraging development for menopause advocacy. This organization
has approximately 38 million members, and is widely considered to be
a "lobbying powerhouse" on issues related to older Americans. In conducting research about various aspects of the menopausal experience[35]—
and in participating in events like the June 2023 Department of Labor
Women's Bureau roundtable—AARP is increasingly drawing attention
to menopause as part of its policy agenda. The AARP "Innovation Labs"
even sponsored a "Hacking Menopause" challenge, with prize money
attached and a goal of finding tech-based solutions for the symptoms of
menopause.[36]

At an initial level, it may seem obvious to treat menopause as an
issue of healthy aging that should be accounted for, both in designing
workplaces and in establishing a public health agenda. Indeed, menopause typically is the result of age-related loss of ovarian function, as

discussed in Chapter 3, and so it clearly is an issue of aging. Furthermore, even if employees are not personally grappling with managing menopause's symptoms while they are at work, menopause-friendly workplaces are consistent with more flexible work policies generally. AARP strongly supports paid family leave and parental leave, because these policies allow employees to "both attend to their own health needs and care for loved ones."[37] The challenge—and aging theories help in understanding why this is difficult—is ensuring that menopause is treated as part of healthy aging.

## POVERTY STUDIES

Poverty studies are concerned with the structural components of poverty and, typically, social justice. Viewing menopause through a poverty lens is important in order to ensure that both its experience and its treatment account for socioeconomic factors. Here, healthcare is particularly salient. Medicaid, the federal health insurance available for low-income individuals, pays for a range of services, including many prescription medicines. Each state is free to set its own precise rules for Medicaid coverage, but generally speaking, menopausal hormone therapy (MHT) is covered by Medicaid if prescribed for the management of menopause symptoms.[38] What Medicaid may not cover, however, are so-called alternative treatments for menopause, such as acupuncture, herbs, biofeedback, and meditation.[39] A federal bill that would have extended Medicaid (and Medicare) coverage to alternative therapies, known as the Menopausal Hormone Replacement Therapies and Alternative Treatments and Fairness Act of 2011, did not advance out of committee and has not been reintroduced.[40]

Despite Medicaid's coverage of MHT, those who are enrolled in public health insurance may not have access to informed menopause care.[41] Compared to patients with private health insurance, a Medicaid patient is 1.6 times less likely to successfully schedule a primary care appointment and 3.3 times less likely to successfully schedule a specialty appointment.[42] Because Medicaid is not as widely accepted as private insurance, its users have not only "less access to choices of primary care providers[,] but likely less access to providers who specialize in menopause treatment" as well.[43] Relatedly, those experiencing perimenopause need menstrual products such as tampons and pads, which in many states are covered neither by Medicaid nor by Supplemental Nutrition Assistance Program (SNAP).

Given the importance and magnitude of issues like food insecurity and lack of affordable housing that poverty lawyers and advocates are attempting to address, it is understandable that issues such as access to effective treatment for menopause might lack salience. Menopause is not, of course, a life-or-death issue in the same way that adequate food and housing are. At the same time, given the relative ease of access to traditionally "male" products like Viagra under state Medicaid programs,[44] the de facto difficulties that low-income people have in accessing informed menopause care and even menstrual products is noteworthy. Greater access to healthcare—in perimenopause, menopause, and beyond—is part of a robust antipoverty agenda.

## INTERSECTIONALITY

As this overview of jurisprudential theories and social movements indicates, fully taking account of menopause-based discrimination requires a distinctly intersectional approach. As Chapter 4 describes, Professor Kimberlé Crenshaw uses the metaphor of a traffic intersection to explain that discrimination can occur along multiple identity axes, all of which meet at one point.[45] And, as Crenshaw explains, intersectional discrimination is not merely additive, but synergistic.[46]

Menopause is a perfect illustration of this phenomenon, and menopause policy therefore requires an intersectional approach along axes of sex and age, and other factors such as disability, race, gender, and socioeconomic status. To discriminate on the basis of menopause is to discriminate on the basis of sex, age, and often disability (in addition to, possibly, gender identity and other factors) simultaneously. Yet current U.S. antidiscrimination law requires the disaggregation of claims, rather than recognizing them as cumulative.

In particular, given evidence of racialized differences in the experience of menopause (while acknowledging that any individual's experience is unique),[47] an agenda for menopause equity must take race into account. Labor force data supports the importance of this approach.[48]

First, the likelihood of having workplace flexibility to address meno-pause may depend on the type of job one has, which in turn may be correlated to race or class. For example, Asian and white women are more likely than Black and Hispanic women to be employed in manage-ment, professional, or related occupations that offer greater workplace flexibility.[49] By contrast, Black and Hispanic women are more likely than Asian and white women to work in lower-wage service industries, which have less flexibility and fewer benefits.[50] Thus, Black and His-panic women are more likely than Asian or white women to be in roles that require uniforms, limit breaks, or lack healthcare insurance and paid leave.[51] Because of these racialized labor-force differentials, laws or policies designed to achieve menopause equity should explicitly take into account different workplace settings, ensuring access to the same means for managing menopause.

Menopause advocacy needs to be sensitive to differences in gender identity and gender expression, too, as discussed in Chapter 6. Statistics show that trans people, for example, have high rates of unemployment, underemployment, and poverty compared to non-trans people.[52] Fur-thermore, other intricacies for trans and gender diverse people involve the nuances of hormonal shifts during the menopause transition, as Chapter 6 describes.

## A MENOPAUSE EQUITY AGENDA FOR CHANGE

Although menopause can draw from all of these movements and ap-proaches, it needs its own advocacy movement and platform. As these different theoretical perspectives show, equality and equity are differ-ent. While equality is grounded in identical treatment for all people, *regardless of* differences, we believe that the ultimate goal is menopause *equity,* which seeks fair treatment *in light* of differences.[53] Moving for-ward means challenging dominant norms and valuing the full diver-sity of each individual menopausal experience. The list of reforms with which this chapter begins is just the starting point. Grounded in a crit-ical perspective, menopause equity insists that law and society must change if it is to become more inclusive. Understanding menopause can improve life and law for everyone.

# ACKNOWLEDGMENTS

This book has been a collaborative project. Throughout, we have shared resources, learning, smiles, edits, and, sometimes, frustrations. We are delighted that this book represents our collective work product.

In writing this book, we received much support and collegiality from many sources.

For helpful comments and conversations, we thank Noa Ben-Asher, Anita Bernstein, Liz Cooper, Jeannette Cox, Marcy Karin, Margaret Johnson, Michelle Simon, Jill Wieber Lens, and Jennifer Weiss-Wolf. For support and inspiration throughout our work on this book, we thank Danielle Citron.

We thank participants in faculty workshops and symposia held at The University of Chicago Law School and Vanderbilt Law School.

We are grateful for research assistance from Mackenzie Kubik, University of Virginia School of Law '25 and Olivia Brenner, Elisabeth Haub School of Law at Pace University '21. The University of Virginia School of Law librarians excelled in tracking down materials for us. We thank our deans, Risa Goluboff at the University of Virginia School of Law and Horace Anderson at the Elisabeth Haub School of Law at Pace University, for their support. Jennifer Allison provided excellent editorial assistance.

We thank Marcela Maxfield for her enthusiasm for this project and generous assistance throughout the publication process.

The preparation of this book's index was supported by a Faculty Book and Performance Completion Award from the Pace University Provost's Office and funding from the University of Virginia School of Law. Portions of this book draw on work that Naomi Cahn published in the *Columbia Journal of Gender and Law* and our prior coauthored work published in the *University of Chicago Legal Forum*, the *Harvard Journal of Law & Gender*, and the *Washington University Law Review*. For each of those coauthored articles, each of us took a "turn" having our name listed as first, second, and third author. For this book, we chose yet another configuration: reverse alphabetical. The ultimate order of the authors' names on this book (or any of our coauthored pieces) in no way reflects unequal contributions. For that reason, we ask that those citing our work use all three names whenever possible.

Naomi Cahn adds thanks to her family for supporting her throughout this project. Emily Gold Waldman adds special personal thanks to Dan, Arielle, and Ben Waldman, Janet and Sandy Gold, and Joan and Larry Waldman. Bridget Crawford adds special personal thanks to Aurora and Jim.

# NOTES

## Introduction

1. *See* Bridget Crawford, *Origins of "Are You There, Law? It's Me, Menstruation" (Columbia Journal of Gender & Law Symposium, April 2021)*, FEMINIST L. PROFESSORS (Apr. 26, 2021), https://perma.cc/MAH8-RB4L; *see generally* JUDY BLUME, ARE YOU THERE GOD? IT'S ME, MARGARET (1970) (the inspiration for the symposium).

2. *10 Celebrities Who Have Spoken Out About Menopause*, GLAMOUR (Oct. 5, 2020), https://perma.cc/LN85-4KRM.

3. *Watch Now: "The Menopause Talk" with Oprah, Drew Barrymore, and Maria Shriver*, OPRAH DAILY (Apr. 5, 2023), https://perma.cc/J2EB-RDCD.

4. *See, e.g.,* Sumathi Reddy, *The Surprising Good News on How Menopause Changes Your Brain*, WALL ST. J. (June 14, 2021), https://perma.cc/RX4J-9DTU; Amy Larocca, *Welcome to the Menopause Gold Rush*, N.Y. TIMES (Dec. 20, 2022), https://perma.cc/9H26-DSWP.

5. *See Largest Women's Health Prevention Study Ever—Women's Health Initiative*, OFF. ON WOMEN'S HEALTH, U.S. DEP'T OF HEALTH & HUM. SERVS., https://perma.cc/PX3D-WP3M (summarizing results of 2002 study); *see also* Writing Group for the Women's Health Initiative Investigators, *Risks and Benefits of Estrogen Plus Progestin in Healthy Postmenopausal Women: Principal Results from the Women's Health Initiative Randomized Controlled Trial*, 288 J. AM. MED. ASS'N 321 (2002).

6. Dobbs v. Jackson Women's Health Organization, 142 S. Ct. 2228 (2022).

7. Roe v. Wade, 410 U.S. 113 (1973).

8. Edmond Coleman et al., *Standards of Care for the Health of Transgender and Gender Diverse People, Version 8*, INT'L J. OF TRANSGENDER HEALTH S1, S11 (2022) (defining "gender diverse").

9. *See Glossary of Terms: LGBT, in* GLAAD MEDIA REFERENCE GUIDE (11th ed.), https://perma.cc/68BQ-NJGW.

**Chapter 1**

1. The Michelle Obama Podcast, *Episode 4: What Your Mother Never Told You* (May 15, 2021), https://perma.cc/5E8D-H6SS.

2. *Id.*

3. Macaela MacKenzie, *1.3 Million Women Enter Menopause Each Year. We Have to Stop Ignoring Them*, GLAMOUR (Oct. 7, 2020), https://perma.cc/AA43 -7BJM.

4. *See Menopause Basics*, OFF. ON WOMEN'S HEATH, U.S. DEP'T OF HEALTH & HUM. SERVS., https://perma.cc/PU9B-TE4B.

5. *See* Deborah Grady, *Management of Menopausal Symptoms*, 355 NEW ENG. J. MED. 2338, 2338 (2006).

6. *See id.* at 2338; *Menopause Basics, supra* note 4.

7. *See* Gail A. Greendale, Nancy P. Lee & Edga R. Arriola, *The Menopause*, 353 LANCET 571, 571 (1999), https://perma.cc/GDS4-TZ7T.

8. *See Menopause Basics, supra* note 4.

9. Jen Gunter, *Menopause Is Something That Almost All Women Go Through— So Why the Silence?*, IDEAS.TED.COM (May 26, 2021), https://perma.cc/38JT -6VNG.

10. *See, e.g., Induced Menopause in Women with Endometriosis—For Patients*, WOMEN'S HEALTH CONCERN (2022), https://perma.cc/2Z95-NMET.

11. *See, e.g., Definition of Menopause, Chemical*, RxLIST (Melissa Conrad Stöppler ed., 2023), https://perma.cc/PZJ8-U4PJ.

12. Rachel Nall, *What Are the Effects of Surgical Menopause?*, MEDICAL NEWS TODAY (May 5, 2023), https://perma.cc/8N72-4TG5.

13. *See, e.g.,* Paula J. Adams Hillard, *Menstruation in Adolescents: What's Normal*, 10 MEDSCAPE J. MED. 295 (2008).

14. *See Amenorrhea*, MAYO CLINIC (2023), https://perma.cc/U7EG-EGXQ.

15. *See, e.g.,* E. Hirvonen, *Etiology, Clinical Features and Prognosis in Secondary Amenorrhea*, 22 INT'L J. FERTILITY 69 (1977); Donna E. Stewart et al., *Infertility and Eating Disorders*, 163 AM. J. OF OBSTETRICS & GYNECOLOGY 1196 (1990); Beatriz Vale et al., *Menstruation Disorders and Adolescents with Eating Disorders— Target Body Mass Index Percentiles for their Resolution*, 12 EINSTEIN 175 (2014).

16. Sam Manzella, *Drew Barrymore's Hilarious Reaction to Her First Hot Flash Is So Relatable*, YAHOO! NEWS (Mar. 29, 2023), https://perma.cc/9N35 -BVW5.

17. *See Menopause FAQs: Hot Flashes*, N. AM. MENOPAUSE SOC'Y (2023), https://perma.cc/J5BJ-S2C8.

18. *Id.*

19. Beth Levine, *What Are Vasomotor Symptoms of Menopause? Symptoms, Causes, Diagnosis, Treatment, and Prevention,* EVERYDAY HEALTH (Dec. 19, 2022), https://perma.cc/UJU7-W56U.

20. *See Dealing with the Symptoms of Menopause,* HARV. HEALTH PUB. (Mar. 21, 2017), https://perma.cc/4SJK-RZVE.

21. *Menopause FAQs, supra* note 17.

22. Nancy E. Avis et al., *Vasomotor Symptoms Across the Menopause Transition: Differences Among Women,* 45 OBSTETRICS & GYNECOLOGY CLINICS OF N. AM. 629 (2018).

23. Ying Sheng et al., *Review of Menopausal Palpitations Measures,* 7 WOMEN'S MIDLIFE HEALTH 5 (2021), https://perma.cc/HD7R-AP6J.

24. *See* Mika Brzezinksi, *How a Menopausal Mystery Landed Mika in the ER,* MSNBC (June 20, 2023, 2:27 PM), https://perma.cc/3HYC-GRT6.

25. JEN GUNTER, THE MENOPAUSE MANIFESTO: OWN YOUR HEALTH WITH FACTS AND FEMINISM 205 (2021).

26. Johns Hopkins Medicine, *Can Menopause Cause Depression?* (2023), https://perma.cc/9JTH-77EP (reviewed by Jennifer Payne).

27. *Id.*

28. *See, e.g., What Is Menopause,* NIH NATIONAL INSTITUTE ON AGING (2021), https://perma.cc/AT4F-UJTK; Hallie Levine, *How Menopause Messes with Your Brain,* AARP BRAIN HEALTH & WELLNESS (Nov. 19, 2021), https://perma.cc/KE63-5VJW.

29. Lisa Mosconi et. al., *Menopause Impacts Human Brain Structure, Connectivity, Energy Metabolism, and Amyloid-Beta Deposition,* 11 SCI. REPS. art. no. 10867 (2021) (June 9, 2021), https://perma.cc/UD43-XYSL.

30. *Id.*

31. *Id.; see also* Sumathi Reddy, *The Surprising Good News on How Menopause Changes Your Brain,* WALL ST. J. (June 14, 2021), https://perma.cc/BK4T-HG64.

32. Reddy, *supra* note 31 (quoting Lisa Mosconi). *See also* LISA MOSCONI, THE MENOPAUSE BRAIN (2024).

33. Laura J. Miller, et al., *Depression and Related Disorders During the Female Reproductive Cycle,* 5 WOMEN'S HEALTH 577 (2009); Liisa Hantsoo et al., *Anxiety Disorders Among Women: A Female Lifespan Approach,* 15 FOCUS 162 (2017).

34. Search results: menopausal symptom lists, GOOGLE (May 19, 2023), https://perma.cc/E89U-TH9N; *compare, e.g.,* Veronica Kirby-Garton, *34 Symptoms of Menopause,* STELLA, https://perma.cc/Y47Q-Z867; *What Are the 34 Symptoms of Menopause?,* UK MEDS (Oct. 21, 2019), https://perma.cc/9H2U-TWYU, *with* Janette M. Perz, *Development of the Menopause Symptom List: A Factor Analytic Study of Menopause Associated Symptoms,* 25 WOMEN & HEALTH 53, 64 (1997), https://perma.cc/J48Q-A4WP.

35. Kamma S. Lund et al., *Measuring Bothersome Menopausal Symptoms: Development and Validation of the MenoScores Questionnaire*, 16 HEALTH & QUALITY OF LIFE OUTCOMES 97 (2018).

36. *See, e.g.*, Lisa Cappelloni, *What Are the Symptoms and Signs of Menopause?*, HEALTHLINE (May 14, 2018), https://perma.cc/RDX2-YMS7.

37. *See* Hannah Devlin, *Breaking the Menopause Taboo: 'There Are Vital Stories We Should Continue to Pursue,'* GUARDIAN (U.K.) (Sept. 21, 2019), https://perma.cc/2ET8-AU8C.

38. Siobán D. Harlow et al., *Disparities in Reproductive Aging and Midlife Health Between Black and White Women: The Study of Women's Health Across the Nation (SWAN)*, 8 WOMEN'S MIDLIFE HEALTH 10-11, 12 (2022), https://perma.cc/AE9F-9KGH; *About SWAN*, STUDY OF WOMEN'S HEALTH ACROSS THE NATION, https://perma.cc/6EGU-8TYU (describing structure and operation of longitudinal study of 3,302 women); Susan D. Reed et al., *Premenopausal Vasomotor Symptoms in an Ethnically Diverse Population*, 21 MENOPAUSE 153, 153 (2014).

39. Harlow et al., *supra* note 38, at 10-11, 12.

40. *See* Adriana Velez, *Menopause Is Different for Women of Color*, ENDOCRINE WEB (Mar. 10, 2021), https://perma.cc/CU44-HCGP; Nancy E. Avis et al., *Duration of Menopausal Vasomotor Symptoms Over the Menopause Transition*, 175 JAMA INTERN. MED. 531, 534, 537 (2015).

41. *See* Reed et al., *supra* note 38, at 153.

42. Alice Callahan, *How Long Does Menopause Last?*, N.Y. TIMES (Apr. 19, 2022), https://perma.cc/J3TH-FAAL.

43. Harlow et al., *supra* note 38, at 11.

44. Ed Yong, *Why Killer Whales (and Humans) Go Through Menopause*, ATLANTIC (Jan. 12, 2017), https://perma.cc/35T9-XGD8.

45. SUSAN MATTERN, THE SLOW MOON CLIMBS 40-67 (2019).

46. *See id.* at 47-49; David P. Barash, *The Evolutionary History of Menopause*, NAUTILUS (Aug. 9, 2022), https://perma.cc/L29N-ZFUC.

47. *Review: Susan Mattern's* "The Slow Moon Climbs: The Science, History, and Meaning of Menopause," LADY SCIENCE (Aug. 25, 2019), https://perma.cc/59PL-JBKD.

48. Ainsley Harris, *Meet the Women Embracing Menopause—and Those Hoping to End It*, FAST CO. (May 4, 2023), https://perma.cc/DGY4-TQ57.

49. Grace Rubenstein, *Is it Time to Cancel Menopause?*, PROTO.LIFE (June 2, 2022), https://perma.cc/VG5D-HBGC.

50. *Roundtable: The Menopause Transition*, WOMEN'S BUREAU, U.S. DEP'T OF LAB. (June 12, 2023), https://perma.cc/K6WV-38H7 (transcript on file with authors).

51. Jill M. Wood, *(In)visible Bleeding: The Menstrual Concealment Imperative*, in THE PALGRAVE HANDBOOK OF CRITICAL MENSTRUATION STUDIES 319-36 (Chris Bobel et al. eds., 2020).

52. *See* Bridget J. Crawford & Emily Gold Waldman, Menstruation Matters 70 (2022).

53. Robert N. Butler, *Age-Ism: Another Form of Bigotry*, 9 The Gerontologist 243, 243 (1969).

54. Bonafide, The State of Menopause: Our First Menopause Survey (2021), https://perma.cc/MA5T-SCTH (survey of 1,039 women).

55. Macaela MacKenzie, *1.3 Million Women Enter Menopause Each Year. We Have to Stop Ignoring Them*, Glamour (Oct. 7, 2020), https://perma.cc/TU5H -GJ82.

56. Elana F. Jaffe, et al., *Experiences of Menopause During Incarceration*, 28 Menopause 829, 829 (2021), https://perma.cc/4TE9-Q4S5.

57. Stephanie Faubion, et al., *Impact of Menopause Symptoms on Women in the Workplace*, 98 Mayo Clinic Proc. 833 (2023), https://perma.cc/VK37-97TE.

## Chapter 2

1. Oprah Winfrey, *Oprah Reveals How Heart Palpitations Led Her to Discover She Was Approaching Menopause*, Oprah Daily (Sept. 18, 2019), https://perma .cc/H4WR-GJT8.

2. *See* Cassie Hurwitz, *Oprah Shares How She Handled Her Scary Menopause Symptom*, Oprah Daily (Dec. 6, 2022), https://perma.cc/8KP3-P9JF.

3. *See* Winfrey, *supra* note 1.

4. *10 Celebrities Who Have Spoken Out About Menopause*, Glamour (Oct. 5, 2020), https://perma.cc/LN85-4KRM (quoting Oprah Winfrey).

5. *See* Laura Woods, *Oprah, Melinda Gates and 8 More of the Richest Women in History*, Yahoo (Aug. 28, 2021), https://perma.cc/2URN-YH3X.

6. *See, e.g., Endocreme—A Cosmetic with a Menace*, 110 J. Am. Med. Ass'n 1194, 1194 (1938) (noting the widespread advertisements "[i]n current periodicals, especially those directed to women" for Endocreme, a topical lotion containing estradiol sold as a cosmetic "in many leading department stores, drug stores and beauty shops").

7. *All in the Family: Edith's Problem* (CBS television broadcast Jan. 8, 1972).

8. *Id.*

9. David Mello, *All in the Family: 10 Things You Didn't Know About the Episode "Edith's Problem*," Screen Rant (Mar. 17, 2020), https://perma.cc/V2HM -3BSQ.

10. That particular episode of *All in the Family* won an Emmy Award in 1972 for Outstanding Writing in Comedy. *See 24th Emmy Awards Nominees and Winners: 1972*, Television Academy, https://perma.cc/U3QR-B7N4.

11. *The Golden Girls: End of the Curse* (NBC television broadcast Sept. 27, 1986).

12. *The Cosby Show: Clair's Liberation* (NBC television broadcast Dec. 6, 1990).

13. *Absolutely Fabulous: Menopause* (BBC One television broadcast Oct. 5, 2001).

14. Anita Gates, *When Middle Age Is Like a Melody*, N.Y. TIMES (Aug. 7, 2009), https://perma.cc/F5CX-EKN4.

15. *See Older Women and Menopause Negatively Stereotyped by the Media, According to UM Research*, MKTG. COMM. NEWS (Sept. 13, 2018), https://perma.cc/XTH3-2PRQ.

16. *House of Cards: Chapter 4* (Netflix Feb. 1, 2013). *See also* June Thomas, *How TV Shows Handle Menopause*, SLATE (Feb. 5, 2013, 2:35 PM), https://perma.cc/2ARQ-A5BW (discussing House of Cards: Chapter 4 episode).

17. *Bombay Begums: Women Who Run with the Wolves* (Netflix Mar. 8, 2021).

18. *See* Paul Chi, *Emma Thompson Is Grateful for Menopause*, PEOPLE (Jan. 8, 2014 3:00 PM), https://perma.cc/WW4D-NDJY.

19. *Fleabag: Series 2, Episode 3* (BBC Three television broadcast Mar. 18, 2019).

20. See Jeff Nelson, *Shania Twain on Posing Topless and "Embracing" Menopause: I'm "So Unashamed of My New Body,"* PEOPLE (Dec. 21, 2022, 9:00 AM), https://perma.cc/LS9N-C6E2.

21. *See Menopause Whilst Black*, https://perma.cc/8RWJ-X8BV.

22. *The Simpsons: Goo Goo Gai Pan* (Fox television broadcast Sept. 13, 2005).

23. *The Big Bang Theory: The Maternal Capacitance* (CBS television broadcast Feb. 9, 2009).

24. Liza Mundy, *The Secret Power of Menopause*, ATLANTIC (Oct. 2019), https://perma.cc/WGV7-QDZB (quoting SIGMUND FREUD, THE DISPOSITION TO OBSESSIONAL NEUROSIS 323-24 (1913)).

25. *See* Tori DeAngelis, *Menopause: The Makeover*, 41 MONITOR ON PSYCH. 40, 40 (2010) (quoting *Feminine Forever*).

26. *See* Ramya NR et al., *Cross Sectional Study to Evaluate the Climacteric Symptoms Using Menopause Rating Scale: In Coastal Karnataka*, 14 J. CARDIOVASCULAR DISEASE RES. 728, 728 (2023) ("Menopause is defined as the permanent cessation of menstruation for 12 months or more due to ovarian failure, and it occurs at an average age of 52 years, with a range of 40 to 58 years.").

27. *See generally* Heather E. Dillaway, *(Un)Changing Menopausal Bodies: How Women Think and Act in the Face of a Reproductive Transition and Gendered Beauty Ideals*, 53 SEX ROLES 1, 4 (2005) ("[M]enopause, or the loss of reproductive capacity, is more symbolically significant as a marker of bodily change than as a general process of aging.").

28. *See id.* at 5.

29. *See* David Bauder, *CNN's Don Lemon Regrets Saying Nikki Haley Past Her "Prime,"* AP NEWS (Feb. 16, 2023), https://perma.cc/H6HH-K7CD.

30. *See* Michael M. Grynbaum et al., *Don Lemon Ousted from CNN in Move That Left Him "Stunned,"* N.Y. TIMES (Apr. 24, 2023), https://perma.cc/5U2B-MFFS (quoting Don Lemon).

31. *See, e.g.*, Giulia Heyward, *CNN's Don Lemon Apologizes for Sexist Remarks About Nikki Haley*, NPR (Feb. 17, 2023, 2:39 PM), https://perma.cc/X95H-ZYW9.

32. Joan Chrisler et al., *Ambivalent Sexism and Attitudes Toward Women in Different Stages of Reproductive Life: A Semantic, Cross-Cultural Approach*, 35 HEALTH CARE FOR WOMEN INT'L 634, 648 (2013); Maria Luisa Marván et al., *Stereotypes of Women in Different Stages of their Reproductive Life: Data from Mexico and the United States*, 29 HEALTH CARE FOR WOMEN INT'L 673, 676–77 (2008).

33. *See* Ann Marcus-Newhall & Suzanne Thompson, *Examining a Gender Stereotype: Menopausal Women*, 31 J. APPLIED SOC. PSYCH. 698, 711, 713–14 (1983).

34. *See 10 Celebrities, supra* note 4 and accompanying text.

35. Elizabeth Gilbert, FACEBOOK (Nov. 25, 2019), https://perma.cc/Z7ZX-FTZJ.

36. *See 10 Celebrities, supra* note 4 (quoting Cynthia Nixon).

37. *Inside Amy Schumer: S3.E1, Last F..able Day* (Comedy Central television broadcast Apr. 22, 2015).

38. Jennifer Kelly, *A Lesbian Feminist Analysis of the Demise of Hormone Replacement Therapy*, 31 WOMEN'S STUD. INT'L F. 300, 306 (2008).

39. ELIZABETH CADY STANTON, EIGHTY YEARS AND MORE (1815–1897): REMINISCENCES OF ELIZABETH CADY STANTON 447 (1898).

40. *Id.*

41. *See Menopause in Different Cultures*, WOMEN'S HEALTH NETWORK, https://perma.cc/34K5-YSNW ("A common belief among traditional shamanic cultures—for example, Mayan women and the Cree women of Canada—is that women must enter menopause to access their shamanic and healing powers.").

42. *See* BOSTON WOMEN'S HEALTH COLLECTIVE, WOMEN AND THEIR BODIES: A COURSE (1970), https://perma.cc/PX2N-SFK2; BOSTON WOMEN'S HEALTH COLLECTIVE, OUR BODIES, OURSELVES: A BOOK BY AND FOR WOMEN 224-235 (1973).

43. *See* Claudia Levy, *"Hot Flashes" Author Barbara Raskin Dies*, WASH. POST (July 24, 1999), https://perma.cc/3ZQW-G95N.

44. *See* North American Menopause Society, *About NAMS* (2023), https://perma.cc/TN2F-U47V.

45. *See* Barbara Ehrenreich, *All Aboard the Raging Hormone Express*, N.Y. TIMES (June 7, 1992), https://perma.cc/3RAQ-XUG8.

46. *See* Mary Jane Minkin et al., *Prevalence of Postmenopausal Symptoms in North America and Europe*, 22 MENOPAUSE: J. N. AM. MENOPAUSE SOC'Y 1231, 1235, 1237 (2015).

47. Lisa Rapaport, *Culture May Influence How Women Experience Menopause*, REUTERS (June 5, 2015, 12:08 PM), https://perma.cc/E3ZV-KF9N (quoting Dr. Mary Jane Minkin of Yale Medical School).

48. *See* IPSOS, GLOBAL VIEWS ON MENOPAUSE 3 (Oct. 19, 2022), https://perma.cc/7KG4-BX5V.

49. *See id.* at 4.

50. *See id.* at 7.

51. *See id.* at 71.

52. Carla Makhlouf Obermeyer et al., *Symptoms, Menopause Status, and Country Differences: A Comparative Analysis from DAMES*, 14 MENOPAUSE 788, 794 (2007).

53. SUSAN MATTERN, THE SLOW MOON CLIMBS: THE SCIENCE, HISTORY, AND MEANING OF MENOPAUSE 337 (2019).

54. *Id.* at 351.

55. *See* Obermeyer et al., *supra* note 52, at 795-96.

56. *See, e.g.*, Margaret Lock & Patricia Kaufert, *Menopause, Local Biologies, and Cultures of Aging*, 13 AM. J. HUM. BIOLOGY 494, 496 (2001).

57. *See id.* at 502 (citing MARGARET LOCK, ENCOUNTERS WITH AGING: MYTHOLOGIES OF MENOPAUSE IN JAPAN AND NORTH AMERICA (1993)).

58. *See id.* at 499.

59. *See* Jing Su et al., *Menopausal Symptoms Among Chinese and Japanese Women: Differences and Similarities*, 29 MENOPAUSE 73, 74-75 (2021).

60. *See* MATTERN, *supra* note 53, at 354 ("Culture partly determines which sensations we interpret as symptoms."); Lynette Leidy Sievert, *Cross-Cultural Comparisons: Methodological Concerns*, 19 MENOPAUSE 1289 (2012) (discussing methodological limitations in certain cross-cultural menopause studies but noting that "the breadth of the study contributes to our understanding of symptom experience, attitudes, and the context of the menopausal transition within each of the populations studied.").

61. Yeou-Lan Duh Chen et al., *Chinese Midlife Women's Perceptions and Attitudes About Menopause*, 5 MENOPAUSE 28-34 (1998) (91.7% held this opinion).

62. *See* Ming-Huei Cheng et al., *Attitudes Toward Menopause Among Middle-Aged Women: A Community Survey in an Island of Taiwan*, 52 MATURITAS 348, 354 (2005).

63. *See* Hsien-An Pan et al. *The Perception of Menopause Among Women in Taiwan*, 41 MATURITAS 269, 273-74 (2002).

64. S Kaur et al., *How Menopause Affects the Lives of Women in Suburban Chandigarh, India*, 7 CLIMACTERIC 175, 175-180 (2004).

65. Vanita Singh & M. Sivakami, *Normality, Freedom, and Distress: Listening to the Menopausal Experiences of Indian Women of Haryana*, in THE PALGRAVE HANDBOOK OF CRITICAL MENSTRUATION STUDIES 985-99, 989 (Chris Bobel et al. eds., 2020).

66. *Id.* at 994.

67. *Id.* at 995.

68. *See* Mary Kruk et al., *Femininity Concerns and Feelings About Menstruation Cessation Among Lesbian, Bisexual, and Heterosexual Women: Implications for Menopause*, 30 J. WOMEN'S HEALTH 1751, 1755-56 (2021).

69. *Id.* at 1753.

70. *Id. See also Child Welfare Nondiscrimination Laws*, MOVEMENT ADVANCEMENT PROJECT, https://perma.cc/REE4-FWM7 (last accessed Aug. 22, 2023) and Ethics Committee of the American Society for Reproductive Medicine, *Access to Fertility Treatment by Gays, Lesbians, and Unmarried Persons: A Committee Report*, 100 FERTILITY & STERILITY 1524 (2013).

71. *See* Kruk et al., *supra* note 68, at 1755-56.

72. *See* Carolyn Ambler Walter, *The Psychosocial Meaning of Menopause: Women's Experiences*, 12 J. OF WOMEN & AGING 117, 119 (2000).

73. *Id.*

74. *See* Dillaway, *supra* note 27, at 11-12 (discussing relationship status and race).

75. *See* Kacey Y. Eichelberger et al., *Black Lives Matter: Claiming a Space for Evidence-Based Outrage in Obstetrics and Gynecology*, 106 AM. J. PUB. HEALTH 1771 (2016); Sarah Vander Schaaf, *Black Women's Problems During Menopause Haven't Been a Focus of Medicine*, WASH. POST (Mar. 6, 2021), https://perma.cc/V8C8-R4J8.

76. *See* Adriana Velez, *Menopause Is Different for Women of Color*, ENDOCRINE WEB, https://perma.cc/FUN2-LEZ6.

77. *See* Susan D. Reed et al., *Premenopausal Vasomotor Symptoms in an Ethnically Diverse Population*, 21 MENOPAUSE 153, 153 (2014).

78. *See* Nanette Santoro et al., *The SWAN Song: Study of Women's Health Across the Nation's Recurring Themes*, 38 OBSTETRICS & GYNECOLOGY CLINICS OF N. AM. 417, 418 (2011).

79. *Compare* Joyce T. Bromberger et al., *Prospective Study of the Determinants of Age at Menopause*, 145 AM. J. EPIDEMIOLOGY 124, 127 (1997), *with* Ellen B. Gold et al., *Factors Associated with Age at Natural Menopause in a Multiethnic Sample of Midlife Women*, 153 AM. J. EPIDEMIOLOGY 865, 870 (2001).

80. *See* Marván et al., *supra* note 32, at 674.

81. *Watch Now: "The Menopause Talk" with Oprah, Drew Barrymore, and Maria Shriver*, OPRAH DAILY (Apr. 5, 2023), https://perma.cc/WYM9-UY53.

82. Morgan Hines, *Oprah, Drew Barrymore, Maria Shriver Get Candid About Menopause: "Shrouded in Stigma,"* USA TODAY (April 5, 2023), https://perma.cc/9E2S-VU8K.

83. Amy Larocca, *Welcome to the Menopause Gold Rush*, N.Y. TIMES (Dec. 20, 2022), https://perma.cc/9H26-DSWP.

84. *See supra* notes 7-10 and accompanying text.

85. *See* Funny Commercials Review, *Astellas Pharma Superbowl Commercial 2023 What's VMS Ad Review*, YOUTUBE (Feb. 12, 2023), https://perma.cc/S48V-NSJA.

86. *See Menopause Awareness: Astellas Pharma Busy Superbowl Commercial Spot to Ask "What's VMS?,"* FEMTECHINSIDER (Feb. 13, 2023), https://perma.cc/FP7B-9TB8.

## Chapter 3

1. *See* Julie Wernau et al., *Millions Awarded in Hormone Suit*, CHI. TRIB. (Nov. 24, 2009, 12:00 AM), https://perma.cc/M6C3-UWEM.

2. *See* Kendall v. Wyeth, Inc., Nos. 936 EDA 2010, 937 EDA 2010, 1154 EDA 2010, 2012 WL 112609, at *2 (Pa. Super. Ct. Jan. 3, 2012).

3. Natasha Singer & Duff Wilson, *Menopause, as Brought to You by Drug Makers*, NBC NEWS (Dec. 13, 2009, 5:12 PM), https://perma.cc/CJ8B-T7QP.

4. Barton v. Wyeth Pharm., Inc., Nos. 694 EDA 2010, 695 EDA 2010, 2012 WL 112613 (Pa. Super. Ct. Jan. 3, 2012) (non-precedential).

5. *Id.* at *3.

6. *Id.* at *2.

7. *Kendall*, 2012 WL at *2.

8. Duff Wilson, *Another Loss for Pfizer in Drug Suits*, N.Y. TIMES (Nov. 23, 2009), https://perma.cc/A7V4-LU36.

9. The Philadelphia Courts, *Civil Docket Access, Kendall v. Wyeth* (last visited Feb. 15, 2023) (on file with authors).

10. *Barton*, 2012 WL at *21 (quoting trial court opinion, Jan. 29, 2010 at 59); *see* Jef Feeley, *Pfizer Paid $896 Million in Prempro Settlements*, BLOOMBERG (June 19, 2012, 4:27 PM), https://www.bloomberg.com/news/articles/2012-06-19/pfizer-paid-896-million-in-prempro-accords-filing-shows-1-?embedded-checkout=truepermalin.

11. Susan Dominus, *Women Have Been Misled About Menopause*, N.Y. TIMES (Feb. 1, 2023), https://perma.cc/6DSG-JL3J.

12. Barry G. Wren, *The History and Politics of Menopause, in* MANAGING THE MENOPAUSE: 21ST CENTURY SOLUTIONS 20, 20 (Nick Pansy et al. eds., 2015).

13. ARISTOTLE, POLITICS bk. VIII, ch. 14, 1335a (Carnes Lord trans., 2d ed. 2013).

14. Michael Stolberg, *A Woman's Hell? Medical Perceptions of Menopause in Preindustrial Europe*, 73 BULL. HIST. MED. 404, 406 (1999) (quoting Giovanni Marinello, *Le Medicine Partenenti Alle Infermità Delle Donne* (1563)).

15. *Id.* at 412.

16. SUSAN P. MATTERN, THE SLOW MOON CLIMBS: THE SCIENCE, HISTORY, AND MEANING OF MENOPAUSE 272 (2019).

17. Christina Boufis, *History, Part II*, WOMAN'S DAY (Sept. 27, 2010), https://perma.cc/H3KN-CQDT.

18. Lucy van de Wiel, *The Time of the Change: Menopause's Medicalization and the Gender Politics of Aging*, 7 INT'L J. FEMINIST. APPROACHES TO BIOETHICS 74, 75 (2014).

19. LOUISE FOXCROFT, HOT FLUSHES, COLD SCIENCE: A HISTORY OF THE MODERN MENOPAUSE 121 (2009).

20. *The History of Menopause*, HENPICKED: MENOPAUSE HUB (Nov. 4, 2022), https://perma.cc/9GR3-4S4A.

21. Alice Smellie, *Misogyny & the Menopause: A Brief History,* PAN MACMILLAN (Mar. 5, 2022), https://perma.cc/2H6M-ATF4.

22. ANDREW F. CURRIER, THE MENOPAUSE; A CONSIDERATION OF THE PHENOMENA WHICH OCCUR TO WOMEN AT THE CLOSE OF THE CHILD-BEARING PERIOD 17 (1897); JUDITH A. HOUCK, HOT AND BOTHERED: WOMEN, MEDICINE, AND MENOPAUSE IN MODERN AMERICA 14 (2008) (discussing Currier's approach).

23. HOUCK, *supra* note 22, at 14–16.

24. *Id.* at 18.

25. *Id.* at 18, 24–25.

26. Grace E. Kohn et al., *The History of Estrogen Therapy*, 7 SEXUAL MED. REV. 416, 418 (2019), https://perma.cc/D8D4-6UY5.

27. ELIZABETH SIEGEL WATKINS, THE ESTROGEN ELIXIR 7 (2007).

28. *See Edward Doisy Sr.; Won Nobel Prize*, N.Y. TIMES (Oct. 25, 1986), https://perma.cc/65BV-XY32 (calling Dr. Doisy's isolation of estrone "the first great accomplishment in a long-term research project" on ovarian function that lasted for twelve years); WATKINS, *supra* note 27, at 11–12 (discussing Doisy's experiments and the patents he received in 1934).

29. James Woods & Elizabeth Warner, *The History of Estrogen*, MENOPAUSE BLOG (Feb. 17, 2016), https://perma.cc/C84A-ASDG.

30. *See* MATTERN, *supra* note 16, at 284.

31. WATKINS, *supra* note 27, at 21.

32. *Id.* (discussing Theelin); August A. Werner et al., *Effective Clinical Dosages of Theelin in Oil*, 109 J. AM. MED. ASS'N 1027 (1937) (addressing process of Theelin administration), https://perma.cc/Y2BN-X469.

33. Kohn, *supra* note 26, at 418; WATKINS, *supra* note 27, at 21.

34. Robert L. Reid, *Menopause Medicine: Past, Present, and Future*, 41 J. OBSTETRICS & GYNAECOLOGY. CAN. S347 (2019), https://perma.cc/JT4G-EGRV.

35. *See, e.g.,* HOUCK, *supra* note 22, at 59.

36. *See* Federal Food, Drug, and Cosmetic Act, ch. 675, 52 Stat. 1040 (1938) (codified as amended at 21 U.S.C. §§ 301–99 (2012 & Supp. 2017)). *See also* PAUL ENRIQUEZ, REWRITING NATURE 294–95 (2021) (discussing development of FDA regulations generally).

37. National Cancer Institute, *Diethylstilbestrol (DES) Exposure and Cancer* (2021), https://perma.cc/AFT5-32VG.

38. Ayerst, McKenna and Harrison (the Canadian company that developed Premarin) eventually became part of Wyeth, which in turn became a wholly owned subsidiary of Pfizer in 2009. Emily Jung et al., *Do Large Pharma*

*Companies Provide Drug Development Innovation? Our Analysis Says No,* STAT (Dec. 10, 2019), https://perma.cc/GXZ8-4RF2.

39. *See, e.g.,* Robert Bazell, *The Cruel Irony of Trying to Be 'Feminine Forever,'* NBC NEWS (Jan. 2, 2007, 5:01 PM), https://perma.cc/FJ6C-K8N4.

40. WATKINS, *supra* note 27, at 35; *id.* at 33 (noting that the medical consensus was also "that only a small proportion of women needed to be treated with estrogen at menopause").

41. *See* Emil Novak, *The Management of the Menopause,* 40 AM. J. OBSTETRICS & GYNECOLOGY 589, 595 (1940), https://perma.cc/T5KKL9UX.

42. *See* HOUCK, *supra* note 22, at 171.

43. *See, e.g., id.* at 175; MATTERN, *supra* note 16, at 286–88.

44. Naomi R. Cahn, Bridget J. Crawford, & Emily Gold Waldman, *Managing and Monitoring the Menopausal Body,* 2022 U. CHI. LEGAL F. 41, 45 (2022).

45. FOXCROFT, *supra* note 19, at 202 (illustration); *Magazine Advertisement for Endocreme Hormone Cream,* THE ADVERTISING ARCHIVES, https://perma.cc/5TJ9-G5SC.

46. Elizabeth Siegel Watkins, *Dispensing with Aging: Changing Rationales for Long-term Hormone Replacement Therapy,* 43 PHARM. HIST. 23, 27 (2001); *see also* WATKINS, *supra* note 27, at 59; Singer & Wilson, *supra* note 3.

47. MATTERN, *supra* note 16, at 286.

48. *See, e.g.,* Angelo Cagnacci & Martina Venier, *The Controversial History of Hormone Replacement Therapy,* 55 MEDICINA 602 (2019).

49. Robert A. Wilson & Thelma A. Wilson, *The Fate of the Nontreated Postmenopausal Woman: A Plea for the Maintenance of Adequate Estrogen from Puberty to the Grave,* 11 J. AM. GERIATRICS SOC'Y 347 (1963).

50. *Id.* at 347 (emphasis added).

51. WATKINS, *supra* note 27, at 47.

52. ROBERT WILSON, FEMININE FOREVER: A REVOLUTIONARY BREAKTHROUGH FOR WOMEN (1966).

53. *See, e.g.,* WATKINS, *supra* note 27, at 49.

54. Tobias Millrood, *The Rise and Fall of Hormone Therapy,* TRIAL, 42, 43 (2003) (quoting Wilson, *supra* note 52).

55. WILSON, *supra* note 52, at 25, 43, 51.

56. *Id.* at 20.

57. *Id.* at 67.

58. *See* TARA PARKER-POPE, THE HORMONE DECISION 27 (2007) (quoting WILSON, *supra* note 52).

59. PARKER-POPE, *supra* note 58, at 26.

60. Kathryn S. Huss, *Feminine Forever,* 197 J. AM. MED. ASS'N 156 (1966).

61. Judith A. Houck, *"What Do These Women Want?": Feminist Responses to Feminine Forever, 1963-1980,* 77 BULL. HIST. MED. 103, 109 (2003).

62. *See* Millrood, *supra* note 54 (discussing the marketing of MHT).

63. *See id.* at 42, n.9 and accompanying text.

64. *See* Liza Mundy, *The Secret Power of Menopause*, ATLANTIC (Oct. 2019), https://perma.cc/DZ6A-3YMS; JEN GUNTER, THE MENOPAUSE MANIFESTO: OWN YOUR HEALTH WITH FACTS AND FEMINISM 219-20 (2021) (identifying Wyeth, the holder of the patent on the prescription drug Premarin, as the sponsor of Dr. Wilson's research).

65. *See* Millrood, *supra* note 54, at 103 n.12 and accompanying text (noting the frequency with which Premarin was prescribed).

66. Singer & Wilson, *supra* note 3.

67. Karen Stabiner, *In the Menopause Market, a Gold Mine of Ads*, N.Y. TIMES (Apr. 4, 1994), https://perma.cc/XX79-AX9B.

68. *See* HOUCK, *supra* note 22 (describing estrone: "The weakest type of estrogen, it's typically higher after menopause. Like all estrogen, estrone supports female sexual development and function. Low or high estrone can cause symptoms such as irregular bleeding, fatigue, or mood swings"); *Estrone*, CLEVELAND CLINIC (2022), https://perma.cc/C7T2-BKAS.

69. Gabrielle Jackson, *The Female Problem: How Male Bias in Medical Trials Ruined Women's Health*, GUARDIAN (Nov. 13, 2019), https://perma.cc/6LNB -9RPH.

70. U.S. FOOD & DRUG ADMINISTRATION OFFICE OF WOMEN'S HEALTH, PROTECTING AND ADVANCING WOMEN'S HEALTH 3 (2006), https://perma .cc/D6SP-Y3F6; *Special Population Clinical Trials Require Special Treatment*, 2 NO. 4 GUIDE TO GOOD CLINICAL PRACTICE NEWSL. 5 (Jan. 1995); Ruth B. Merkatz, *Inclusion of Women in Clinical Trials: A Historical Overview of Scientific, Ethical, and Legal Issues*, 27 J. OBSTET. GYNECOL. NEONATAL NURS. 78, 78 (1998).

71. HOUCK, *supra* note 22, at 182.

72. WATKINS, *supra* note 27, at 137.

73. 42 Fed. Reg. 37636, 37642 (July 22, 1977) (codified at 21 C.F.R § 310.515). The labeling was required to include the importance of minimizing the estrogen dose and length of time because of a risk of endometrial cancer, and other risks, such as gall bladder disease, abnormal blood clotting, and other potential side effects. *Id.*

74. *See* Adam L. Hersh et al., *National Use of Postmenopausal Hormone Therapy: Annual Trends and Response to Recent Evidence*, 291 J. AM. MED. ASS'N 47, 47-48 (2004), https://perma.cc/KR97-9L5S.

75. *See* HOUCK, *supra* note 22, at 230 (noting that the number of prescriptions increased "from 13.6 million in 1982 to 31.7 million in 1992"); *see, e.g.*, Cynthia A. Stuenkel, *Hormone Therapy for Postmenopausal Women: A Brief History of Time*, 23 HASTINGS WOMEN'S L.J. 45, 54 (2012) (noting that the ability of hormone therapy to reduce menopausal symptoms "had previously been unequivocally demonstrated").

76. In addition, Wyeth "inundat[ed] doctors and patients with a sea of positive preventive health messages." Singer & Wilson, *supra* note 3.

77. *See* Deborah Grady et al., *Hormone Therapy to Prevent Disease and Prolong Life in Postmenopausal Women*, 117 ANN. INTERNAL MED. 1016 (1992); Gretchen Wells and David M. Herrington, *The Heart and Estrogen/Progestin Replacement Study: What Have We Learned and What Questions Remain?*, 15 DRUGS & AGING 419, 419 (1999), https://perma.cc/D28W-S872.

78. *See* WATKINS, *supra* note 27, at 149–50.

79. Cahn, Crawford, & Waldman, *supra* note 44; *see also* WATKINS, *supra* note 27, at 240–41.

80. Sheldon Krimsky, *Reviewed Work: The Greatest Experiment Ever Performed on Women: Exploding the Estrogen Myth by Barbara Seaman*, 24 J. PUB. HEALTH Pol. 479, 482 (2003).

81. Julie Steenhuysen, *Wyeth Paid Writers to Promote Hormone Therapy: Study*, REUTERS (Sept. 7, 2010, 6:14 PM), https://perma.cc/9YAU-8WPM.

82. Katherine Drabiak, *The Impact of a Developing Regulatory Framework Governing LDTs in Precision Oncology: Reenvisioning the Clinical Risk Assessment Paradigm*, 13 J. HEALTH & BIOMEDICAL L. 1, 72 (2017).

83. *See* WATKINS, *supra* note 27, at 148 (citing prescription rates).

84. Neel U. Sukhatme & M. Gregg Bloche, *Health Care Costs and the Arc of Innovation*, 104 MINN. L. REV. 955, 1040 (2019).

85. *See* HOUCK, *supra* note 22, at 231.

86. Erin N. Marcus, *When TV Commercials Play the Doctor*, N.Y. TIMES (Jan. 3, 2003), https://perma.cc/WN9X-CDUX.

87. *See* HOUCK, *supra* note 22, at 231.

88. WATKINS, *supra* note 27, at 246 (explaining that progesterone had been shown to play some role in reducing the risk for endometrial cancer).

89. WATKINS, *supra* note 27, at 231.

90. *See* MATTERN, *supra* note 16, at 298 (citing prescription statistics).

91. Stephen Hulley et al., *Randomized Trial of Estrogen Plus Progestin for Secondary Prevention of Coronary Heart Disease in Postmenopausal Women*, 280 J. AM. MED. ASS'N 605 (1998).

92. WATKINS, *supra* note 27, at 265–66.

93. *See Women's Health Initiative*, NAT'L HEART, LUNG, & BLOOD INST., https://perma.cc/7648-CVXT (last visited June 4, 2023).

94. Karin B. Michels, *The Women's Health Initiative—Curse or Blessing?*, 35 INT'L J. EPIDEMIOLOGY 814, 814 (2006); WATKINS, *supra* note 27, at 227.

95. WOMEN'S HEALTH INITIATIVE, 2021 ANNUAL PROGRESS REPORT 1-1 (2021), https://perma.cc/Q2J2-4C7W. The Initiative has been extended until 2025, relying on both medical and self-reports. *Id.*

96. The Women's Health Initiative Study Group, *Design of the Women's Health Initiative Clinical Trial and Observational Study*, 19 CONTROL CLINICAL TRIALS 61 (1998); Rebecca Chesler et al., *What the Women's Health Initiative Has Taught Us About Menopausal Hormone Therapy*, 41 CLINICAL CARDIOLOGY 247, 247 (2018).

97. *See* Chesler et al., *supra* note 96. One group, which included women with a uterus, took a combination of estrogen and progestin; the second group, which included women without a uterus, took estrogen alone; and the third group received a placebo; *see* HOUCK, *supra* note 22, at 229; JoAnn Manson et al., *Menopausal Hormone Therapy and Health Outcomes During the Intervention and Extended Poststopping Phases of the Women's Health Initiative Randomized Trials*, 310 J. AM. MED. ASS'N 1353 (2013). Manson was the lead investigator. *See id.*

98. *See* MATTERN, *supra* note 16, at 298–99 (explaining that the combination estrogen and progestin hormone replacement trial was stopped prematurely in 2002 for multiple reasons and that the estrogen replacement trial was stopped prematurely in 2004 because of an increased risk of stroke).

99. *See Largest Women's Health Prevention Study Ever—Women's Health Initiative*, OFF. ON WOMEN'S HEALTH, U.S. DEP'T OF HEALTH & HUM. SERVS. (2020), https://perma.cc/PX3D-WP3M (summarizing results of 2002 study); *see also* Writing Group for the Women's Health Initiative Investigators, *Risks and Benefits of Estrogen Plus Progestin in Healthy Postmenopausal Women: Principal Results From the Women's Health Initiative Randomized Controlled Trial*, 288 J. AM. MED. ASS'N 321 (2002), https://perma.cc/9BLQ-7ZQA.

100. *Largest Women's Health Prevention Study, supra* note 99.

101. JoAnn E. Manson et al., *Menopausal Hormone Therapy and Long-term All-Cause and Cause-Specific Mortality*, 318 J. AM. MED. ASS'N 927 (2017), https://perma.cc/RU4D-KFLF.

102. *The Greatest Experiment Ever Performed*, TODAY (July 11, 2003, 5:53 AM), https://perma.cc/DK6V-ZVF2.

103. Nancy Shute, *The Last Word on Hormone Therapy from the Women's Health Initiative*, NPR (Oct. 4, 2013, 4:19 PM), https://perma.cc/2GLX-8PLH.

104. Gina Kolata with Melody Petersen, *Hormone Replacement Study a Shock to the Medical System*, N.Y. TIMES (July 10, 2002), https://www.nytimes.com/2002/07/10/us/hormone-replacement-study-a-shock-to-the-medical-system.html.

105. Dominus, *supra* note 11.

106. Shute, *supra* note 103.

107. Susan R. Johnson, *Hormone Replacement Therapy: Applying the Results of the Women's Health Initiative*, 69 CLEVELAND CLINIC J. MED. 682 (2002).

108. Susan J. Landers, *Hormone Therapy Guide Issued by ACOG Task Force*, AMEDNEWS.COM (Nov. 15, 2004), https://perma.cc/G3AV-Z47X; *Summary of Balancing Risks and Benefits*, 104 OBSTETRICS & GYNECOLOGY 18 (Oct. 2004) (withdrawn), https://perma.cc/9W3W-XR2N.

109. Manson, *supra* note 101, at 928.

110. Scott Gottlieb, *FDA Insists Oestrogen Products for Menopause Carry a Warning*, 326 BRIT. MED. J. 126 (2003), https://perma.cc/75Y9-GSWK.

111. Pfizer Form 10-Q, at 26 (2012) (on file with authors).

112. *See, e.g.*, Krueger v. Wyeth, Inc., 396 F. Supp. 3d 931 (S.D. Cal. 2019); *see also* In re Prempro Prods. Liab. Litig., 254 F. Supp. 2d 1366 (J.P.M.L. 2003); Pfizer Form 10-Q, *supra* note 111, at 25; Jef Feeley, *Pfizer Said to Pay $330 Million in Prempro Settlement*, BLOOMBERG NEWS (Feb. 9, 2011, 4:42 PM), https://perma.cc/Y2FP-ZFNK.

113. *In re* Prempro Prod. Liab. Litig., 591 F.3d 613 (8th Cir. 2010); Pfizer Form 10-Q, *supra* note 111, at 25 (noting that some cases involved ovarian cancer and heart disease); *see also* Kate Miller, *Hormone Replacement Therapy in the Wake of the Women's Health Initiative Study: An Opportunity to Reexamine the Learned Intermediary Doctrine*, 12 WM. & MARY J. RACE, GENDER, & SOC. JUST. 239 (2005) (discussing early cases).

114. Pfizer Form 10-Q, *supra* note 111, at 27.

115. JoAnn V. Pinkerton, *After the Women's Health Initiative—Menopausal Women and Hormone Therapy*, 7 ETHICS J. AM. MED. ASS'N 751 (2005), https://perma.cc/V3QA-VRXK.

116. GUNTER, *supra* note 64, at 225.

117. Dominus, *supra* note 11.

118. Carolyn J. Crandall et al., *Management of Menopausal Symptoms: A Review*, 329 J. AM. MED. ASS'N 405, 409 (2023), https://perma.cc/3JFC-RA24.

119. Deborah Copaken, *How to Hack Insurance so You Can Get the Hormones You Need*, OPRAH DAILY (Apr. 5, 2023), https://perma.cc/6LXT-ABKN.

120. *Thinking of Menopausal Hormone Therapy? Here's What You Can Expect from Your GP* (Jan. 12, 2020, 3:14 PM), https://perma.cc/VM3H-GS3H; North American Menopause Society, *The 2022 Hormone Therapy Position Statement of the North American Menopause Society*, 29 J. N. AM. MENOPAUSE SOC'Y 767 (2022).

121. North American Menopause Society, *supra* note 120, at 785.

122. Jennifer Weiss-Wolf et al., *Menopause Doesn't Have to Be Miserable*, L.A. TIMES (June 5, 2023), https://perma.cc/Y237-YHEF.

123. Cleveland Clinic, *Premature and Early Menopause*, CLEVELAND CLINIC HEALTH LIBR. (2022), https://perma.cc/5U4Y-W9ET.

124. The North American Menopause Society, *The Experts Do Agree About Hormone Therapy* (2023), https://perma.cc/9E38-FT4E.

125. Dominus, *supra* note 11.

126. Reid, *supra* note 34, at S348.

127. GUNTER, *supra* note 64, at 326; *see* Nancy Boone, *Why It's So Hard to Talk About "Down There": The Doctor Who Is Normalizing Menopause*, L.A. TIMES (June 10, 2021), https://perma.cc/M7MT-F9SJ.

128. Katharine Gammon, *It's Time to Rethink Hormone Therapy for Women, Says Health Scientist*, USC TROJAN FAMILY (2021), https://perma.cc/K4TJ-YVHE.

129. CENTERS FOR DISEASE CONTROL, NATIONAL HEALTH AND NUTRITION EXAMINATION SURVEY: USE OF HORMONE REPLACEMENT THERAPY AMONG

POSTMENOPAUSAL WOMEN IN THE UNITED STATES, 1988–1994 (2003), https://perma.cc/J9H5-CG8H.

130. Adrianna Rodriguez, *Why Some Doctors Shy Away from Hormone Therapy for Menopause—and What to Know About Risks*, USA TODAY (Feb. 15, 2023, 1:47 PM), https://perma.cc/T9AP-RYUR.

131. Amy Larocca, *Welcome to the Menopause Gold Rush*, N.Y. TIMES (Dec. 20, 2022), https://perma.cc/E3JG-KR7P; Juliana M. Kling et al., *Menopause Management Knowledge in Postgraduate Family Medicine, Internal Medicine, and Obstetrics and Gynecology Residents: A Cross-Sectional Survey*, 94 MAYO CLINIC PROC. 242 (2019), https://perma.cc/3F4N-53KN.

132. GUNTER, *supra* note 64, at 246.

133. Stephanie S. Faubion & Andrew M. Kaunitz, *Stopping Systemic Menopausal Hormone Therapy: Why, When and How*, 89 MATURITAS 3 (2016).

134. *Menopause and Midlife Clinic to Launch*, BRIGHAM BULLETIN, https://perma.cc/5YQY-MQ5L; Dominus, *supra* note 11; Sandy Cohen, *New Comprehensive Menopause Program Gives Patients "The Care They Truly Deserve,"* UCLA HEALTH (Sept. 13, 2023), https://perma.cc/69L9-5HHT.

135. Menopause Research Act of 2022, H.R. 8774 (2022), https://www.congress.gov/bill/117th-congress/house-bill/8774?s=1&r=13.

136. *5 Things to Know About Menopause and Hormone Therapy*, N.Y. TIMES (Feb. 1, 2023), https://perma.cc/C3A8-27A9.

137. Femtech Insider, *Menopause Awareness: Astellas Pharma Busy Superbowl Commercial Spot to Ask "What's VMS?"* FEMTECH INSIDER (Feb. 13, 2023), https://perma.cc/CMK6-RQPW; Selena Yeager, *Menopause Therapies to Watch in 2023*, FEISTY MENOPAUSE (Jan. 4, 2023), https://perma.cc/KSS7-MB3K.

138. Alisha Haridasani Gupta, *What to Know About the New Treatment for Hot Flashes*, N.Y. TIMES (May 12, 2023), https://perma.cc/V5WN-38Y5.

139. *See, e.g.*, Linda C. Andrist, *Conceptual Models for Women's Health Research: Reclaiming Menopause as an Exemplar of Nursing's Contributions to Feminist Scholarship*, 19 ANN. REV. NURSING RSCH. 29, 29 (2001).

140. *See, e.g.*, GUNTER, *supra* note 64, at 336.

## Chapter 4

1. Deposition of Georgia Sipple at 323, Sipple v. Crossmark, No. 2:10-CV-00570 (E.D. Cal. June 27, 2011).

2. Declaration of Cindy Slinker in Support of Defendants' Motion for Summary Judgment at Exhibit 7, Sipple v. Crossmark, No. 2:10-CV-00570 (E.D. Cal. Sept. 7, 2011).

3. *Id.* at ¶ 8.

4. *Id.* at Exhibit 8.

5. Declaration of Carla Hemyari in Support of Defendants' Motion for Summary Judgment at Exhibit E, Sipple v. Crossmark, No. 2:10-CV-00570 (E.D. Cal. Sept. 7. 2011).

6. Sipple v. Crossmark, 2012 WL 2798791, at *5 (E.D. Cal. July 9, 2012).

7. *See, e.g., 10 Celebrities Who Have Spoken Out About Menopause*, GLAMOUR (Oct. 5, 2020), https://perma.cc/2DFW-RZDB] (quoting Michelle Obama, Oprah Winfrey, and Gwyneth Paltrow speaking about their experiences with menopause).

8. Stephanie S. Faubion et. al., *Impact of Menopause Symptoms on Women in the Workplace*, 98 MAYO CLINIC PROC. 845 (2023).

9. BANK OF AMERICA, BREAK THROUGH THE STIGMA: MENOPAUSE IN THE WORKPLACE (2023), https://perma.cc/NSA4-QSF7

10. Amanda Griffiths et al., *Menopause and Work: An Electronic Survey*, 76 MATURITAS 155, 156–157 (2013). A study of Australian women similarly found that "hot flushes were more difficult to cope with when working in hot or unventilated work environments." Martha Hickey et al., *No Sweat: Managing Menopausal Symptoms at Work*, 38 J. PSYCHOSOMATIC OBSTETRICS & GYNECOLOGY 202, 207 (2017).

11. Philip Sarel et al., *Incremental Direct and Indirect Costs of Untreated Vasomotor Symptoms*, 22 MENOPAUSE: J. N. AM. MENOPAUSE SOC'Y 260, 262 (2014).

12. Heather Yoeli et al., *Menopausal Symptoms and Work: A Narrative Review of Women's Experiences in Casual, Informal, or Precarious Jobs*, 150 MATURITAS 14, 16 (2021).

13. Pragya Gartoulia et al., *Menopausal Vasomotor Symptoms Are Associated with Poor Self-Assessed Work Ability*, 87 MATURITAS 33, 35 (2016).

14. KAYE ADAMS & VICKY ALLAN, STILL HOT: 42 BRILLIANTLY HONEST MENOPAUSE STORIES 52 (2020).

15. Amanda Griffiths, Sara Jane MacLennan, & Juliet Hassard, *Menopause and Work: An Electronic Survey*, 76 MATURITAS 155, 156–157 (2013).

16. Coleman v. Bobby Dodd Institute, Inc., 2017 WL 2486080 (M.D. Ga. June 8, 2017).

17. Initial Brief of Plaintiff-Appellant at 4, Coleman v. Bobby Dodd Inst., No. 17-130-23 (11th Cir. Aug. 14, 2017), https://perma.cc/GJL5-YE8S.

18. Risa Kagan et al., *Impact of Sleep Disturbances on Employment and Work Productivity Among Midlife Women in the US SWAN Database: A Brief Report*, 28 MENOPAUSE: J. N. AM. MENOPAUSE SOC'Y 1176, 1178 (2021).

19. James A. Simon & Kathleen Z. Reape, *Understanding the Menopausal Experiences of Professional Women*, 16 MENOPAUSE 73, 75 (2009).

20. ADAMS & ALLAN, *supra* note 14, at 44 (quoting Pippa Marriott).

21. Lisa Mosconi et al., *Menopause Impacts Human Brain Structure, Connectivity, Energy Metabolism, and Amyloid-Beta Deposition*, 11 SCI. REP. 10867 (2021).

22. Alex Bryson et al., *The Consequences of Early Menopause and Menopause Symptoms for Labour Market Participation*, 293 SOC. SCI. & MED. 114676, at 8 (2022).

23. *Id.*

24. Simon & Reape, *supra* note 19, at 74.

25. Keiko Hashimoto et al., *Relationship Between Number of Menopausal Symptoms and Work Performance in Japanese Working Women*, 28 MENOPAUSE: J. N. AM. MENOPAUSE SOC'Y 175, 177 (2020).

26. Belinda Steffan, *Managing Menopause at Work: The Contradictory Nature of Identity Talk*, 28 GENDER, WORK, & ORG. 195, 205 (2021).

27. *Menopause Killing Careers of Women, Reveals AMS and AIA Australia Study*, BUSY CONTINENT (Dec. 20, 2022), https://perma.cc/44YY-XST7; *see also* Anna Kelsey-Sugg & Maria Tickle, *Menopause Can Make Everyday Work a Struggle. So Why Aren't We Talking About It?*, ABC NEWS AUST. (Mar. 28, 2021), https://perma.cc/PZ3G-P6AC.

28. *Menopause Killing Careers, supra* note 27.

29. Cruz-Aponte v. Caribbean Petroleum Corp., 123 F. Supp. 3d 276, 278–79 (D.P.R. 2015).

30. Sidhu v. State of California, 2021 WL 411149, at *4 (E.D. Cal. Feb. 5, 2021).

31. Dault v. Georgia Urology, P.A., 2021 WL 2517373, at *2 (N.D. Ga. Feb. 1, 2021).

32. Rayburn v. United Airlines Inc., 2021 WL 8893645, at *2 (C.D. Cal. July 2, 2021).

33. Schmalz v. Northrop Grumman Corp., 2012 WL 1813095, at *5 (S.D. Ohio May 17, 2012). Another case involved similar remarks by colleagues about the plaintiff's "assumed menopause-related moodiness." Doerfler-Casner v. Placer Cnty. Dept. Pub. Works, 2006 WL 1581856, at *2 (E.D. Cal. June 2, 2006).

34. Bailey v. Henderson, 94 F. Supp. 2d 68, 72 (D.D.C. 2000).

35. EEOC v. Massey Yardley Chrysler Plymouth, Inc., 117 F.3d 1244 (11th Cir. 1997).

36. Nancy Fugate Woods et al., *Perimenopause Meets Life: Observations from the Women Living Better Survey*, 29 MENOPAUSE: J. N. AM. MENOPAUSE SOC'Y 1388, 1392 (2022).

37. Emily Bariola et al., *Employment Conditions and Work-Related Stressors Are Associated with Menopausal Symptom Reporting Among Perimenopausal and Postmenopausal Women*, 24 MENOPAUSE: J. N. AM. MENOPAUSE SOC'Y 247, 250 (2016).

38. *Id.*

39. Claire Hardy et al., *What Do Working Menopausal Women Want? A Qualitative Investigation into Women's Perspectives on Employer and Line Manager Support*, 101 MATURITAS 37, 39 (2017).

40. *Id.*

41. ADAMS & ALLAN, *supra* note 14, at 44.

42. BANK OF AMERICA, *supra* note 9, at 10.

43. Hilary Osborne, *A Third of Women Hide Menopause Symptoms at Work*, GUARDIAN (Mar. 8, 2021), https://perma.cc/G8CQ-7P43; Alice Broster, *Why*

*One-Third of People Experiencing Menopause Hide It at Work,* FORBES (Mar. 31, 2021), https://perma.cc/G7L5-S7QY.

44. Amanda Griffiths et al., *Menopause and Work: An Electronic Survey,* 76 MATURITAS 155, 157 (2013); Alicia A. Grandey, *Research: Workplace Stigma Around Menopause Is Real,* HARV. BUS. REV. (Dec. 20, 2022), https://perma.cc/Z86W-LVX3.

45. Grandey, *supra* note 44.

46. 42 U.S.C. § 2000-e2(a)(1).

47. 42 U.S.C. § 2000-e2(k).

48. 29 U.S.C. § 623(a)(1).

49. *Id.* § 623(a)(1)-(2).

50. ADA Amendments Act of 2008, Pub. L. No. 110-325, 122 Stat. 3553 (2008) (codified as amended in scattered sections of 42 U.S.C.).

51. 42 U.S.C. § 12102(1)(A).

52. *Id.* § 12102(1).

53. *Id.* § 12102(2).

54. *Id.* § 121.

55. Both the Pregnant Workers Fairness Act (PWFA) and the Providing Urgent Maternal Protections for Nursing Mothers Act (PUMP for Nursing Mothers Act) were included in the appropriations act for fiscal year 2023, which was signed into law on December 29, 2022. Consolidated Appropriations Act 2023, Pub. L. 117-328, 136 Stat. 4459, 6084, 6093 (2022).

56. Meritor Sav. Bank v. Vinson, 477 U.S. 57 (1986).

57. *Id.* at 67.

58. SANDRA F. SPERINO & SUJA A. THOMAS, UNEQUAL: HOW AMERICA'S COURTS UNDERMINE DISCRIMINATION LAW 31 (2017).

59. Burkhart v. Am. Railcar, 2009 WL 10695340 (E.D. Ark. Apr. 28, 2009); *see also, e.g.,* Schmalz v. Northrop Grumman Corp., 2012 WL 1813095 (S.D. Ohio May 17, 2012) (holding, in case where supervisor repeatedly leered at plaintiff and made sexually suggestive comments, while also commenting about her possible PMS or menopause, that the alleged conduct did not rise to the requisite level of severity or pervasiveness required to establish a hostile work environment).

60. Massey Yardley, 117 F.3d at 1244.

61. Dault v. Georgia Urology, P.A., 2020 WL 10139416 (N.D. Ga. Dec. 18, 2020) (containing magistrate judge's report and recommendation), *adopted by* 2021 WL 2517373 (N.D. Ga. Feb. 1, 2021).

62. White v. Twin Falls Cnty., 2016 WL 1275594 (D. Idaho Mar. 31, 2016).

63. Coleman v. Bobby Dodd Inst., 2017 WL 2486080, at *2 (M.D. Ga. June 8, 2017).

64. *Id.*

65. Betancourt v. Margaritaville Hollywood, Beach Resort, L.P., 2019 WL 2119611, at *4 (S.D. Fla. Mar. 29, 2019).

66. Flores v. Va. Dep't of Corr., 2021 WL 668802 (W.D. Va. Feb. 22, 2021).

67. Baskerville v. CBS News, Inc., 2022 WL 612608, at *3 (D.D.C. Mar. 2, 2022).

68. Sipple v. Crossmark, Inc., 2012 WL 2798791, at *6 (E.D. Cal. July 9, 2012).

69. *Baskerville*, 2022 WL 612608, at *6.

70. *See, e.g.*, Scheidt v. Floor Covering Associates, Inc., 2018 WL 4679582, at *6 (N.D. Ill. Sept. 28, 2018) (citing multiple cases holding that typical and normal symptoms of pregnancy do not constitute a physical disability); *cf.* Stark v. Atwood Good Samaritan Center, 2016 WL 4076203 (Ct. App. Kan. 2016) (holding that typical and normal psychological and psychiatric responses to experiencing chronic physical pain did not constitute a mental disability); Lanci v. Arthur Andersen, LLP, 2000 WL 329226, at *4 n.1 (S.D.N.Y. Mar. 29, 2000) (holding that an employee's "day-to-day symptoms" of Tourette's Syndrome "do not constitute a disability"); Boren v. Wolverine Tube, Inc., 966 F. Supp. 457, 461 n.4 (N.D. Miss. 1997) (rejecting the disability claim of a plaintiff who suffered typical symptoms of contact dermatitis, including "itching, redness and some swelling and blistering of the skin," following the plaintiff's exposure to a chemical at work, all of which "cleared quickly with treatment[.]").

71. U.S. Equal Emp. Opportunity Comm'n, Enforcement Guidance on Pregnancy Discrimination and Related Issues (June 25, 2015), https://perma.cc/7NHD-NB29.

72. Consolidated Appropriations Act 2023, Pub. L. 117-328, 136 Stat. 4459, 6084 (2022).

73. Mullen v. New Balance Athletics, 2019 WL 958370 (D. Me. Feb. 27, 2019).

74. *Sipple*, 2012 WL 2798791, at *5.

75. Saks v. Franklin Covey Co., 117 F. Supp. 2d 318 (S.D.N.Y. 2000). This case was cited in support of a court's ruling that menopause-related infertility is not a disability as recently as February 2023. *See* Blanchard v. Arlington Cty., 2023 U.S. Dist. LEXIS 31334, at *37 n.37 (E.D. Va. Feb. 24, 2023).

76. 42 U.S.C. § 12111(9)–(10).

77. *See, e.g., Mullen*, 2019 WL 2798791, at *6. According to the court,

> [T]he Plaintiff has presented sufficient facts to support a finding that she had an actual disability of her endocrine function. The Plaintiff's doctor warned her that her oophorectomy would impact her endocrine system by limiting her ability to produce hormones including estrogen, that after the surgery "she w[ould] be in menopause," and that she would experience symptoms including hot flashes and becoming emotionally overwhelmed.

*Id.*

78. *Sipple*, 2012 WL 2798791, at *6.

79. Coleman v. Bobby Dodd Inst., 2017 WL 2486080, at *2 (M.D. Ga. June 8, 2017) (emphasis added).

80. Kimberlé Crenshaw, *Demarginalizing the Intersection of Race and Sex: A Black Feminist Critique of Antidiscrimination Doctrine, Feminist Theory and Antiracist Politics*, 1989 U. CHI. LEGAL F. 139, 149.

81. Equality Act 2010 c. 15, Explanatory Notes, at ¶ 10 (U.K.).

82. *Id.* at pt. 2, c. 1, §§ 4–12 (U.K.).

83. *Id.* at pt. 2, c. 2, §§ 13–27.

84. *Id.* at § 26(1)(b).

85. *Id.* at § 6(1).

86. A. v. Bonmarche Ltd. [2019] E.T. Z4 (WR), Case No. 4107766/2019 (Scot.), https://perma.cc/K529-U88Z.

87. *Id.*

88. *Id.*

89. Maria Rooney, *Social Worker Takes Council to Court for Menopause Discrimination*, CROWDJUSTICE (Nov. 18, 2022), https://perma.cc/5JLE-HK63.

90. Ms. M. Rooney v. Leicester City Council [2019] Employment Tribunal, Case No. 2600242/2019 (Nov. 1, 2019) (Eng.), https://perma.cc/AS5D-HJ6N.

91. Ms. M. Rooney v. Leicester City Council [2021] Employment Appeal Tribunal, Appeal No. EA-2020-000070-DA & EA-2021-000256-DA (Oct. 7, 2021) (Eng.), https://perma.cc/D8XW-8TTV.

92. Ms. M. Rooney v. Leicester City Council [2022] Employment Tribunal, Case. No. 2600242/2019 & 2600243/2019, *Judgment* (Mar. 25, 2022) (Eng.), https://perma.cc/FE47-KM5M.

93. Jog Hundle, *EAT Gives First Ruling on Menopausal Symptoms and Disability*, MILLS & REEVE (Oct. 18, 2021), https://perma.cc/HQX5-5GVA.

94. *See, e.g.*, Sanika Karandikar & Alison Sneddon, *How Should Employers React to the UK Government's Recent Announcements Around Menopause?* (Aug. 26, 2022), https://perma.cc/6PYL-HWCF.

95. *Menopause at Work: A Guide for People Professionals*, CHARTERED INST. OF PERSONNEL & DEV. (Aug. 9, 2022), https://perma.cc/BFY8-UP94.

96. *Menopause at Work*, Advisory, Conciliation & Arb. Serv. (ACAS) UK (Mar. 25, 2022), https://perma.cc/B2AH-KQA4.

97. Sue Westwood, *How Well Does Current UK Legislation Protect Older Women from Menopause Discrimination in the Workplace?* 1 (draft on file with authors, 2022).

98. WOMEN AND EQUALITIES COMMITTEE, HOUSE OF COMMONS (U.K.), MENOPAUSE AND THE WORKPLACE: FIRST REPORT OF SESSION 2022–23 (2022), https://perma.cc/WP92-GV4H.

99. WOMEN AND EQUALITIES COMMITTEE, HOUSE OF COMMONS (U.K.), MENOPAUSE AND THE WORKPLACE: GOVERNMENT RESPONSE TO THE COMMITTEE'S FIRST REPORT OF SESSION 2022–2023 (Jan. 24, 2023), https://perma.cc/9RW5-84AT; *see also* Olivia Konotey-Ahulu, *Government Rejects UK Menopause Law, Citing Potential Discrimination Against Men*, BLOOMBERG (Jan. 23, 2023), https://perma.cc/3RBZ-F84Y.

**Chapter 5**

1. *News Release: Channel 4 Launches Dedicated Menopause Policy,* CHANNEL 4 (Oct. 18, 2019), https://perma.cc/3RAQ-TLV4.

2. *Menopause Policy,* CHANNEL 4, https://perma.cc/JM2M-XDSC.

3. NAT'L HEALTH SERV. (ENG.), SUPPORTING OUR NHS PEOPLE THROUGH MENOPAUSE: GUIDANCE FOR LINE MANAGERS AND COLLEAGUES, Pub. No. PR1329 (Dec. 2, 2022), https://perma.cc/F4VQ-8F34.

4. *The Menopause at Work: A Guide for People Professionals,* CHARTERED INST. OF PERS. & DEV. (CIPD) (May 18, 2021), https://perma.cc/8FVH-8FA9.

5. *Menopause Workplace Pledge,* WELLBEING OF WOMEN, https://perma.cc/HM4M-44SN.

6. *Menopause, in* SEC'Y OF STATE FOR HEALTH & SOC. CARE (ENG.), WOMEN'S HEALTH STRATEGY FOR ENGLAND (Aug. 30, 2022), https://www.gov.uk/government/publications/womens-health-strategy-for-england/womens-health-strategy-for-england#menopause.

7. BANK OF AMERICA, BREAK THROUGH THE STIGMA: MENOPAUSE IN THE WORKPLACE (2023), https://perma.cc/NSA4-QSF7.

8. *See, e.g.,* Alicia A. Grandey et al., *Tackling Taboo Topics: A Review of the Three Ms in Working Women's Lives,* 46 J. OF MGMT. 7, 8 (2020).

9. An act to amend title VII of the Civil Rights Act of 1964 to prohibit sex discrimination on the basis of pregnancy, Pub. L. No. 95-555, 92 Stat. 2076 (1978) (codified at 42 U.S.C. § 2000e).

10. General Electric Co. v. Gilbert, 429 U.S. 125 (1976).

11. 42 U.S.C. § 2000e(k).

12. Pregnant Workers Fairness Act, Pub. L. No. 117-328, 136 Stat. 4459 (2022) (codified at 42 U.S.C. § 2000gg).

13. H.R. COMM. ON EDUC. & LAB., REPORT TO ACCOMPANY H.R. 1065: PREGNANT WORKERS FAIRNESS ACT, H.R. Rep. 117-27 (2021).

14. 29 U.S.C. § 2612(a)(1).

15. EEOC v. Houston Funding II, 717 F.3d 425, 428 (5th Cir. 2013); Hicks v. City of Tuscaloosa, 870 F.3d 1253, 1259-60 (11th Cir. 2017); *see also, e.g.,* EEOC v. Vamco Sheet Metals, 2014 WL 2619812, at * 6 (S.D.N.Y. June 5, 2014); Mayer v. Pro. Ambulance, LLC, 211 F. Supp. 3d 408, 417 (D.R.I. 2016).

16. U.S. EQUAL EMP. OPPORTUNITY COMM'N, ENF'T GUIDANCE ON PREGNANCY DISCRIMINATION AND RELATED ISSUES (June 25, 2015), https://perma.cc/Y5D6-JLXV [hereinafter EEOC PREGNANCY DISCRIMINATION GUIDANCE].

17. 29 U.S.C. § 207(r).

18. 40 U.S.C. § 3318.

19. Providing Urgent Maternal Protections for Nursing Mothers Act, Pub. L. No. 117-328, 136 Stat. 4459 (2022) (codified at 29 U.S.C § 218d).

20. *See, e.g.,* Bruce Feiler, *Lights, Camera, We're Having a Baby,* N.Y. TIMES (May 29, 2016), https://perma.cc/UNP4-BUSV (noting that when couples learn they are having a baby, they could write notes, make phone calls, or "send a

mass email? So 1990s. These days . . . they often whip out their cellphones, shoot a video and post it on social media.").

21. ELIZABETH HOFFMAN, LACTATION AT WORK 180 (2021).

22. Meghan Boone, *Lactation Law*, 106 CAL. L. REV. 1827, 1850 (2018).

23. Tara Siegel Bernard, *Divided Over Abortion, but Joining Forces for Women's Workplace Rights*, N.Y. TIMES (July 12, 2019), https://perma.cc/2BSM -GNWW.

24. H.R. COMM. ON EDUC. & LAB., REPORT TO ACCOMPANY H.R. 3110: PROVIDING URGENT MATERNAL PROTECTIONS FOR NURSING MOTHERS ACT, H.R. Rep. 117-102 (2021).

25. Meritor Savings Bank v. Vinson, 477 U.S. 57 (1986).

26. *Combatting Sexual Harassment in the Workplace: Frequently Asked Questions*, N.Y. STATE GOV'T, https://perma.cc/EY29-DN4C ("Q. How serious does the harassment have to be before I can file a complaint? A5. New York State no longer requires harassment be severe or pervasive before it is considered illegal. Harassment or discrimination is anything more than 'petty slights or trivial inconveniences.' Every instance of harassment is unique to those experiencing it, and there is no single boundary between petty slights and harassing behavior. Generally, any behavior where a worker is treated worse because of their gender is gender discrimination.").

27. *Sexual Harassment Prevention Training*, N.Y.C. COMM'N ON HUM. RTS., https://perma.cc/5D2W-J3FN.

28. Margaret Rees et al., *Global Consensus Recommendations on Menopause in the Workplace: A European Menopause and Andropause Society (EMAS) Position Statement*, 151 MATURITAS 55, 59 (2021).

29. BANK OF AMERICA, *supra* note 7.

30. Flores v. Va. Dep't of Corr., 2021 WL 668802 (W.D. Va. Feb. 22, 2021).

31. U.S. DEP'T OF ED. OFF. FOR CIV. RTS., SUPPORTING THE ACADEMIC SUCCESS OF PREGNANT AND PARENTING STUDENTS UNDER TITLE IX AND THE EDUCATION AMENDMENTS OF 1972, Rep. No. OCR-00069, at 17 (2013), https:// perma.cc/6ASE-JAB4.

32. EEOC Pregnancy Discrimination Guidance, *supra* note 16.

33. MAYA DUSENBERY, DOING HARM: THE TRUTH ABOUT HOW BAD MEDICINE AND LAZY SCIENCE LEAVE WOMEN DISMISSED, MISDIAGNOSED, AND SICK 215–16 (2018).

34. 42 U.S.C. §12102(1)–(4).

35. *See, e.g.*, Samuel R. Bagenstos, *Subordination, Stigma, and "Disability,"* 86 VA. L. REV. 397, 401 (2000); Adam M. Samaha, *What Good Is the Social Model of Disability?*, 74 U. CHI. L. REV. 1251 (2007); Andrew Gerst & Tara Schwitzman-Gerst, *Disabling Inequity: How the Social Model of Disability Resists Barriers to Social Security Disability Benefits*, 44 N.Y.U. REV. L. & SOC. CHANGE 145 (2020).

36. *See, e.g., Pregnancy and All Things Heat-Related (You, the Weather, Your Bath Water, and More)*, HEALTHLINE.COM (Dec. 20, 2019), https://perma.cc/ KLX6-Y6Q6 ("hot flashes during pregnancy are usually hormonal"); Rebecca C. Thurston et al., *Prospective Evaluation of Hot Flashes During Pregnancy and Postpartum*, 100 FERTILITY & STERILITY 1667, 1667 (2013).

37. *See, e.g.*, Elie Sader & Melissa Rayhill, *Headache in Pregnancy, the Puerperium, and Menopause*, 38 SEMINARS IN NEUROLOGY 627 (2018) (noting associations between migraines and all three conditions or processes).

38. Laura J. Miller et al., *Depression and Related Disorders During the Female Reproductive Cycle*, 5 WOMEN'S HEALTH, 577, 577 (2009).

39. *See* Liisa Hantsoo & C. Neill Epperson, *Anxiety Disorders Among Women: A Female Lifespan Approach*, 15 FOCUS 162, 162–168 (2017), https://perma.cc/ C65Q-N35K.

40. Jessica L. Barnack-Tavlaris et al., *Taking Time to Bleed, Perceptions and Attitudes Toward Menstrual Leave Policy*, 40 HEALTH CARE FOR WOMEN INT'L 1355, 1361 (2019).

41. Rachel B. Levitt & Jessica L. Barnack-Tavlaris, *Addressing Menstruation in the Workplace: The Menstrual Leave Debate*, *in* THE PALGRAVE HANDBOOK OF CRITICAL MENSTRUATION STUDIES, 561, 570–71 (Chris Bobel et al. eds., 2020).

42. Ari Ne'eman, *What If Disability Rights Were for Everyone?* N.Y. TIMES (Oct. 1, 2021), https://perma.cc/MR7U-HPYK.

## Chapter 6

1. ERICA RAND, THE SMALL BOOK OF HIP CHECKS: ON QUEER GENDER, RACE AND WRITING ix (2021).

2. *Id.* at 112, 113.

3. Sarah Marloff, *Do Transgender Women Experience Menopause?* HEALTHYWOMEN (Oct. 26, 2020), https://perma.cc/9494-9WJ8 (quoting artistic director and activist Lisa Scheps).

4. Melissa Giannini, *The Change*, DAMN JOAN (Nov. 13, 2017), https://perma .cc/REX8-Y2DU (quoting Mike Funk, age 27).

5. Tania Glyde, *How Can Therapists and Other Healthcare Practitioners Best Support and Validate Their Queer Menopausal Clients*, SEXUAL & RELATIONSHIP THERAPY 510, 512–13 (Feb. 17, 2021) (quoting "Bret," a pseudonym for a 46-year-old nonbinary, pansexual project manager).

6. We borrow the phrases "people with ovarian systems" and "people with testicular systems" from London psychotherapist Tania Glyde. *See What Is the Non-Binary Experience of Menopause?* QUEER MENOPAUSE (Oct. 13, 2021), https://perma.cc/V9US-VHCZ [hereinafter *Non-Binary Experience*]. As this site explains,

> If you want to be more specific, you could say *people with ovarian systems* (as opposed to *people with testicular systems*). As people start to question and

dismantle the gender binary, you will hear constructions like 'people with
vaginas' or 'vulva-havers', which may well feel clunky (and don't forget
some trans and non-binary people don't wish to use those words for their
genitals in the first place), but it's a sign of humans trying to bust their way
out of an outdated and restrictive framework.

*Id.* (emphasis in original).

7. *Glossary of Terms: Transgender, in* GLAAD MEDIA REFERENCE GUIDE
(11th ed.), https://perma.cc/X98T-PP74.

8. Edmond Coleman et al., *Standards of Care for the Health of Transgender
and Gender Diverse People, Version 8,* 23 INT'L J. OF TRANSGENDER HEALTH S1,
S11 (2022) (defining "gender diverse" and "transition"), https://perma.cc/
QEH8-JR7G [hereinafter Coleman et al., *SOC-8*]. "Gender diverse" is the term
that international human rights lawyers use, too. *See, e.g.,* Rep. of Vincent
Madrigal-Borloz, Independent Expert on Protection Against Violence and Discrimination Based on Sexual Orientation and Gender Identity, U.N. DOC. NO.
A/73/152, at 4 (Jul. 12, 2018) (explaining that the term "gender diverse" is used
in the report to represent "persons whose gender identity, including their
gender expression, is at odds with what is perceived as being the gender norm in
a particular context at a particular point in time.").

9. *See* Coleman et al., *SOC-8, supra* note 8, at S12.

10. *See Glossary of Terms: LGBTQ, in* GLAAD MEDIA REFERENCE GUIDE
(11th ed.), https://perma.cc/68BQ-NJGW.

11. *See, e.g.,* Rosa Lauretta et al., *Gender in Endocrine Diseases: Role of Sex
Gonadal Hormones,* INT'L J. OF ENDOCRINOLOGY (Oct. 21, 2018).

12. *See, e.g.,* André Guay & Susan R. Davis, *Testosterone Insufficiency in
Women: Fact or Fiction,* 20 WORLD J. UROLOGY 106 (2002); Cathy Garrard, *Testosterone and Women's Health,* EVERYDAY HEALTH (Oct. 20, 2022), https://
perma.cc/PGZ7-DZQV.

13. *See, e.g.,* Rex A. Hess, *Estrogen in the Adult Male Reproductive Tract: A
Review,* 1 REPRODUCTIVE BIOLOGY & ENDOCRINOLOGY 52 (2003).

14. *See, e.g.,* Michael Schulster et al., *The Role of Estradiol in Male Reproductive Function,* 18 ASIAN J. OF ANDROLOGY 435 (2016).

15. *See Patient Resources: Menopause,* ENDOCRINE SOC'Y (Jan. 24, 2022),
https://perma.cc/A6NF-JPUY.

16. In some publications, the term "andropause" is used to describe "decreasing testosterone levels in men or people assigned male at birth (AMAB)." *See, e.g.,*
*Menopause,* CLEVELAND CLINIC (Oct. 5, 2021), https://perma.cc/K2XG-KNR3.

17. *See* Duncan C. Gould & Richard Petty, *The Male Menopause: Does It
Exist?,* 173 WESTERN J. MED. 76, 76 (2000).

18. *See Male Menopause: Myth or Reality?,* MAYO CLINIC (May 24, 2022),
https://perma.cc/X7U4-N43M; Carl G. Heller & Gordon B. Meyers, *The Male
Climacteric, Its Symptomatology, Diagnosis and Treatment,* 126 J. AM. MED.
ASSOC. 472, 472 (1944).

19. *See* Gould & Petty, *supra* note 17, at 76 (specifying that "abnormally low" testosterone levels are below 11 nmol/L).

20. *See id.* at 76–77. *See also* Vito A. Giagulli et al., *Pathogenesis of the Decreased Androgen Levels in Obese Men*, 79 J. CLINICAL ENDOCRINOLOGY & METABOLISM 997 (1994); Yoshishige Ida et al., *Effects of Acute and Repeated Alcohol Ingestion on Hypothalamic-Pituitary Gonadal and Hypothalamic-Pituitary-Adrenal Functioning in Normal Males*, 31 DRUG & ALCOHOL DEPENDENCE 57 (1992).

21. *See Glossary of Terms: Transgender, supra* note 7.

22. *Id.*

23. *See, e.g.,* Amanda A. Deeks & Marita McCabe, *Sexual Function and the Menopausal Woman, The Importance of Age and Partner's Sexual Functioning*, 38 J. SEX RESEARCH 219 (2001); Phyllis K. Mansfield et al., *Predictors of Sexual Response Changes in Heterosexual Midlife Women*, 19 HEALTH VALUES 10 (1995); Keith Hawton et al., *Sexual Function in a Community Sample of Middle-Aged Women with Partners: Effects of Age, Marital, Socioeconomic, Psychiatric, Gynecological and Menopause Factors*, 23 ARCHIVES SEXUAL BEHAV. 375 (1994).

24. *See, e.g.,* Mary Kruk et al., *Feminist Concerns and Feelings About Menstruation Cessation Among Lesbian, Bisexual, and Heterosexual Women: Implications for Menopause*, 30 J. WOMEN'S HEALTH 1751, 1756–57 (2021) (describing study population); Julie A. Winterich, *Sex, Menopause, and Culture: Sexual Orientation and the Meaning of Menopause for Women's Sex Lives*, 17 GENDER & SOC'Y 627, 632 (2003) (explaining research focus on "surgically induced menopausal women because these women have a sudden and often more difficult menopause").

25. *Cf.* Glyde, *supra* note 5.

26. Jennifer Kelly, *A Lesbian Feminist Analysis of the Demise of Hormone Replacement Therapy*, 31 WOMEN'S STUD. INT'L F. 300, 305 (2008).

27. *Id.* at 301.

28. *See* Kruk et al., *supra* note 24, at 1751.

29. Kelly, *supra* note 26, at 301 (2008) (quoting interviewee "Andy").

30. *Id.* at 305 (quoting "Elizabeth").

31. *Id.*

32. *See Midlife in the United States*, NAT'L INST. AGING, https://perma.cc/A5P2-92BX.

33. Kruk et al., *supra* note 24, at 1754.

34. *Id.* at 1755.

35. *Id.* at 1755–56.

36. *Id.* at 1753.

37. *Id.*

38. *See* Winterich, *supra* note 24.

39. *Id.* at 636 (quoting "Susan").

40. *Id.* at 637.

41. *Id.* at 638 (quoting "Marcia").

42. *Id.* at 628.

43. *See, e.g.,* Cécile A. Unger, *Hormone Therapy for Transgender Patients*, 5 TRANSLATIONAL ANDROLOGY & UROLOGY 877, 878 (2016).

44. *See id.*

45. *See* Georg S. Kranz et al., *High-Dose Testosterone Treatment Increases Serotonin Transporter Binding in Transgender People*, 78 BIOLOGICAL PSYCHIATRY 525 (2015) (reporting results of a study of both men assigned female at birth and women assigned male at birth who received hormone treatment as part of their gender-affirming care). *See also* Joanna Moncrieff et al., *The Serotonin Theory of Depression: A Systematic Umbrella Review of the Evidence*, MOLECULAR PSYCHIATRY 11 (Jul. 20, 2022), DOI:10.1038/s41380-022-01661-0 ("there is no convincing evidence that depression is associated with, or caused by, lower serotonin concentrations or activity"); Dana G. Smith, *Antidepressants Don't Work the Way Many People Think*, N.Y. TIMES (Nov. 8, 2022), https://perma.cc/296Z-8SMZ.

46. *See* Marco Colizzi et al., *Hormonal Treatment Reduces Psychobiological Distress in Gender Identity Disorder, Independently of the Attachment Style*, 10 J. SEXUAL MED. 3049 (2013) (reporting decreased self-perceived stress levels after receiving hormone therapy).

47. *See* Marloff, *supra* note 3.

48. *See, e.g.,* Unger, *supra* note 43. *See also* Corinne O'Keefe Osborn, *Your Guide to Anti-Androgens*, HEALTHLINE (May 18, 2022), https://perma.cc/ BWM8-4DV7.

49. *See* Brendan J. Nolan & Ada S. Cheung, *Estradiol Therapy in the Perioperative Period: Implications for Transgender People Undergoing Feminizing Hormone Therapy*, 93 YALE J. BIOLOGY & MED. 539 (2020).

50. *See* Marloff, *supra* note 3.

51. Sophie Mohamed & Myra S. Hunter, *Transgender Women's Experiences and Beliefs About Hormone Therapy Through and Beyond Mid-Age: An Exploratory UK Study*, 20 INTL. J. TRANSGENDERISM 98, 105 (2018).

52. *See* Coleman et al., *SOC-8*, *supra* note 8, at S12.

53. *See* Unger, *supra* note 43.

54. *See* Erik J. Giltay & Louis J. Gooren, *Effects of Sex Steroid Deprivation/ Administration on Hair Growth and Skin Sebum Production in Transsexual Males and Females*, 85 J. CLINICAL ENDOCRINOLOGY & METABOLISM 2913 (2000); Katrien Wierckx et al., *Long-term Evaluation of Cross-sex Hormone Treatment in Transsexual Persons*, 9 J. SEXUAL MED. 2641 (2012); Michael S. Irwig, *Testosterone Therapy for Transgender Men*, 5 LANCET DIABETES ENDOCRINOLOGY 301 (2017).

55. *See* Seema Shah, *Q&A: LGBTQIA+ Menopause Experience with Dr. Shah*, KINDRA (Aug. 24, 2021), https://perma.cc/X9VY-M2XF.

56. *See Transgender Health*, ROCK MY MENOPAUSE, https://perma.cc/JU6W -6S5D.

57. *See* Rachel Reese, *How Do Hormonal Changes Affect the Trans and Non-binary Community?*, HENPICKED (Jul. 21, 2020), https://menopauseintheworkplace.co.uk/articles/how-do-hormonal-changes-affect-the-trans-and-non-binary-community.

58. Quispe López, *You Don't Have to Constantly Take Hormones to Be Trans, 3 People Who Have Gone On and Off Hormones*, INSIDER (Nov. 4, 2021, 8:00 AM), https://perma.cc/Q33P-F66F (quoting Simon Moore, age 27, who is nonbinary and uses them/they pronouns).

59. *See id.*

60. *Non-Binary Experience, supra* note 6.

61. *Id.*

62. *See* Alice Scott & Louise Newson, *Should We Be Prescribing Testosterone to Perimenopausal and Menopausal Women? A Guide to Prescribing Testosterone for Women in Primary Care*, 70 BRITISH J. GEN. PRAC. 203, 203 (2020) ("A recent systematic review and meta-analysis of testosterone treatment in women has provided robust support for a trial of testosterone in women when clinically indicated. In postmenopausal women, testosterone supplementation improved several domains of sexual response, including sexual desire, pleasure, arousal, orgasm, and self-image.").

63. *Id.*

64. *See Non-Binary Experience, supra* note 6 ("[I]t should be way more straightforward to get a microdose prescription of T than it is already.").

65. *See* Shah, *supra* note 55 (explaining the reasons for the absence of research on the trans experience with menopause: "This is both a consequence of not only the understandable hesitancy of community members to be further scrutinized, but also the current lack of focus in the medical community in this area.").

66. SANDY E. JAMES ET AL., NTL. CTR. FOR TRANSGENDER EQUALITY (NCTE), REPORT OF THE 2015 U.S. TRANSGENDER SURVEY 5 (2016), https://perma.cc/N8TE-FV2S.

67. *See* Obergefell v. Hodges, 576 U.S. 644 (2015). *But see* Annah K. Bender & Janet L. Lauritsen, *Violent Victimization Among Lesbian, Gay, and Bisexual Populations in the United States: Findings from the National Crime Victimization Survey, 2017–2018*, 111 AM. J. PUB. HEALTH 326 (2021) (reporting higher rate of victimization among lesbian, gay, and bisexual individuals compared to heterosexuals).

68. *See* Shabab Ahmed Mirza & Caitlin Rooney, *Discrimination Prevents LGBTQ People from Accessing Health Care*, CTR. FOR AM. PROGRESS (Jan. 18, 2018), https://perma.cc/LUC2-9C4E.

69. *See id.* (quoting Bow as saying, "Thinking of us only as transgender means doctors can often miss basic health needs—vaccinations, colon cancer screenings, or vaginal exams.").

70. Glyde, *supra* note 5, at 511, 515, 518 (quoting Katie, age 56, a cis feminine asexual survivor of sexual abuse, and Lucas, age 52, who uses unique words to refer to his clitoris).

71. *See* Megan Sutton, *We Need to Talk About the LGBTQ+ Menopause Experience*, GOOD HOUSEKEEPING (UK) (Feb. 16, 2021), https://perma.cc/3TKA -VMUM (quoting "Sam").

72. *See* Marloff, *supra* note 3 (quoting trans woman Claire Bow, age 55).

73. *Non-Binary Experience*, *supra* note 6.

74. Glyde, *supra* note 5, at 516 ("Three participants were cis, three non-binary, two transmasculine, one agender, one genderfluid, one genderqueer, and one transfeminine. Six identified as queer, three as pansexual, one as asexual, one as bisexual, and one as lesbian.").

75. *Id.* at 520.

76. *See id.* at 521, 522 (quoting Bret).

77. *See Non-Binary Experience*, *supra* note 6.

78. Tania Glyde, *Dear Menopause Community*, QUEER MENOPAUSE (May 5, 2021), https://perma.cc/R7HW-XAZ7.

79. *See Non-Binary Experience*, *supra* note 6.

80. *See, e.g.*, Kyveli Angelou et al., *The Genitourinary Syndrome of Menopause: An Overview of the Recent Data*, 12 CUREUS e7586 (2000).

81. *How Sex Changes After Menopause*, JOHNS HOPKINS HEALTH (2023), https://perma.cc/SFF4-VJU8.

82. *See* Sutton, *supra* note 71 (quoting "Jane").

83. *Id.*

84. *Id.*

## Chapter 7

1. *See* Amy Larocca, *Welcome to the Menopause Gold Rush*, N.Y. TIMES (Dec. 20, 2022), https://perma.cc/Z27G-LDLV (including Alloy founder Anne Fulenwider's retelling of Ankur Jain's reaction to her description of her company); *About Us*, ALLOY, https://perma.cc/L7LF-GAJ7.

2. *See, e.g.*, Maneet Ahuja, *Meet Ankur Jain, The Under 30 Founder Tackling Some of the Biggest Challenges Facing the Millennial Generation—Like Rent Relief Amid the Pandemic*, FORBES.COM (Nov. 20, 2020), https://perma.cc/A6TM -NGA7. *See also* Larocca, *supra* note 1; *Alloy Raises $3.4 Million in Seed Funding Round for Telehealth, Prescription, and Community Platform to Address Health of Women Over 40*, CISION PR NEWSWIRE (Oct. 14, 2021), https://perma.cc/ K3WN-QDFN.

3. *See, e.g.*, Eliza Haverstock, *Narrative Change: VCs Are Finally Ready to Talk About Menopause*, PITCHBOOK (May 28, 2020), https://perma.cc/9Q6E-VPVH (reporting that worldwide menopause start-up companies have raised $254 million in capital since 2009).

4. *See* Larocca, *supra* note 1. *See also* Fiorella Valdesolo, *Once a Taboo Topic, Menopause Is (Finally) Having Its Wellness Moment,* VOGUE (June 1, 2022), https://perma.cc/X247-WW7S; Vivian Manning-Schaffel, *Rebranding Midlife,* THE CUT (Nov. 25, 2022), https://perma.cc/YK67-WXCZ.

5. The United Nations Population Division in its 2022 revision of *World Population Prospects* reported female population percentages across several age brackets. *See Population Ages 40-44, Female (% of Female Population),* WORLD BANK (2022); https://perma.cc/X3TU-Z57K (estimating 6% of all females are in this age demographic); *Population Ages 45-49, Female (% of Female Population),* WORLD BANK (2022), https://perma.cc/AV7Y-FHHA (estimating 6% of all females in this age demographic); *Population, Female,* WORLD BANK (2022), https://perma.cc/H95G-TR8G (estimating that there are 3.92 billion females worldwide).

6. *See Labor Force Statistics from the Current Population Survey 2022,* U.S. BUREAU LAB. STATS. (Jan. 25, 2023), https://perma.cc/S2YE-ZZYV.

7. *See Trend: The Rise of Menopause Retreats,* GLOBAL WELLNESS SUMMIT (Oct. 2022), https://perma.cc/H6A9-GZB8 (citing Andrea Petersen, *The Rise of the Menopause Vacation,* WALL ST. J. (Sept. 4, 2022), https://perma.cc/3ABK -KJ9B).

8. *See* Cheryl R. Lampkin, *Menopausal Symptoms: There's a Place for Tech-Related Solutions,* AARP (Jan. 8, 2020), https://perma.cc/3FUE-VCZG.

9. Anna Altman, *Mommy and Data,* NEW REPUBLIC (Jan. 14, 2019), https://perma.cc/VE65-Z3EU (describing reach of femtech companies). *See also* Ida Tin, *The Rise of a New Category: Femtech,* CLUE (Sept. 14, 2016), https://perma.cc/NJG7-4DBQ.

10. *See* Naomi R. Cahn, Bridget J. Crawford, & Emily Gold Waldman, *Managing and Monitoring the Menopausal Body,* 2022 U. CHI. LEGAL F. 41, 81 n.105.

11. *See, e.g.,* Miriam Partington, *These Are Europe's Top Startups Tackling Menopause,* SIFTED (Oct. 25, 2021), https://perma.cc/9PGP-BYNN.

12. *See* Cahn, Crawford, & Waldman, *supra* note 10, at 43 (containing our first use of the term "menopause capitalism").

13. Admittedly, the companies we discuss in this chapter are not the only illustrative ones, and this chapter is not meant to serve as a directory of all menopause-related companies.

14. *See The Essential Bundle,* KINDRA, https://perma.cc/9AQY-R5ZH (retailing for $98 for a one-time purchase or $77 for a subscription delivered every thirty to sixty days). Its primary ingredients are water, glycerin, vitamins, and alcohol. *Id.* (listing ingredients).

15. *See id.*

16. *See, e.g., Soothe Bath Soak,* KINDRA, https://perma.cc/K7WB-4BZV (retailing for $30 for a one-time purchase or $24 for a subscription delivered every fifteen to thirty days).

17. *See, e.g., The Daily Vaginal Lotion,* KINDRA, https://perma.cc/9TF4-MES6 (retailing for $54 for a one-time purchase or $39 for a subscription delivered every thirty or sixty days).

18. *See Find Your Kindra,* KINDRA, https://perma.cc/N4N2-J2FD.

19. *See, e.g., The Core Supplement,* KINDRA, https://perma.cc/ABF6-EBCC (retailing for $49 for a 30-capsule supply, or $39 for a subscription delivered every thirty or sixty days).

20. *All Products,* I AM STRIPES, https://perma.cc/3KMV-MNJ5 (selling "The Power Move Ectoine Hydrating and Plumping Facial Serum" for $85; "Dew as I Do Ectoine + Vitamin C Brightening and Hydrating Cream" costs $25 for a travel size 0.5 ounces, or $80 for 1.7 ounces).

21. *See Vag of Honor Hydrating Gel,* I AM STRIPES, https://perma.cc/U8TA-59C3.

22. *See The Inside Addition Daily Menopause Symptom Support Supplement,* I AM STRIPES, https://perma.cc/U8A8-3B4P (urging potential customers to "[s]how yourself love from the inside, out[.]").

23. *See* Anna Starostinetskaya, *Serena Williams Invests in Vegan Menopause Brand to Support Women in Their Prime,* VEGNEWS (May 4, 2022) https://perma.cc/H9VD-KUPD.

24. *See Homepage,* STRIPES, https://perma.cc/7SVP-XTFH.

25. *About,* KINDRA, https://perma.cc/DAM6-THVT.

26. *Id.*

27. *See Homepage,* KINDRA, https://perma.cc/444D-FHWD; *Private Group: Menopause Support & Straight-Talk,* FACEBOOK, https://perma.cc/RQ8L-P8ZX.

28. *See* India Roby, *Naomi Watts Launches Stripes, a Beauty and Wellness Brand Focused on Menopause Health,* FASHIONISTA (Oct. 18, 2022), https://perma.cc/KNY9-FY6J (linking to company's Instagram page).

29. *Id.*

30. *See, i.e., Vag of Honor Hydrating Gel, supra* note 21 and accompanying text.

31. *See, e.g.,* Barrett J. Brunsman, *P&G Launches New Brand for Women Coping with Menopause,* BIZWOMEN: THE BUSINESS JOURNALS (Nov. 15, 2019), https://perma.cc/58WF-L2R5; *Brands,* PROCTER & GAMBLE U.S., https://perma.cc/36H2-UBA3.

32. YourExtraLife, *"In Menopause and Hotter Than Ever" T-Shirt,* ETSY, https://perma.cc/8JPR-S9A7 (selling for $25.00).

33. RandomCornerUS, *"Smoking Hot" T-Shirt,* ETSY, https://perma.cc/G4TA-2RPJ (selling for $25.95).

34. *Homepage,* BECOME BY FEMOGRAPHY, https://perma.cc/7K4G-LNLV.

35. *Shop Menopause Clothing,* BECOME BY FEMOGRAPHY, https://perma.cc/RN38-N4WL.

36. *See* Fibre2Fashion News Desk, *Apparel Using US' NASA-Funded Technology Can Ease Menopause Symptoms,* TECHNICAL TEXTILE (Sept. 6, 2022),

https://perma.cc/HBJ3-L5JZ (discussing company's name) [hereinafter Fibre-2Fashion, *NASA-Funded Technology Apparel*].

37. *See Pyjama Set Combination—Iris Cami and Billie Jogger*, Fifty One Apparel, https://perma.cc/KG9T-ABPL (selling for $93.00).

38. *See* Fibre2Fashion, *NASA-Funded Technology Apparel, supra* note 36; *How It Works*, Fifty One Apparel, https://perma.cc/M2DD-CWEU.

39. *See Anti-Flush Low Rise Brief*, Become by Femography, https://perma.cc/MS7K-NCSF.

40. *See Leakproof Panties*, Become by Femography, https://perma.cc/75B6-2WY9 (selling two different models of underwear for $25 and $26).

41. *Menopause—What to Wear?* Cucumber Clothing, https://perma.cc/FZ6F-WXNW.

42. *Menopause Clothing Designed to Help with Hot Flushes*, Fifty One Apparel, https://perma.cc/8XHF-26UP.

43. *See, e.g., About*, Hello Hazel, https://perma.cc/P4ME-3XTU; *The Anti-Stick Stick*, Hello Hazel, https://perma.cc/TNZ9-ZVS6.

44. *How Our Menopause Clothing Works*, Become by Femography, https://perma.cc/4RDJ-DN7B (advertising clothing with these features).

45. *See* Bernd Schäfer et al., *Nanosilver in Consumer Products and Human Health: More Information Required!*, 45 Env't Sci. & Tech. 7589 (2011).

46. *See* Elsie M. Sunderland et al., *A Review of the Pathways of Human Exposure to Poly- and Perfluoroalkyl Substances (PFASs) and Present Understanding of Health Effects*, 29 J. Exposure Sci. & Env't Epidemiology 131, 138–40 (2019); Kristen M. Rappazzo et al., *Exposure to Perfluorinated Alkyl Substances and Health Outcomes in Children: A Systematic Review of the Epidemiologic Literature*, 14 Int'l J. Env't Rsch. & Pub. Health 691 (2017); Melanie Buser et al., U.S. Dep't of Health & Hum. Servs., Toxicological Profile for Perfluoroalkyls (2021), https://perma.cc/AVN5-5GUR.

47. *See, e.g.*, Pat Rizzuto, *"Staggering" Impact Foreseen on US Firms from EU PFAS Ban*, Bloomberg Law (Feb. 14, 2023), https://perma.cc/PUZ5-KJKX.

48. *See the Facts on PFAS*, 3M (2019), https://perma.cc/UZ27-BJGJ (describing the company 3M's decision to phase out production of PFOA and PFOS, two types of PFAS, because of potential adverse health and environmental impacts).

49. *See, e.g.*, Dean Scott, *Dozens of States Seek to Regulate PFAS, Other Chemicals in 2022*, Bloomberg Law (Feb. 3, 2022), https://perma.cc/7993-8FVR; Zach Bright, *PFAS Bans, Restrictions Go into Effect in States in 2023*, Bloomberg Law (Jan. 4, 2023), https://perma.cc/A89V-8JYQ.

50. *See* Press Release, UL Research Institutes, Chemical Insights Research Institute, and Emory University's Rollins School of Public Health Team to Study the Human Health Impact of PFAS Chemical Exposure (Feb. 21, 2023), https://perma.cc/RJG6-BGXT.

51. *See Ultra Absorbent High Waist Brief*, BECOME BY FEMOGRAPHY, https://perma.cc/EL7K-LC9F ("Certified PFAS-free by external labs").

52. *See* Jessian Choy, *What You Need to Know About "Nontoxic" Menstrual Underwear*, SIERRA MAG. (Mar. 18, 2020), https://perma.cc/666X-ALUG; BRIDGET J. CRAWFORD & EMILY GOLD WALDMAN, MENSTRUATION MATTERS: CHALLENGING THE LAW'S SILENCE ON PERIODS 154-55 (2022).

53. *See* Alisha Haridasani Gupta, *What to Know About PFAS in Period Underwear*, N.Y. TIMES (Jan. 20, 2023), https://perma.cc/PU3M-K7SK.

54. *See id.* (quoting statement from Thinx) (emphasis added).

55. *See* Complaint at ¶ 56, Dickens v. Thinx, Inc., 1:122-cv-04286 (S.D.N.Y. May 25, 2022), https://perma.cc/J9BE-KK2U; Amended Complaint at ¶ 60, Dickens v. Thinx, Inc., 1:122-cv-04286 (S.D.N.Y. Aug. 8, 2022), https://perma.cc/J2XG-PSVV; Settlement Agreement at ¶ 3.4, Dickens v. Thinx, Inc., 1:122-cv-04286 (S.D.N.Y. Nov. 21, 2022), https://perma.cc/Q7HK-6HXP.

56. *What's Thinx for All Leaks?*, THINX, https://perma.cc/95UJ-J7LC.

57. *How We Ensure Thinx Are Body-Safe*, THINX (Jan. 14, 2020) (no longer available on the company's website, archived at https://perma.cc/AUY7-GKAR).

58. *See* Laurene Rey-Millet, *Kelly Newton's BP3 Underwear: The Eco-Friendly Alternative*, GRAMERSI (Mar. 3, 2022), https://perma.cc/N3FY-BFZE.

59. *See* Lampkin, *supra* note 8.

60. *See Frequently Asked Questions*, SLEEP.ME, https://perma.cc/8E2V-SDVB (responding to the question, "Can the Cube sleep system help with reducing my hot flashes and night sweats?"); *Cube Sleep System*, SLEEP.ME, https://perma.cc/F26Y-6UGA (showing the price of a half-king mattress pad as $749.99, reduced to $699.99); Joshua Lyon, *This Bed Cooling System Isn't Cheap. But It Might Beat Washing Your Sweaty Sheets*, WIRECUTTER (Aug. 10, 2023), https://perma.cc/85VW-2SXY (explaining the change in the name of the product from "Chilipad" to the "Cube Sleep System").

61. *See Embr Wave 2*, EMBR WAVE, https://perma.cc/G2BN-XLXX (selling wristband that "gives you immediate relief from hot flashes and improves sleep" for $299).

62. *See, e.g., Homepage*, GRACE, https://perma.cc/LZQ2-LLU5 ("the bracelet to get you through hot flushes").

63. *See Madorra Announces Publication of Positive 12-Week and 12-Month Pilot 1 Randomized Controlled Trial Results*, CISION PR NEWSWIRE (Feb. 9, 2023), https://perma.cc/7DQ3-QTAS (describing 2021 approval by FDA).

64. *See* Martha Hickey et al., *Safety and Effectiveness of a Novel Home-Use Therapeutic Ultrasound Device for the Treatment of Vaginal Dryness in Postmenopausal Women: A Pilot Study*, MENOPAUSE: J. N. AM. MENOPAUSE SOC'Y (2023). *See also Madorra's Device Could Offer a New, Nonhormonal Treatment Option for Post-Menopausal Women with Vaginal Atrophy*, FEMTECH INSIDER (Feb. 15, 2023), https://perma.cc/ECS8-NCWX.

65. *See* Rossella E. Nappi et al., *Female Sexual Dysfunction (FSD): Prevalence and Impact on Quality of Life (QoL),* 94 MATURITAS 87 (2016).

66. *About Madorra,* MADORRA, https://perma.cc/5WFV-CJ9Z.

67. *See Embr Wave 2, supra* note 61.

68. *Homepage,* GRACE, *supra* note 62.

69. *Moona 2: The First Precision Cooling Pillow Just Got Better,* KICKSTARTER, https://www.kickstarter.com/projects/moona/moona-2-precision-cooling -pillow-pad, https://perma.cc/CSV7-5B6R.

70. *See, e.g., Menopause Support with Peppy,* PEPPY, https://perma.cc/N6KN -J8PA; *Homepage,* MYSYSTERS, https://perma.cc/BVZ2-PC6K.

71. *See* Kate Bunyan, *A Guide to Using the Stella App,* STELLA, https://perma .cc/UD29-7A3V.

72. *See* Partington, *supra* note 11 (calling Femilog an "AI menopause health tracker" and quoting Femilog founder and CEO Samina Usman).

73. *See* MYSYSTERS, *supra* note 70 (the company mySysters "is a social and self-care mobile app to help women manage perimenopause and menopause. Women can track symptoms, print a chart of what they've tracked, and share advice with other women in discussion forums.").

74. Menolabs, LLC, *Menolife: Menopause Tracker,* APPLE APP STORE, https:// perma.cc/8EN4-J8DB.

75. Andrea Ford et al., *Hormonal Health: Period Tracking Apps, Wellness, and Self-Management in the Era of Surveillance Capitalism,* 7 ENGAGING SCI., TECH. & SOC'Y 48, 50 (2021).

76. holy snack GmbH, *perry: Perimenopause Community,* APPLE APP STORE, https://perma.cc/X8E3-K72P; *see also Explore Other Groups* screen on the perry app (screen capture image from smartphone, archived at https://perma.cc/ NKA3-DL94).

77. *See* Peanut App Limited, *Peanut App: Find Mom Friends,* APPLE APP STORE, https://perma.cc/497A-FVYT.

78. *See Suggested Groups for You* screens on the Peanut app (screen capture images from smartphone, archived at https://perma.cc/W7FL-VGTT & https:// perma.cc/B68S-MTR8).

79. *See* Lizzie Widdicombe, *At Last, An App for Menopause,* NEW YORKER (Sept. 25, 2021), https://perma.cc/MPA4-QY37 (recounting a 2019 appearance by the actor Viola Davis on the Jimmy Kimmel talk show in which Kimmel pretended not to know what menopause is and Davis explains, "Menopause is hell, Jimmy. Menopause is a dark hole. That's what menopause is. And that's where I'm at right now.").

80. *Homepage,* PERRY, https://perma.cc/K9R8-K4XA.

81. *See* PEANUT, https://perma.cc/H45W-CYLM (permitting download of app and then creation of a user profile where one self-identifies a life stage).

82. *See* PERRY: PERIMENOPAUSE COMMUNITY, https://perma.cc/3VAW -34TD (permitting download of app and then creation of a user profile that asks

user to answer the question, "What is your biggest WTF peri/menopause symptom?").

83. Fani Gkrozou et al., *Mobile Health (mHealth) Apps Focused on Menopause: Are They Any Good?*, 25 POST REPROD. HEALTH 191, 196 (2019).

84. *Terms & Conditions*, CARIA (2020), https://perma.cc/UB9V-S9EQ.

85. The level of FDA oversight of over-the-counter drugs is far lower than for prescription medicines. *See generally* AGATA DABROWSKA & SUSAN THAUL, CONG. RES. SERV., HOW FDA APPROVES DRUGS AND REGULATES THEIR SAFETY AND EFFECTIVENESS, REP. NO. R41983 (May 8, 2018).

86. *See Embr Wave2, supra* note 61 and accompanying text.

87. *Embr Labs Privacy Policy*, EMBR WAVE, https://perma.cc/5V23-ZXZ6.

88. *The Story of Dmitry Gurski, Co-founder and CEO of Flo Health: How Two Self-Taught Brothers Founded a Women's Health App Worth $800 Million*, UNICORNS LITHUANIA (March 4, 2023), https://perma.cc/5EXU-8MTF; *US Fem-Tech Market Leader Flo Health Completes $12M Series A; Scores $200M Valuation*, CISION PR NEWSWIRE (Oct. 11, 2018), https://perma.cc/SWV4-222L.

89. *Privacy Policy*, FLO HEALTH, https://web.archive.org/web/20181208022938/https:/flo.health/privacy-policy (effective Aug. 6, 2018).

90. Sam Schechner & Mark Secada, *You Give Apps Sensitive Personal Information. Then They Tell Facebook.*, WALL ST. J. (Feb. 22, 2019), https://perma.cc/MR82-QSGB.

91. *See* Press Release, U.S. Fed. Trade Comm'n, Developer of Popular Women's Fertility-Tracking App Settles FTC Allegations That It Misled Consumers About the Disclosure of Their Health Data (Jan. 13, 2021), https://perma.cc/T8JK-NTW9 [hereinafter F.T.C., Flo Health Press Release]; John D. McKinnon, *FTC Reaches Settlement with Flo Health over Fertility-Tracking App*, WALL ST. J. (Jan 14. 2021), https://perma.cc/L8EA-DQQR.

92. Complaint, Flo Health, Inc., No. C-474 (F.T.C. June 17, 2021), https://perma.cc/8YDW-CQCV.

93. *See* F.T.C., Flo Health Press Release, *supra* note 91.

94. *See* Sara Merken, *Fertility App Maker Flo Health Faces Consolidated Privacy Lawsuit*, REUTERS (Sept. 4, 2021), https://perma.cc/WA73-GLQ2.

95. *Id.*

96. *See Homepage*, PEPPY, https://perma.cc/8N8Y-UJLL.

97. *How It Works*, PEPPY, https://perma.cc/5WWF-XAXY.

98. *See Product*, B-WOM, https://perma.cc/4HU9-WRX8; *Partners*, B-WOM, https://perma.cc/QT8K-7BSC.

99. *See Partners*, B-WOM, *supra* note 98.

100. *See Q&A: A Deep Dive into Ovia Health's New Menopause Program*, OVIA HEALTH (Dec. 8, 2022), https://perma.cc/2JTZ-REL2.

101. *See* Aphrodite Papadatou, *Menopause Costs UK Economy 14 Million Working Days per Year*, HRREVIEW (UK) (Apr. 19, 2019), https://perma.cc/6PMP-RTJ2.

102. *See* Stephanie S. Faubion et al., *Impact of Menopause Symptoms on Women in the Workplace*, MAYO CLINIC PROC. 1, 5-6 (2023), https://perma.cc/3WLE-3UY7.

103. *See, e.g.*, Hiromi Ariyoshi, *Evaluation of Menopausal Interventions at a Japanese Company*, 57 AM. ASS'N OF OCCUPATIONAL HEALTH NURSING J. 106 (2009).

104. *Why Do We Ask for This?*, OVIA HEALTH, https://perma.cc/MD54 -B8CA. HIPAA, enacted by Congress in 1996, included several amendments to existing federal law regarding the regulation and provision of health-care services. Health Insurance Portability and Accountability Act of 1996, Pub. L. 104-191, 110 Stat. 1936 (1996) (codified as amended in scattered sections of the U.S.C.). Among HIPAA's provisions is a privacy law that gives people "rights over [their] health information and sets rules and limits on who can look at and receive [their] health information." *Your Rights Under HIPAA*, U.S. DEPT. OF HEALTH & HUM. SVCS. (Jan. 19, 2022), https://perma.cc/5JBK-VWB6. Regarding HIPAA's current applicability when it comes to protection of health-care data, specifically in the femtech space, see, e.g., Laura Travis, *Who Will Regulate Privacy in Femtech After* Dobbs?, BLOOMBERG LAW (Nov. 13, 2022), https://perma.cc/X6H6-3VGC.

105. *See* Tatum Hunter & Jeremy B. Merrill, *Health Apps Share Your Concerns with Advertisers. HIPAA Can't Stop It.*, WASH. POST (Sept. 22, 2022), https://perma.cc/57G2-DMY6.

106. *See* Drew Harwell, *Is Your Pregnancy App Sharing Your Intimate Data with Your Boss?*, WASH. POST (Apr. 10, 2019), https://perma.cc/B8DM-LETB.

107. *About Us*, GENNEV, https://perma.cc/JN4L-GRBW; *Homepage*, GENNEV, https://perma.cc/N48S-J2MS.

108. *See Homepage*, GENNEV, *supra* note 107 (then follow links to "Create"); Jessica Hagen, *Unified Women's Healthcare Acquires Gennev to Become the Leader in Menopause Care in the U.S.*, MOBIHEALTHNEWS (Oct. 24, 2022), https://perma.cc/FW43-JZVE.

109. *See Plans*, GENNEV, https://perma.cc/QH4Q-GFL6.

110. *See id.*

111. *See Symptoms*, GENNEV, https://perma.cc/G5HN-3ZBT.

112. *See Menopause Education: Articles and Resources*, GENNEV, https://perma.cc/FF27-5F9L; *Programs*, GENNEV, https://perma.cc/AUG2-FS6Z.

113. *See Shop*, GENNEV, https://perma.cc/CV2C-MMQ9.

114. *Homepage*, ALLOY, https://perma.cc/ZY52-QM6U.

115. *Id.*

116. MY ALLOY (images on file with the authors).

117. *Terms of Use*, ALLOY (Sept. 20, 2022), https://perma.cc/7S42-W7GK.

118. *Contact Us*, ALLOY, https://perma.cc/R8C4-48DC.

119. *See Telemedicine*, GENNEV, https://perma.cc/8KZP-UYRF.

120. *See* MY ALLOY, *supra* note 116.

121. *See Alva's Annie Coleridge: "Learning to lead a team is a time of intense personal development, reflection and learning,"* FEMTECH INSIDER (Dec. 21, 2020), https://perma.cc/6DY4-HMRB (quoting menopause company Alva co-founder Katie Coleridge exhorting others to find their passion: "Make improving the experience of menopause important to me personally. These reasons spur me on every day.").

122. *Homepage,* ALLOY, https://perma.cc/ZY52-QM6U.

123. *About Us,* BIA CARE, https://perma.cc/HB4M-LR85.

124. *See Your Rights Under HIPAA, supra* note 104, and Travis, *supra* note 104.

125. DANIELLE CITRON, THE FIGHT FOR PRIVACY: PROTECTING DIGNITY, IDENTITY, AND LOVE IN THE DIGITAL AGE 97 (2022).

126. *See* Jennifer Nou & Julian Nyarko, *Regulatory Diffusion,* 74 STAN. L. REV. 897, 946 (2022). *See also* U.S. Fed. Trade Comm'n, Statement of the Commission on Breaches by Health Apps and Other Connected Devices (Sept. 15, 2021), https://perma.cc/55FA-LSQA; Press Release, U.S. Fed. Trade Comm'n, FTC Warns Health Apps and Connected Device Companies to Comply with Health Breach Notification Rule (Sept. 15, 2021), https://perma.cc/7SPG-CBF3.

127. *See* Michele Estrin Gilman, *Periods for Profit and the Rise of Menstrual Surveillance,* 41 COLUM. J. GENDER & L. 100 (2021).

128. *See, e.g.,* Daniel J. Solove & Paul M. Schwartz, *ALI Data Privacy: Overview and Black Letter Text,* 68 UCLA L. REV. 1252, 1271 (2022); Ryan Calo, *Against Notice Skepticism in Privacy (and Elsewhere),* 87 NOTRE DAME L. REV. 1027, 1039 (2012).

129. Danielle Keats Citron, *The End of* Roe *Means We Need a New Civil Right to Privacy,* SLATE (June 27, 2022), https://perma.cc/HR7C-UVSJ.

130. *See* Danielle Citron, *Intimate Privacy in a Post-*Roe *World,* 75 FLA. L. REV. 1033, 1068 (2023).

131. *See* CITRON, *supra* note 125, at 156–161.

132. *Mobile Health App Developers: FTC Best Practices,* U.S. FED. TRADE COMM'N (Dec. 2022), https://perma.cc/SM96-9Q85.

133. CITRON, *supra* note 125, at 5.

## Chapter 8

1. *Roundtable: The Menopause Transition at Work,* WOMEN'S BUREAU, U.S. DEPT. OF LABOR (June 12, 2023), https://perma.cc/7KXG-LKFA.

2. *See* Stephanie Faubion et al., *Impact of Menopause Symptoms on Women in the Workplace,* 98 MAYO CLINIC PROC. 833 (2023), https://perma.cc/VK37 -97TE; BANK OF AMERICA, BREAK THROUGH THE STIGMA, MENOPAUSE IN THE WORKPLACE (2023), https://perma.cc/3CXV-J6RS.

3. BANK OF AMERICA, *supra* note 2.

4. Faubion et al., *supra* note 2, at 840.

5. *See generally* MARTHA CHAMALLAS, INTRODUCTION TO FEMINIST LEGAL THEORY (3d ed. 2012).

6. *See* Bridget J. Crawford, Emily Gold Waldman, & Naomi R. Cahn, *Working Through Menopause*, 99 WASH. U.L. REV. 1531, 1574 (2022).

7. Sharon Malone & Jennifer Weiss-Wolf, *America Lost Its Way on Menopause Research. It's Time to Get Back on Track*, WASH. POST (Apr. 28, 2022), https://perma.cc/Y958-HGSR.

8. *See* Exec. Order No. 14,120, 89 Fed. Reg. 20095 (Mar. 18, 2024).

9. *Id.*

10. Zolan Kanno-Youngs, *Biden Signs Executive Order to Boost Women's Health Research*, N.Y. TIMES (Mar. 18, 2024), https://perma.cc/U7P8-RSZ4 (quoting Maria Shriver).

11. *See, e.g., What Is an Executive Order?*, AM. BAR ASS'N (Jan. 25, 2021), https://perma.cc/53ZG-L2W3.

12. Jennifer Weiss-Wolf, *No Tax on Tampons: Stop Taxing Our Periods! Period*, CHANGE.ORG, https://perma.cc/5WTK-H5JS (petition started Oct. 10, 2015).

13. *See generally* BRIDGET J. CRAWFORD & EMILY GOLD WALDMAN, MENSTRUATION MATTERS: CHALLENGING THE LAW'S SILENCE ON PERIODS 34–58 (2022).

14. The website of periodlaw.org, which has worked with volunteer attorneys throughout the country to fight the tampon tax, keeps a "state scoreboard" to enable easy tracking of the movement's progress. *See Homepage*, PERIOD LAW, https://perma.cc/6UDR-B2KX.

15. First Step Act of 2018, Pub. L. No. 115-391, § 611, 132 Stat. 5194, 5247 (2018) (codified at 18 U.S.C. § 4042).

16. CRAWFORD & WALDMAN, *supra* note 13, at 91.

17. Press Release, Congresswoman Grace Meng, Meng Introduces Whole-of-Government Approach to Combat Period Poverty and Improve Access to Menstrual Products (May 30, 2023), https://perma.cc/F3B6-VRDT.

18. *See* CRAWFORD & WALDMAN, *supra* note 13, at 31.

19. *Id.* at 88.

20. *See* CHAMALLAS, *supra* note 5 at 4, 8.

21. *See, e.g.*, Katharine T. Bartlett, *Feminist Legal Methods*, 103 HARV. L. REV. 839, 851 (1990).

22. *See* Deborah A. Widiss, *Equalizing Parental Leave*, 105 MINN. L. REV. 2175, 2226 (2021) (illustrating how the sameness-difference debate plays out in the context of pregnancy and employment law).

23. *See, e.g.*, Wendy W. Williams, *Notes from a First Generation*, U. CHI. LEGAL F. 99, 108 (1989).

24. *See, e.g.*, Aya Gruber, *Neofeminism*, 50 HOUSTON L. REV. 1325, 1338 (2013).

25. *See, e.g.*, CATHARINE A. MacKINNON, SEXUAL HARASSMENT OF WORKING WOMEN 117 (1979).

26. *Id.* at 118.

27. Joan Chalmers Williams, *Dissolving the Sameness/Difference Debate: A Post-Modern Path Beyond Essentialism in Feminist and Critical Race Theory*, 1991 DUKE L.J. 296, 298 (1991).

28. *See* Martha Albertson Fineman, *What Vulnerability Theory Is and Is Not*, VULNERABILITY AND THE HUMAN CONDITION (Feb. 1, 2021), https://perma.cc/8NPW-QSC7.

29. *See* Samuel R. Bagenstos, *Subordination, Stigma, and "Disability,"* 86 VA. L. REV. 397, 428 (2000).

30. *See* Adam Samaha, *What Good Is the Social Model of Disability?*, 74 U. CHI. L. REV. 1251, 1251–52 (2007).

31. ROBERTA NULL, UNIVERSAL DESIGN: PRINCIPLES AND MODELS 12 (2013) ("Universal [D]esign asks that designers create spaces and products that adapt to people as individuals and that strengthen their sense of themselves as capable and independent[.]").

32. *See* Michael Ashley Stein, *Same Struggle, Different Difference: ADA Accommodations as Antidiscrimination*, 153 U. PA. L. REV. 579, 642 (2004).

33. *See Confronting the Taboo Surrounding Menopause in the Workplace*, BLOOMBERG (Jan. 28, 2022), https://perma.cc/BBE8-LYLR.

34. Nina A. Kohn, *A Framework for Theoretical Inquiry into Law and Aging*, 21 THEORETICAL INQUIRIES L. 187, 195 (2020).

35. *See, e.g.*, Vicki Gelfeld & Oscar Anderson, *Menopause Experiences: Providers Can Do Better in Educating, Starting the* Conversation, AARP (Jul. 31, 2018), https://perma.cc/XH9P-FX8M.

36. Press Release, AARP Announces "Hacking Menopause Challenge" Winners, AARP (June 16, 2020), https://perma.cc/JJ25-TMSE.

37. Jennifer Millea, *AARP Testimony in Support of Paid Family Medical Leave Insurance* (March 13, 2013), https://perma.cc/4JF5-RJJD (reprinting testimony of Connecticut AARP State Director Nora Duncan from a March 13, 2013, hearing before the Connecticut General Assembly's Labor and Public Employees Committee on *An Act Establishing a Task Force to Study Family Leave Insurance*, H.B. 6553.).

38. *See, e.g.*, Irene O. Aninye et al., *Menopause Preparedness: Perspectives for Patient, Provider, and Policymaker Consideration*, 28 MENOPAUSE 1186, 1188 (2021).

39. *See* Alisa Johnson et al., *Complementary and Alternative Medicine for Menopause*, 24 J. EVIDENCE BASED INTEGRATIVE MED. 1 (2019).

40. *See* Menopausal Hormone Replacement Therapies and Alternative Treatments and Fairness Act of 2011, H.R. 383, 112th Cong. (2011); *see also* email from Gregory Whitmore to Naomi Cahn (July 17, 2023) (on file with authors) (finding no comparable bills introduced since 2011).

41. *See, e.g.,* ROBIN A. COHEN ET AL., NAT'L CTR. FOR HEALTH STAT., HEALTH INSURANCE COVERAGE: EARLY RELEASE OF ESTIMATES FROM THE NATIONAL HEALTH INTERVIEW SURVEY, 2022 (2022), https://perma.cc/6MXH-KDX8.

42. *See* Walter R. Hsiang et al., *Medicaid Patients Have Greater Difficulty Scheduling Health Care Appointments Compared with Private Insurance Patients: A Meta-Analysis,* 56 INQUIRY 1, 1 (2019).

43. Team Verywell Health, *Health Divide: Menopause and Black Women,* VERYWELL HEALTH (May 25, 2023), https://perma.cc/SX7P-LWLE.

44. *See, e.g.,* Letter from Sally K. Richardson, Dir., Dept. of Health & Hum. Svcs., to State Medicaid Dirs. (Nov. 30, 1998), https://perma.cc/37T6-WHXU.

45. *See* Kimberlé Crenshaw, *Demarginalizing the Intersection of Race and Sex: A Black Feminist Critique of Antidiscrimination Doctrine, Feminist Theory and Antiracist Politics,* 1989 U. CHI. LEGAL F. 139, 148-50; *see also* Kimberlé Crenshaw, *Mapping the Margins: Intersectionality, Identity Politics, and Violence Against Women of Color,* 43 STAN. L. REV. 1241, 1249 (1991).

46. *See, e.g.,* Kimberlé Crenshaw (@sandylocks), TWITTER (June 26, 2020, 1:41 PM), https://perma.cc/YA2V-UXSA ("Intersectionality is not additive. It's fundamentally reconstitutive. Pass it on.").

47. *See* Lisa Cappelloni, *What Are the Symptoms and Signs of Menopause?,* HEALTHLINE (May 14, 2018), https://perma.cc/RDX2-YMS7 (indicating that some people have no experience of negative symptoms of menopause).

48. *See, e.g.,* U.S. BUREAU OF LAB. STAT., WOMEN IN THE LABOR FORCE: A DATABOOK, REPT. NO. 1084, at 7-8 tbl.1 (Dec. 2019), https://perma.cc/LJA2 -CHYJ (providing data based on race, occupation, and industry).

49. *See id.,* at 46-64, tbl. 11. We use the terms "women," "Asian," and "Hispanic" here because the U.S. Bureau of Labor Statistics employs this terminology. Such managerial and professional occupations include software development, chief executive roles, attorneys, accountants, nurses, and teachers. *See id.*

50. *See id.* at 64-65, tbl.12.

51. *E.g.,* Usha Ranji et al., *Difficult Tradeoffs: Key Findings on Workplace Benefits and Family Health Care Responsibilities from the 2020 KFF Women's Health Survey,* KFF (Apr. 21, 2021), https://perma.cc/7JGB-33ZL (finding that Asian women are most likely to have access to paid family and medical leave and health insurance).

52. *See, e.g., Transgender Workers at Greater Risk for Unemployment and Poverty,* NAT'L LGBTQ TASK FORCE (Sept. 6, 2013), https://perma.cc/3A64-S6RP.

53. *See generally* Bridget J. Crawford et al., *The Ground on Which We All Stand: A Conversation about Menstrual Equity Law and Activism,* 26 MICH. J. GENDER & L. 341, 343-344 (2020).

# INDEX

camphor, 38
Canada, 27, 39, 48, 136
cancer (organ nonspecific), 11, 39,
	41-43, 46, 48, 62, 98, 116
cancer, breast, 2, 35-37, 39, 44-46, 48
cancer, colorectal, 35, 46
cancer, endometrial, 42
capitalism. *See* menopause
	capitalism
cardiac issues, 2, 12, 15, 35, 37,
	43-45
Caria (app), 122
carpal tunnel syndrome, 67
Center for American Progress, 105
change, the, 21, 113
Change.org, 136
Channel 4 (U.K.), 78-79
Chartered Institute for Personnel
	and Development (CIPD)
	(U.K.), 75
Chemical Insights Research
	Institute, 117
chest pains. *See* cardiac issues.
children, raising, 15
China, 28, 29
chloroform, 38
cis-women. *See* women, cisgender
Citron, Danielle, 130-31
Civil Rights Act of 1964, Title VII of,
	60, 72, 81, 86, 87
class, socioeconomic, and health
	disparities, 134
class action lawsuits, 124, 136-37
climate-controlled workplaces. *See*
	temperature
clinical trials, 42, 44-47, 130
clothing. *See* dress codes; menopause
	clothing; t-shirts, novelty
clothing, antimicrobial, 116
clothing, odor control, 116
cognitive behavioral therapy, 49
cognitive symptoms, 55-56. *See also*
	menopause, symptoms of

Coleman, Alisha, 54, 61, 63-64,
	69-71, 87
community. *See* menopause, support
	groups for
Comprehensive Menopause Care
	Program (UCLA), 49
concentration, mental. *See* brain fog
confidence, erosion of, 55, 59
Congress, 42, 49, 81, 83, 88, 135
consumerism. *See* menopause
	capitalism
consumer protection, 124
continuing medical education, 134
contraception, 85
cooling devices. *See* menopause-
	related devices
coronary heart disease. *See* cardiac
	issues
correctional facilities, 64-65, 137
*Cosby Show, The*, 21
*Cosmopolitan Magazine*, 136
COVID-19, 93
cows, 38
crabbiness. *See* anger.
Crenshaw, Kimberlé, 72, 144
criminal justice reform, 137
crying. *See* tearfulness
Cucumber Clothing (company), 116
cultural depictions. *See* menopause,
	cultural or societal view of
Currier, Andrew, 38

data privacy, 6, 18, 112, 123-31, 136
data tracking. *See* menopause
	symptom tracking
Dault, Jackie, 57, 60-61, 62, 65
de Gardanne, Charles-Pierre-
	Louis, 37
de Togni, Guilia, 121
*Decisions at Menopause Study*, 28
Delaney, Janelle, 56
Department of Education Office of
	Civil Rights, 88